Contents

*An asterisk next to the name of an organisation in the text indicates that the address or website can be found in this section.

Introduction

Working from home is a positive choice being made by more and more people each year. Some people do it because they are starting up a new business and do not want separate premises until they have a going concern. Others, perhaps with small or not-so-small children, just want to work as many or as few hours as suits them. Many are self-employed people who have left commuting behind them to re-purpose their skills. Some are not fully mobile and therefore cannot easily travel to a workplace outside the home. Yet others work from home because the property itself provides a source of income. In the next few years a new category of home-based worker may well emerge – the retired person whose pension has not lived up to expectations and who finds some form of continuing work necessary. There appear to be no age limits on the home-based worker. Some of the organisations that give grants to young people to start their own businesses report that they are receiving applications from entrepreneurs as young as 14 who are operating fledgling enterprises from the computers in their bedrooms!

New government legislation has made it compulsory for employers to think positively about flexible working and to be flexible themselves when approached by staff who wish to organise some of their work from home. Many large companies are now seeking to save money by slimming down their headquarters and using the latest technology to create a mobile workforce that operates from a home base. Numerous statistics, all conflicting, predict how many people in the UK will work from home or outside of a traditional office environment in ten years' time. All show a definite upwards trend in the numbers of people choosing to take this route in their working lives.

This guide provides an entrée for all of these sections of the workforce, alerting them to the pitfalls as well as the advantages of being a home-based worker. It has been updated to include an overview of the latest technology which has, without a doubt, made working from home very much simpler. Even the smallest business, partnership or lone entrepreneur can now do business globally through the Internet. Many self-employed teleworkers can work for clients on the other side of the world, thanks to the World Wide Web and the ease of email communication. The latest generation of mobile phones makes it possible to download text, graphics, photographs and even video clips on your handset, no matter how remote your location.

However, modern technology has brought with it new problems, as we have highlighted in Chapter 4. The ease and scope of the Internet has benefited the fraudsters as well as the honest. Internet scams are on the rise each year and homeworkers need to beware of dubious schemes. The good news is that you can avoid being taken in by following the advice in this guide.

All in all, working from home is a constructive choice. A lot of support and advice is available for those who start up a small business. Government and other organisations are still mindful of the fact that many 'micro-businesses', as they are called, have a high failure rate in the first two years and need to be supported through that period. Once established, they make a significant contribution to the national economy. Although it may seem that the UK government and the EU spend most of their time devising legislation to impede the lone entrepreneur, much of it, in recent years, has been created to protect businesses and the general public from inadequate and harmful products and services. Reforming employment legislation, in particular, has been the remit of the present government, as well as the regulation of many professions that were previously open to abuse, such as those that care for children, the elderly and animals, or offer health and beauty treatments.

Many of the questions that need to be answered when you start to work from home – How do I organise myself? How do I raise money? Where do I get advice? What do I have to do when I become an employer? – have not changed. The book continues to address these vital issues in full. It may not have all the answers to all the questions, but it provides an invaluable research tool for anyone about to drop out of the rat race and start afresh.

Chapter 1
Working from home

Each year, more and more of the working population work from home. Most reports, surveys and statistics over the last couple of years point towards the fact that economic trends and changes in employment and work patterns – together with transport and office-space costs in the UK's major cities – are reinforcing the present trend towards working from home as a deliberate strategy by major employers. Equally, many individuals have made a lifestyle choice and have opted to escape from the traditional role of the employee to become self-employed or to start up a small business, and many of them make the home their working environment. Statistics released in 2002 by various organisations show a significant surge in the number of people electing to work from home: the Office of National Statistics has estimated that, by 2006, almost a third of the UK's working population will be working from home for some or all of the working week either as employees, self-employed or running a small business.

Changes in society and the job market

Why has there been such a significant move away from traditional work practices to using the home as a workplace? In 2002, a survey commissioned by the *Evening Standard*, the London daily newspaper, found that almost one in ten workers had become homeworkers and 80 per cent of them cited the stress and strain of the daily commuting to London as a major factor in their decision to work from home.

Rising divorce statistics, and the demise of the traditional two-parent family, have meant that there are more single parents who are turning to home-based occupations which provide extra money while allowing them to continue to be an active parent.

A more recent development is that of the early retiree who gives up full-time work in his or her fifties and needs an occupation which will provide continued stimulation as well as bring in revenue. Often, early retirement provides an excellent opportunity for someone to develop a totally new home-based profession. Many colleges which run training courses for alternative therapy practitioners, for example, have reported an increasing number of mature students in their fifties.

CASE HISTORY: Norman

Norman was made redundant in his late forties and, after eight months of unsuccessful job-hunting, decided to use his redundancy money to train as a driving instructor and to buy an adapted car. He now runs his own one-man driving school from his home. The demand has proved so high locally that his wife is undergoing similar training so that she can come into the business.

Less fortunate are those who are made redundant in mid-life and find the job market has closed ranks against them. For such people, retraining or developing an existing skill into a home-based business can be a lifesaver.

New catalysts

The most recent development in society, aided and abetted by the sophisticated technology now on offer, is that of the 'half and half' worker. The National Association of Estate Agents reports that, since the turn of the millennium, there has been a noticeable rise in families buying properties far away from urban areas, but with good road or rail links, because the main wage earner of the family chooses to commute to and live in a city for 'half' of the week and work at home for the remainder. What were once holiday home areas in the UK are rapidly turning into main residence areas.

In the past two years, the UK government has been promoting flexible working to companies through its 'Managing Diversity' initiative and the Department of Trade and Industry (DTI)*'s Work–Life Balance campaign. From June 2000 to March 2002, the government made a fund of £81.5 million available for employers to enable them to receive free consultancy advice to develop flexible working practices in their companies. The new legislation, *Flexible Working – the Right to Apply*, that came into effect in April 2003, will probably have a profound effect on working practices. As mentioned earlier in the chapter, it will make it a legal duty for employers to consider applications for flexible working from employees who are parents of young or disabled children. Commerce and industry watchdogs expect that it will tip the balance for those large companies that have been teetering on the edge of a decision to introduce teleworking practices among their workforces.

However, it is probably the reality of economic factors that will really fuel the explosion in tele/remote/flexible and e-working. According to the City University in London, the cost of putting a worker at a desk in the UK has now reached £10,000 a year, while the cost of supporting a worker at home is estimated at £3,000. Another piece of research, by The RAC Foundation and the Telework Association*, shows that some workers spend a third of their salary and a third of their day on travelling to work.

If you add in the emergence of what is now being called 'm-commerce' (mobile commerce) to the equation, then working away from an office becomes the best solution, economically.

The Institute of Directors* predicts that, in the next two years, mobile technology will provide an even greater range of services, such as still images and video, bringing a uniformity to the applications, interfaces and programming of mobile phones, and their interaction with the Internet. The practical application of this for a homeworker would be that it would allow images from a digital camera to be downloaded via a PC to a client's or employer's phone.

Broadband – the newest form of connection to the Internet, which processes data ten times faster than older connections – could be of benefit to people who are trying to run home-based businesses that market goods or services on the Web.

But more about technology in Chapter 10.

CASE HISTORY: Sundeep

Sundeep is a consultant engineer. He was working for a very large consultancy in central London but found that he was spending a great deal of time commuting and was also working on projects which he did not feel he was best suited to manage. He began to make enquiries among his contacts and discovered that there was a place in the freelance marketplace for his particular skills. He drew up a business plan and managed to secure a bank loan to equip his home office with the necessary technology and to have brochures printed. The loan was made easier by the fact that he had managed to capture a contract with a large company before officially starting up. He now earns more than he did as an employee and he is able to work mainly in the field of petro-chemicals, which interests him most.

Restrictions on enterprise

For anyone earning money at home today, the fact is that legislation imposes more restrictions than ever on the budding entrepreneur. Even the earner of modest 'pin money' who makes jam and cakes to sell at bazaars has to meet a barrage of food regulations designed to ensure maximum food safety and hygiene for the buying public.

Banks, unfortunately, are far less inclined today to lend money to assist business start-ups than they were 20 years ago. Much of the grant aid that was on offer in certain areas for developing industries has dried up. However, loan facilities may be available (see Chapter 6).

Despite all that, the picture is not gloomy: sources of finance do exist, and the legislation can be coped with. For those who have a PC and access to the Internet, it is now possible to market products and services worldwide with relative ease

For those who wish to remain employees, there are now many home-based technology jobs available. Joining the Telework Association★ is one way of getting regular details of teleworker jobs on offer and various online employment agencies have special sections for those who want to work from home. Advice on obtaining unskilled homeworking is detailed in Chapter 3.

Why work from home?

The reasons why people choose to work from home are as diverse as the ways they choose to earn their money. For some, the desire to opt out of the rat race, the pressures of daily commuting, the personality clashes in the office or factory take precedence over the security of a monthly salary cheque. The tradition of staying in a job 'man and boy' is virtually moribund, and this, combined with the growing popularity and success of working from home, has profoundly affected the way in which people view their jobs.

A first analysis of the motives for earning money from home may point to ultimate success or failure. If, for example, the prime motive for working at home is so that you can have more free time, this could point to a lack of the self-discipline that any self-employed person needs by the spadeful.

Typical reasons why people work from home are: _(advantages)_

- they have small children and need some extra income, but do not wish to leave the home to work
- they have small children and cannot afford nursery care
- they have no means of transport and commuting to work would be difficult
- they are disabled and either housebound or unable to find employment out of the home
- they manufacture products, in a small way, in their home and have always done so; to rent extra premises would be expensive
- they can save three hours a day by not travelling to and from a job – this means they can see more of their family and save travel costs
- they cannot get a job on the open market because of age, lack of qualifications or other factors
- they have an illness which, although it does not totally disable them, restricts the number of hours they can work or gives them 'good' days and 'bad' days
- they have skills that can be easily practised from home, for example book-keeping or dressmaking
- they want an interest in life which will provide some income but also allow them time to devote to family and home

- they are members of the working community who can earn more money working for themselves, using their home as a base, than they can working for an employer – for example, builders, consultants and so on
- they have worked for a succession of companies where the company politics and policies have affected their enjoyment of work
- they have entered the job market after university and found it impossible to get a good and fulfilling job, despite their qualifications
- they *can* work at home now because of the ease of communications created through email and mobiles etc.
- they have been given the opportunity to work at home by their employer.

CASE HISTORY: Barry

Barry is paraplegic and, although he is a qualified teacher, finds the demands of daily school life too great. He decided to set up at home as a private tutor in maths and has a full client list. The pupils come to him for their lessons, and most of his work is in the early evenings and at weekends. He also makes extra income by invigilating at examinations, marking the papers and proof-reading maths textbooks.

New breed of homeworker

The sections of the homeworking marketplace which have seen the largest growth are teleworking, remote working, flexible working and e-working.

Teleworkers

The definition of a teleworker, supplied by the Telework Association*, is 'working at a distance from the people who can pay you, either at home, on the road, or at a locally based centre. Teleworkers use email, phone and fax to keep in touch with their employers or customers.' According to the Office of National

Statistics, there were 2.2 million teleworkers in the UK in 2001 – a 65 per cent rise in four years. Teleworkers can either be employed or freelance.

Remote workers

There has been a significant growth in the number of remote workers in the UK – people who, by design, work for a large organisation from home or a locally based centre. This is primarily due to the rise in the use of call centres. Many organisations now farm out their telephone services to remote communities (such as areas of the Scottish Highlands). These people deal with customer queries, operate advice lines, process orders and offer other telephone services.

Flexible workers

The practice of flexible working is when employees are able to organise their work and working hours so that some portion of the working week is spent at home, or work is undertaken outside the traditional nine to five hours. Apparently more than two million people now work at home at least one day a week (Office of National Statistics again). This practice will undoubtedly increase with the new employment legislation, *Flexible Working – the Right to Apply*, that came into effect in April 2003 (see 'New catalysts', on page 10).

E-workers or m-workers

E-workers or m- (mobile) workers are people who have no head office base and use the latest technology (WAP/Java phones, in-car faxes, laptops etc.) to communicate with employers or clients. E-workers tend to be home-based, m-workers tend to be on the road a lot. As technology advances, it affords the opportunity for more and more people to work in this way.

Other types of homeworkers

While the sections of the homeworking community mentioned above have expanded, the two mentioned below have remained fairly static.

Outworkers

This category of homeworkers covers the semi-skilled or unskilled people who work at home, either as employees or, more likely, self-employed, doing labour-intensive work for manufacturing or services companies such as assembling items, packing, sewing, stuffing envelopes etc. The wages are usually low. Statistics are patchy on this section of the working community because some of the work is, sad to say, cash-based and tax-dodging. Few representative bodies are interested in the conditions and contracts under which outworkers operate. Those that are may be concerned with only a certain section of the outworker community, for example, women from ethnic minorities who may be exploited doing work in the clothing industry. A few Low Pay Units were set up in the UK to advise upon and monitor the employment of homeworkers, and several local authorities have a special interest in helping homeworkers in their area. These are referred to in greater detail in Chapter 3 and contact details appear in the back of the book.

CASE HISTORY: Sharon

Sharon is a young mother with one baby. Money is a bit tight and she needed to get some sort of job. However, she has no relatives who can look after her baby, and when she investigated the cost of nursery care in her area she realised that if she worked full-time in a shop she would barely be able to make enough money to pay for her baby to be looked after, let alone make some extra money to pay bills. She saw an advertisement in the local paper for homeworkers and when she telephoned the number given was told that the work was packing greetings cards. Sharon took the job and has found that in a good week she can make about £108, which pays some of the bills. The work is repetitive but not unpleasant; she can do quite a lot in the evenings while watching television, and sometimes her husband helps. The company requested that she should be self-employed and therefore take care of her own tax and National Insurance. Because of her low earnings she has not yet paid tax but she voluntarily pays Class 2 NI.

Small businesses

Many people choose to set up a home-based business, either turning an existing skill or hobby into an income or by buying a new business, such as a small franchise.

Sadly, a large proportion of small businesses fail each year, but various sources report that these statistics seem to relate to the businesses that have expanded beyond the one-man/-woman band and moved on from using the home as a base. It could be that the greater risks involved in paying for working premises and employing staff contribute to the demise of small companies. A healthy percentage of people seem to survive self-employment and continue to have happy and profitable careers. And those who survive expansion into a fully-fledged business do so because each step of the way is planned and built into the balance sheet from the beginning – something that is discussed in Chapters 7 and 8.

Employment options

The at times uncertain job market and the expansion in numbers of early retirees and active pensioners have had the result that anyone considering embarking upon self-employment today has an unprecedented number of training schemes, diploma courses and business courses on offer, a large percentage of which are available during the day as opposed to the evenings.

Other developments in the marketplace have enabled many people to start working for themselves in a small way. Franchising, developed in the USA in the 1960s and 1970s, has taken quite a hold in the UK, employing well over 300,000 people. The British Franchise Association (BFA)* represents over 200 franchise brands, and has thousands of members. Franchising is, basically, a way of purchasing the good name and experience of a business that has proved that it works. A franchisee usually buys a package which should include the right to trade under the name of the parent company, the right to use its proven equipment and products and to be given training and business support, at least in the initial stages. Many of these franchises are very big operations indeed, but some are one-man/woman operations, such as carpet and upholstery cleaning systems, mobile fast-food outlets and business services.

Most national newspapers regularly carry pages of adverts for franchises and large exhibitions of franchising opportunities are held around the UK on a frequent basis.

CASE HISTORY: Peter

Peter is a retired accountant in his early sixties who was formerly employed by a large firm of accountants in Bradford. When he retired he was financially very secure but was bored and frustrated by not having any work to do. At his daughter's suggestion he visited a franchise exhibition and found several one-man/woman franchises that appealed to him. Being an accountant he was able to investigate the financial viability of the various proposals, and took professional advice from his bank's franchise department and a friend in a marketing consultancy. He then purchased a printing franchise which specialises in printing business stationery and similar products, and which he could operate from home. It has proved so successful that he now employs his daughter and one other member of staff.

Still with us, although less popular, are 'network marketing' schemes, also called 'multi-level selling' (formerly called 'pyramid selling'). Network marketing is a method of selling goods or services to the general public – usually door to door, to individuals or through 'parties' (a gathering of friends or neighbours). These goods or services are purchased by the participants from a central source or from other participants in the 'pyramid' or 'network'. Participants not only make commissions on the sales that they personally generate, but also on the sales of any other 'agents' they have recruited. These multi-level marketing schemes acquired a bad reputation and caused the government to legislate to protect participants. The Pyramid Selling Regulations 1989 and the Pyramid Selling Schemes (Amendment) Regulations 1990 are both part of the Third Trading Act 1973. As a result of this legislation some very fair network marketing schemes are now in existence and it is possible to make a reasonable income from them. However, caution should still be exercised. Often, unscrupulous companies that offer 'get rich quick' schemes are only seeking to offload stock.

In China, network marketing is now illegal after thousands of people lost their life savings through their involvement with such companies. Network marketing has also moved into the realm of the Internet and, unfortunately, some operations have already appeared on the hit list of Internet scams compiled by various watchdog organisations. Network marketing is explored further in Chapters 2 and 4.

Weighing up the pros and cons

If you are seriously contemplating working from home in one capacity or another, then it is worth thinking about the advantages and, more importantly, the disadvantages, before making such an important decision.

The advantages

- **It is cheap** You save a considerable amount of money by not travelling to your place of work and, if you are self-employed, by not having to rent or buy other premises.
- **There are tax benefits** By using part of your own home for work you are allowed to claim part of the costs of the mortgage or rent, heating, lighting and telephone. Any alterations or repairs done to the premises which are directly related to improving your working conditions can also be put through your accounts.
- **It saves time** The hours that you would otherwise spend in travelling can be devoted to work.
- **It is flexible** If you are a parent, you can take advantage of certain types of work that can be fitted into school hours. If you have pre-school children you may be able to work when they are in bed in the evening. Alternatively, you may just want to work unconventional hours because they suit you better; if you function best in the mornings you can start work early and finish early or, if you are a night owl, you can work late. The flexibility of working hours obviously depends upon the type of occupation and whether it relies upon interaction with people who work normal office hours. The self-employed insurance salesman may find that he or she has to make all his or her calls

in the evening because that is when most working people are at home. The craftworker or writer may be able to work any hour of the day or night, whereas a mobile hairdresser may find that his or her clients demand appointments during the daytime only.

CASE HISTORY: Hilary

Hilary is a single parent of two school-age children. Although she receives adequate maintenance from her ex-husband she felt that she needed to generate some extra money, but did not want to go out to work and have her children looked after by someone else after school hours. Her greatest love has always been cooking, and she has a Cordon Bleu diploma which she gained before her marriage. She decided that she could put this skill to use during school hours and hit upon the idea of business lunches. She approached all the local businesses and offered a boardroom luncheon service. Her own kitchen was inspected and approved by the local Environmental Health Department so that she could prepare the food there and transport it to the clients. For those offices that do not have any means of heating food she uses a variety of portable methods – slo-cookers, small microwaves, electric rings and so on. She prepares anything from sandwiches and salads to full Cordon Bleu meals.

- **It is comfortable** Working in your own home can be relaxing. You can wear whatever you like, you have control over your environment – the temperature, the lighting, the décor. You can drink as many cups of tea and coffee as you like and when you like, and time your breaks to suit yourself.
- **You see more of your family** No more being a weekend parent because you are usually on your way to work when the kids get up and you don't get back until they are in bed.
- **You can have family support** It may be possible to enlist the help of those members of your family who have the time to assist you to get tasks completed, for example, a parent or teenage children, who might be available at weekends to help.
- **You can sometimes work at your own pace** From the start you can decide just how much work you want to take on. You

may simply be trying to generate a little extra money for your family rather than providing the main income. You may be disabled or ill and so only capable of coping with a certain amount of concentrated physical or mental effort. You may be an early retiree or a pensioner who just wants an occupation to fill in the spare time, or your whole lifestyle may depend upon your making a go of self-employment and therefore you are prepared to work every hour there is in order to make a success of things. Whatever your situation, you now have the choice – you can run your working life.

- **Technology will help you to communicate with others** Whether it is just communicating with the employer that has allowed you to work from home, communicating with your own clients, running a home-based business, or actually marketing your goods or services internationally on the Internet – you should be able to conduct business as effectively as anyone who has the benefit of working in a large office or factory.

The disadvantages

- **Restrictions by your landlord or mortgage lender** Restrictions could prevent you from using your home as a base for business. If you have a quiet and unobtrusive occupation, such as hand-knitting or book-binding, this may not be classified as a 'business' under the terms of whatever contract covers your residence. However, when an occupation substantially encroaches on the domestic use of a house – say a mail-order business for which half the house is filled with boxes and packages, a carpentry workshop in the basement filled with flammable materials, wood and chemicals, or a motorbike repair service which litters up your front and back garden and garage with dismantled bikes, then your building society or landlord and, certainly, your insurer will take a dim view of such proceedings. Before starting on any venture you should check the details of all leases, deeds, charges and covenants to see whether running a business in your home is prohibited.
- **Restrictions by local authorities** Similarly, local bylaws may prohibit any occupations in a residential area which involve a fire risk, noisy machinery or frequent deliveries by large vehicles.

21

- **You may need planning permission** This is required if your home-based occupation changes the use of a building, for example converting your living room into a tea shop, using two rooms in your house as a waiting room and treatment room, or turning your garden into a cattery.

   There is a general rule that if you are using less than half your house as office space, or your shed as a workshop, then you do not have to apply for planning permission. However, this rule is not hard and fast. The key to it all is unobtrusiveness. You could run a very small office from one room in your house without any problem, but if you suddenly started receiving frequent visits from customers who parked their cars outside and prevented residents from parking in a residential area you could find yourself falling foul of the local authority.

   Check with the local authority before starting your new venture because they will be concerned not just over the change of use of a house, but also whether your business will contribute to noise or air pollution, whether you are planning any structural alterations to your house and whether your activities come under the scrutiny of the department concerned with health and safety.

- **You will need extra insurance** Your home contents policy will certainly have to be extended to cover your work materials, records and also outbuildings if you are using them for storage or as workshops. You may need to consider other forms of insurance – public liability, professional indemnity (see Chapter 7) and some form of private health insurance and pension.

- **You need to pay greater attention to home security** If your whole livelihood is housed in your home you cannot afford to be burgled. You may have high-value, easily portable equipment such as computers, fax machines, specialist tools and so on. You may work with valuable materials such as gold and silver. You will almost certainly have to use your home address, or at least your telephone number, in advertising and publicity, even if only on business cards. This, unfortunately, does make your home a target.

   Outbuildings, of course, are at greater risk. You need to make the garden and the buildings as secure as possible. It is best to seek advice on this from the local police.

- **You may be too easily distracted at home** If the work that you are doing requires great concentration you may find working in a home environment is too noisy, family life is too intrusive, or you are too easily tempted to break off from work and do other things.

- **You may get lonely** If you do not have a family, or the family are out at work all day, you may find the solitude of working at home unbearable. If you are engaged in some sort of craftwork which is easily portable, you may find that the answer is to team up with like-minded people in your area and work together in each other's houses. Other solutions are listed under the 'What if..?' section below.

- **It could adversely affect your family life** Because you cannot leave the pressures of work at an office and calm down on the way home, or expect your children to talk in whispers all day or your partner to refrain from using noisy household appliances, resentments may build up on both sides. You have to be sure that you have a personality that can adapt to working at home. You may have decided to pursue an occupation which is home-based but, in fact, gets you out and about most of the time, in which case conflict between you and the family should not arise. But people who have sedentary home-based jobs need to be self-disciplined yet relaxed, and able to work as many hours as needed, then to shut work off and give the family some time too. It is not an easy juggling act.

- **Running your own business can mean insecurity** This applies to self-employed freelancers too. Will enough money come in to pay next month's bills? Will customers pay on time or will you have to chase them? Can you get the work done on time? Will the demand for your product or service continue? These questions will probably occupy a good deal of your attention from time to time. If you are a second-income generator the pressure may not be so great, but many people find that coping with the cash-flow worries of self-employment can be too much.

- **Working for someone else can also mean insecurity** This may not apply if, say, you are a home-based employee of a large company, with a properly negotiated contract of employment; however, you may feel insecure about missing out on promotion or other opportunities if you are not working at the head office. Teleworkers or freelancers on short-term contracts often worry about where the next job is going to come from – especially if they do not have the time or resources to market their services/skills as well as fulfil their obligations. Out-workers rarely have the sort of contracts that offer some compensation if their services are no longer required. It is always best not to put all your eggs in one basket. Have one or two sources of part-time work on the go at once, so that if one fails you can perhaps increase the hours on another, without too much loss of income.

- **Working for someone else can sometimes mean boring and poorly paid work** The work may be easy and possible to do while watching television, but it may also be tiring and pay very little. Do you have the patience to stuff envelopes all day long? Or sew millions of buttons on clothes? Your home may also be cluttered with dozens of boxes or bags of work waiting to be done. You may have to process thousands of pieces a week to make a living wage. This type of work can be very repetitive and time-consuming.

- **You may only be earning a commission and do long hours of work for no return at all** There are home-based jobs, such as telephone canvassing, where the employee has the telephone bill paid but only earns commission on successful conversions into sales. This can mean making hundreds of telephone calls (sometimes receiving abuse from the people you are calling) without earning anything at all.

- **You may have to traipse the street in all weathers, delivering and collecting catalogues, orders, directories or leaflets** Many network-marketing schemes involve delivering catalogues to houses over quite large areas and then knocking on doors to get them back a few days later, with orders if you are lucky. Some people deliver phone directories, local newspapers or leaflets. Others do house-to-house surveys. All these jobs have to be done whatever the weather and, quite often, during the evenings.

- **Your work could be dangerous** Collecting money door-to-door for football pools, Christmas clubs, debt collectors or catalogues can be hazardous. Walking the streets at a regular time each week with large amounts of cash on your person is an invitation to muggers.

- **Your technology could let you down** If it is your lifeline – for example, you may be marketing through the Internet, or totally reliant on your mobile phone – you must equip yourself with the help of a very good supplier who will organise repairs, maintenance and back-up systems at the time of purchase. (More about this in Chapter 10.) If you cannot afford new equipment and have to make do with existing hardware then you must organise your own back-up mechanisms. Try to establish from the outset a good dialogue with someone local who is a techno-wizard and can repair any hardware, re-install software or re-establish connections at any time of the day or night. This may involve paying someone a retainer, to keep them 'on-call' for you, if at all possible. You also need that person to organise someone to take his or her place if they are away or ill. Discuss with a professional, before starting your business, exactly what your technology requirements are and how to organise a fail-safe system.

Preparation is the key to success

Once you have analysed your motives for working from home and weighed up the advantages and disadvantages, you are halfway to preparing yourself for a fruitful and satisfying working life.

Every business should work out a business plan before starting up to make sure that every possible eventuality is covered in its scheme of operation for the first few years. If you are contemplating earning money from home, however modestly, you should do the same thing. You must analyse every step you plan to take in the future and prepare yourself for any direction in which your chosen occupation may take you.

This may seem unnecessary at first – after all, you're only decorating a few wedding cakes for your friends, aren't you? But what happens if one of your wedding cakes is so admired by a professional baker that he or she offers you a contract to decorate 50 cakes a week? You can't resist the money, the challenge and the security but suddenly you are catapulted from a paying hobby into a small business. You hadn't planned on it; you didn't actively market yourself, it just happened. Without preparation you are lost – the effort of meeting the orders leaves you no time to sort out accounts, get some back-up help and deal with the authorities if necessary.

If you had investigated every possible business scenario before you even started your venture, gathered the information needed for possible expansion and sorted out a fail-safe mechanism should things go wrong, then you would have laid the foundations for success or, at the very least, a painless withdrawal from something that did not work out as you had hoped.

What if . . . ?

This is the question you should ask yourself at the preparation stage and then discuss the answers with your family, friends, investors or advisers.

What if . . .

- **No one wants my product or services?** Have you researched the marketplace to gauge demand? Can you adapt your product or service in some way to appeal to a different market sector? Can you diversify and provide something else using the same materials/skills?
- **I can't make enough money from each piece of work to make a profit?** Perhaps you are concentrating on items that are too expensive and too time-consuming. If the market is not there, can you produce smaller, cheaper items that are less labour-intensive and have a higher profit margin? Would you make more money if you offered your skills for part of the process rather than for all of it? Or would it be still more profitable to write about or teach your skill rather than practising it?
- **I get more work than I can handle?** This is where the preparation comes in handy. You have to set up a back-up infrastructure at the beginning. This may be no more than getting to know people in your area with similar or related skills, finding out their availability and discussing with them the possibility that you may need their help at some time in the future and that you would be willing to reciprocate.

  Before you start up you can decide, as a family, which members would be available, capable and interested enough to help you if the orders came thick and fast. You may have friends who would be able to help you now and then on a part-time basis – several part-time helpers add up to at least two full-time pairs of hands.

Of course, in order to pay for extra help you will have to take a cut in profit and perhaps adjust your price structure to customers. This also has to be planned ahead; many rapidly expanding companies get caught off-guard when they are suddenly offered a large contract and grab it too quickly without adjusting prices first to allow for the employment of extra staff.

- **I get sick?** Again, you need to have back-up mechanisms set in place wherever possible to take care of the business side of things. On the personal side, however, it is a matter of adequate insurance cover. If you want to protect yourself (and your family) from loss of your income as a result of illness or death, consider topping up your life insurance and taking out permanent health insurance and perhaps critical illness insurance. You could also consider private medical insurance which would give you some control over the timing of an operation, so that you could either speed up the time it would take to get treated or organise it to coincide with a slack business period. You may also want to consider what is known as 'key person' insurance which can cover you against any business losses incurred by accident or unforeseen ill health.

- **My children get sick and I can't work because I am looking after them?** This depends on the economics of your business. How much money will you lose if you look after them yourself? In the early stages of your enterprise, probably not much. However, if you have a deadline to meet, or a new contract that is worth a lot of money to you, perhaps you can have grandparents to stay for the period of the illness or you can pay a friend to child-sit while his or her own children are at school. If this scenario is discussed with the parties concerned at a very early stage in your venture you will know that you have their agreement in principle and it is not something you have to worry about. (Those with live-in or live-out nannies for pre-school children won't have to worry anyway.) If you have no available grandparents or friends to bail you out, if the

27

finances can stand it and the work is that important, you could always hire an agency nurse for a week. After all, you will be in the house yourself, albeit shut away in another room, and available if there are problems.

- **I need more equipment?** If you can, budget at the beginning for future expansion. If you cannot put money away you will have to borrow the money to buy equipment outright, or investigate leasing or hire terms. Talk to your bank at the beginning – you will need to show them some sort of business plan and discuss what they may be able to offer you in the future and what they will charge for loans or overdraft facilities. Obtain information from the equipment manufacturers or hire centres – you may find that it works out cheaper to lease than to have a bank loan. But make all the enquiries at the beginning so that you know what your future outgoings are likely to be.

- **I need more space to cope with increased business?** Again, talk it over with your family, local authority and neighbours long before you need to do anything. Could you afford to build an extension to your house? You can even go through the whole process of drawing up plans and getting planning permission – the permission is valid for five years before it has to be resubmitted. But do discuss it with neighbours; it may be that they would object to any planned extension. It may also be the case that the local authority would refuse planning permission. If you investigate all these things at the outset you may discover that at a certain point in your business expansion you will either have to rent space outside the home, move to a bigger house, convert the cellar or loft, or move your work into a very large garden shed.

- **Customers won't pay their bills?** First, you have to be very strict about payment terms, invoicing and following up invoices. Don't do commissioned work such as a wedding dress, a painting or a piece of furniture on credit; ask for payments along the way. Find out what your local solicitor will charge for sending intimidating letters to bad payers – some solicitors now offer a cheap service for this. Make a resolution, from the beginning, that if anyone defaults on a bill more than twice you will no longer carry out work for them. If all else fails you can go to a factoring company or a specialist debt-collecting agency. They will undertake to collect the monies owed to you in return for a percentage.

- **Employers don't pay me?** Make sure at the outset that you don't get a job with one of the blacklisted companies that have a reputation for very low pay and defaulting on wages. Various organisations can advise you on this (see Chapter 3). Once an employer has defaulted, the first thing is to find out why. If it is because of bankruptcy you will be contacted by the Official Receiver and asked to put in your bid for monies owed to you. If it is for some other reason, you may need the advice of ACAS★ and perhaps a solicitor. It is best to know your rights before seeking home employment.
- **My source of supplies dries up?** You should never totally rely on one supplier. Right from the beginning you should investigate and source from more than one supplier as an insurance policy in the event of a supplier going bust or being unable to get materials from a certain part of the world.

CASE HISTORY: Reuben

Reuben, a single man who recently completed an MA at university, started up his own business as an online translator. He speaks seven European languages and he offers a fast translation service of business documents via email. Although he was very happy and successful running this business he found that he felt very isolated not having a family around him, so decided to get planning permission to convert the ground floor of his house into a group of small offices and rent out the space to like-minded individuals. There are now four individuals operating small e-businesses from Reuben's house and he is able to interact with others during the day but still remain independent.

- **I get too lonely and don't like working by myself but I don't want to go back to working for someone else?** Many people have found themselves in this situation and have solved it by 'renting a desk' locally. If you feel that you want to work for yourself, but you need interaction with others during the working day, then the best solution is to rent some space near your home in a local office building, or industrial estate, or to offer space in your homeworking environment to a friend who is in a similar situation. Don't abandon a potentially better way of life just because you are the sort of person who finds it difficult to work alone. Organisations such as Women in Business★, The Home Business Alliance★ and the Telework Association★ may be able to put you in touch with people in a similar position in your area.

Ready to start?

Preparation is essential before you start to earn money from home. Choose your line of work, then do your market research. Next, you have to sort out your finances – start-up costs, running costs, banking and accounting methods. And you have to cost your work correctly, if you are to cover all your outgoings and make a profit. The following chapter will set you off on the right path.

Chapter 2

What can you do?

Having analysed your motives, needs and personality you have decided that you are suited to working from home. You may, of course, already know what you want to do, or you may have absolutely no idea. It's worthwhile looking at the options. As you will see, there is plenty of choice for those seeking a home-based occupation – perhaps even too much. It is essential to take time to decide exactly what is right for you; it is best not to rush into anything.

If you are starting with a clean slate you need to do as much research as possible. Talk to people, listen to conversations, read the local newspapers and magazines, browse the notices in your local library, shop windows, leisure centre and parish magazine. Keep a file of information, articles and comments which will contribute towards pointing you in the direction of your new career. Browse on the Internet and look at the sort of home-based jobs that are on offer through reputable agencies. By all means look at some of the dotcom businesses on offer, but ask your local Trading Standards Department if it has any knowledge or advice regarding some of these operators before you make any commitments.

If you want to work for someone else, get as much advice as possible about what work is available, how to apply for it and how to safeguard your rights.

Once you know how you are going to earn money at home, you need to start organising the business side of things and gathering information for the future (see Chapters 5, 6 and 7). First, though, you need to look at the assets you have, in the way of skills, specialist knowledge, qualifications etc., that will play a role in your decision about what work to do.

What will actually earn you money?

Is it your **skill**? Do you know whether your skill is in demand, whether it has scarcity value, or whether it represents a luxury purchase or a need in today's society? Think of a skill that is in demand – invisible mending, perhaps. Commuters damage expensive suits travelling to and from the big city and they need to be repaired. Most dry cleaners offer invisible mending and this is usually done by homeworkers. All you have to do is offer your services to every dry cleaning shop in your area. If they do not need you now, they may keep your details on file for later.

Think of a skill that is rare. There is a lack of watch and clock repairers in towns today, for example. Obviously, jewellers employ such craftspeople but, again, they are usually homeworkers. You could offer them your services, but you may think that there are enough people around with watch and clock problems to make it worth your while to advertise locally.

Perhaps you are a management consultant, highly skilled at assessing a company's problems and coming up with the appropriate solutions. But does the current economic climate affect your value? Are you, as a management consultant, a necessity, or have you become a luxury that no one can afford until times get better?

Perhaps what you are really selling is your **time**? Your skills may be limited, and your most valuable asset is that you can serve those busy customers who do not have the time to perform certain tasks themselves, such as ironing, lawnmowing, window-cleaning, dog-walking, housework, laundry, cooking, preparation for a party, typing, envelope stuffing, mailshots, and so on. When you think about ways in which you can save other people time, the list is quite long.

Then, again, perhaps it is your **effort** that is most valuable? You can do all the heavy or unpleasant jobs that your customers cannot manage – digging, building and repairs, tree-felling, cleaning stonework, laying patios, cleaning out drains, pest control, roof and gutter repair, chimney sweeping and so on. If you are strong, don't mind heights or smells, are not afraid of rats or getting yourself dirty and sweaty, then you could be in great demand!

CASE HISTORY: Esther

Esther lives in a rural community within commuting distance of a large metropolitan area. Her children have grown up and left home and she has recently been widowed. She has no need to work from a financial point of view, but she has a need to get out of the house. Her greatest pleasure is walking her two dogs, whatever the weather. She noticed, to her distress, that many of the people in her village kept dogs but were out at work all day, leaving the dogs shut indoors for long periods. Esther decided to start up a dog-walking service. She had some leaflets printed and put them through every door in her village and the two neighbouring ones, offering to walk dogs twice a day for half an hour for a fairly modest sum. The response was tremendous. Because she is well-known in the area, people are happy to give her their door keys. She lets herself in, takes the dog out for a walk and then takes it back home again. She makes a fair amount of money because she walks several dogs at once, piling them all in the back of her estate car and taking them to the nearest open area.

Perhaps your **ingenuity, analytical skills and creative flair** are valuable to your customers. They come to you when they want a problem solved, a new image, a new direction. You may be a consultant, a graphic artist, an advertising agent or a PR genius, an interior designer, a garden designer, a clothes designer or a milliner.

Or is it your **specialist knowledge** which will really earn you the money? Others might benefit from your knowledge in certain areas because you do research for them, you give them health and beauty therapy or you advise them on insurance and pension plans. Perhaps you drive a taxi or are a local tourist guide – both professions requiring intimate knowledge of the local area. You can write books and articles, give lectures and demonstrations on your specialist subject. You pass your knowledge on to other people and they pay for your services.

You may have **qualifications** which equip you to train others. You are a private tutor in your own home to schoolchildren who need extra tuition in certain subjects; you perhaps teach the piano or some other musical instrument; or you train people to drive cars or ride bikes safely. Perhaps you are involved in a literacy programme, you teach English to foreigners or you are fluent in another language. Cookery and needlework can be taught in the home, as can carpentry, silver- and goldsmithing and many other crafts.

Perhaps your familiarity with **technology** will enable you to earn money as a remote IT worker. Many large companies need large quantities of data processed – to enable them to function as an international mail-order publisher, for example. It doesn't matter to them where their data processors are based as long as they can receive and transmit the relevant material when required.

Maybe it's your **personality** that earns you money. It could enable you to sell effectively, to keep small children amused, to look after the sick and the elderly, or to soothe people's troubles away with a massage and an attentive manner. You may have the skills and qualifications to be an excellent hairdresser or chiropodist but very few customers will invite you into their homes if you do not have a warm personality. It's just as important as any diploma.

CASE HISTORY: Malcolm

Malcolm lives in a remote area of Scotland where jobs are scarce. However, a large financial organisation did a recruiting campaign in his area to enrol staff to sell financial products over the telephone. The company held 'auditions' to find personable people with clear speaking voices and Malcolm was successful. After a two-day training programme he now sells the products to people all over the UK. The parent company provides him with the contacts – individuals who have filled in enquiry forms in the national press – so he is only telephoning people who have displayed an initial interest in the product. He is paid a low basic wage plus commission on every sale achieved and, obviously, his telephone bill is paid by the company.

Your business options

When weighing up the choices, look at your existing skills, new skills you may need to acquire, and opportunities you feel the marketplace may offer. You may decide that you want a complete change of direction in life. Whatever you are planning, this chapter may give you some options that you had not considered before.

Translate an existing job into a home-based one

As mentioned in Chapter 1, many teleworkers have done just that –
and many more, thanks to the new legislation regarding flexible
working patterns, will be able to join them. Employers increasingly
allow their employees to contribute to the corporate workload from
their home base. This is an ideal scenario because you are doing a
job which probably suits you very well in terms of skills and
aptitude and you are still an employee, with the attendant financial
security. However, only a small percentage of the working population will be able to take advantage of this option.

CASE HISTORY: Hardip

Hardip worked for a large entertainment organisation in the
computer section. His job was to amend the huge mailing list that
was held on computer. Hardip's section of the organisation was
sold to another group and some of the workforce were offered the
chance to work from home. Hardip has a young family and he
relished the chance to spend more time with them, so he opted for
the teleworker offer. His salary decreased slightly but this was
offset by the fact that he no longer had to pay fares. All his other
benefits – pension, medical insurance and so on – stay the same.
Because he is an employee, the computer hardware and modem
belong to his employers and his contract forbids him to use them to
do any other work or to introduce any unauthorised software or
disks because of the risk of viruses. He works from 9a.m. until
3.30p.m., which exactly coincides with his children's school hours.
The job is working out so well that Hardip's wife is considering
getting a part-time job because Hardip is able to take the children
to school, fetch them home and look after them.

With the technological explosion of the Internet, it has become
possible for those who have the appropriate skills to work for themselves and use their knowledge to set up a home-based business or
consultancy, or become freelancers. The Internet and electronic
mail (email) have become powerful business tools for finding and
distributing information, advertising, selling products and services

and conducting business globally without the need to step outside your front door. Many employment agencies have set up Internet divisions which deal purely with home-based job opportunities. Many companies are now looking at the widespread use of remote workers who may be employees or self-employed.

It is not just office-based employees who may choose to leave employment. Other professions whose practitioners can easily set up at home include hairdressers, beauticians, masseurs, chiropodists and upholsterers, for example. All can offer a visiting service to clients in their own homes or have clients come to them.

Translate existing employment knowledge into your own venture

Many people who have worked for years in particular industries find that now, with the aid and support of computer technology, they can set up their own business or consultancy at home, using the knowledge they have gained over many years. Take publishing, for example – it is now possible to become a modestly successful one-man/-woman publisher of books, pamphlets and magazines at home by using desktop packages to create professional products. Teaching from home has become a popular option for retired or disabled teachers who have a thorough knowledge of the National Curriculum and can offer specialist tuition. Some people now run their own small agencies from home, capitalising on expertise gained when in the employ of large agencies: these agencies offer anything from domestic staff to travel or public relations.

Develop new skills by training part-time

This is a popular route to a new career for people who are approaching retirement and for anyone who is returning to the job market. Many younger people, bored and frustrated in full-time employment that does not offer any stimulation, have also turned to adult education classes to provide them with new qualifications to restart a career, and the range and diversity of courses (part-time, day release, evening classes) on offer is surprising.

Training does not have to be lengthy or demanding – it is possible to acquire certain skills, provided one has a talent for them, in just a few months. Cake decorating, picture framing and keyboard skills are examples.

Sometimes people are already highly skilled in certain areas but feel that they need the appropriate diplomas or certificates to give extra confidence to their customers. In this case it may be possible, by arrangement with the local adult education institute, to sit the examinations without attending classes. Provided you can satisfy the principal of the institute that you are skilled in the relevant field (perhaps by producing testimonials from past employers) there should be no problem.

Develop an interest into a service

Some popular money-making ventures do not require any particular skills, just a keen interest in the subject. Many people who love animals and children begin a profitable home-based career by pet-sitting or baby-sitting. Looking after pets or children for a short period in the homes where they live requires no qualifications. Take note, however, that if you were to open a kennel or cattery in your garden or take children into your home every day you would have to be registered with the appropriate authorities, abide by the existing regulations and be subject to regular inspections.

A love of libraries, a familiarity with library systems and an interest in certain topics have led many people to offer their services as researchers for authors and academics. No particular qualifications need to be obtained by a would-be researcher other than an extensive knowledge of a particular subject matter and the ability to locate the necessary sources of information.

CASE HISTORY: Matthew

Matthew has been interested in genealogy all his life and has done volunteer research work for various people since he was a teenager. He knows his way so well around the Public Record Office in Kew that someone recommended him to an American writer who needed to do some research in England but did not have the time. Matthew enjoyed the work and was quite well paid, so he decided to advertise his availability as a researcher in various publications. The response was very encouraging and he is now a full-time researcher of English social history.

Gardening is one area where many people have made an interest into a profitable career. No one asks the jobbing gardener whether he or she has trained at a horticultural college. Someone who sets themselves up as a garden designer or offers landscaping services or tree surgery, though, will find that customers are likely to be a little more particular.

CASE HISTORY: Anne

Anne is approaching early retirement at the age of 57 and feels that although she will be financially secure, she does not want to give up a working life. For the last two years she has been attending a part-time course in horticulture, with the intention of becoming a garden designer when she finally retires from her full-time job. Already an avid gardener with an extensive knowledge of horticulture, she nevertheless wants to get the formal qualifications in order to inspire her future customers with confidence.

Develop a hobby into a business

It is not unusual to make a hobby pay in some small way, even if you have no intention of turning it into a business. Materials are so expensive nowadays that very few people can afford to, say, make picture frames or small pieces of furniture without occasionally offering them up for sale so that they can afford to buy new materials.

Sometimes skilled hobbyists are spurred along the road to self-employment after donating a piece of work to a charitable sale and being surprised at how quickly and profitably it sells. After you decide to charge for items, an appraisal has to be done regarding the demand for the work, the price the customer is prepared to pay, and how much the work is realistically worth after time, labour and materials have been properly costed. Sadly, many beautiful crafts are greatly undervalued when one considers the time and effort that are put into them. However, the materials may not be expensive and although you should always approach self-employment with the intention of making enough money to cover all overheads, you cannot strictly apply the rule if you are a second-income generator with a great love for your craftwork. Satisfaction is worth a great deal in life and, as one happy and fulfilled needlewoman says, 'I regard my little business as therapy that pays for itself!'

CASE HISTORY: Stanley

Stanley's lifelong hobby has been breeding budgerigars and his birds have won many awards in shows. Various people at the shows kept asking him if they could buy some of his birds and, eventually, he decided to make this a full-time job. He sells the birds through the hobby magazine and to reputable pet shops and garden centres (which he personally inspects). He also writes articles on the subject and has just finished writing his first book.

Do unskilled work at home for someone else

This may be the only option open to you if you have no skills or hobbies to develop nor the time to train for a new career.

Many of the people who work at home for an outside employer are doing the type of work generally done in a factory, assembling anything from watch straps to fire extinguishers, making toys or lampshades, filling Christmas crackers, or finishing textile products. A lot of such work is done for the clothing industry. Much of the work is repetitive, requires little skill (but calls for attention) and does not lead to the satisfaction of seeing the finished product.

Finding such work and ensuring that you are getting a fair deal is not easy. It has to be approached with some caution and it is best to be aware of possible pitfalls before answering advertisements for unskilled homework (see Chapter 3).

Do skilled work at home for someone else

This is a more promising line of work to pursue, because if you have a skill that is in demand you will be paid a reasonable rate by an employer.

This type of work may be more difficult to find and may require some marketing on your part. For example, if you are a skilled hand – or machine – knitter but you do not want the insecurity or the hassle of working for yourself, you may have to approach local wool shops, haberdashers or clothes shops to see if they would be interested in paying you for garments.

CASE HISTORY: Donald

Donald is an unskilled homeworker. He has learning disabilities and cannot easily find a job. However, his mother answered an advertisement for homeworkers in the local paper and found that the work was simple, consisting of filling Christmas crackers with paper hats, mottoes and toys. Donald quite enjoys this work and has become good at it. It doesn't pay very much but it is enough to give him some independence.

Wool manufacturers are always looking for skilled knitters, but bear in mind that there are only a handful of manufacturers and many thousands of good knitters.

People in the Scottish Highlands and Islands have, of course, been homeworkers or outworkers for centuries, producing sweaters, tartan cloth and so on for clothing manufacturers who pay them by the piece. Many clothing manufacturers employ homeworkers to sew small parts of garments together or to finish or inspect them. Most employers are honest and fair but the textile and clothing industries have borne a bad reputation in the past for taking advantage of homeworkers.

CASE HISTORY: Sandra

Sandra is a skilled homeworker. She hand-knits beautiful Fair Isle sweaters for a Scottish company which sells them mainly through tourist shops in Scotland and abroad. She has actually seen some of her sweaters in a Scottish shop in an international airport. Sandra got the job because she lives near the company and she was able to show them some samples of her knitting. She is a fast worker and is paid a good rate for the sweaters, which sell for quite a high price. The company supplies the wool and specifies the pattern she is to knit. She enjoys the work and knits five days a week for a good eight hours in between the hours of 10a.m. and 10p.m., with frequent breaks.

Crafts are not the only skills that can be turned into businesses. Looking after children is a skill in great demand today, and in most areas there would be no shortage of customers for a registered child-minder. Computer skills too are much sought after, and many small companies will subcontract their computer repair, maintenance and training work to a suitably qualified person who works from home. Often distance is no barrier. Teleworkers work for very remote employers. Companies based in North America often advertise for teleworkers anywhere in the world. Many smaller companies and publishing houses often seek the services of keyboard operators to type and correct documents and manuscripts on disk.

Work as a salesperson via the Internet

This type of work has to be approached with caution. There are many companies nowadays offering dotcom 'business opportunities' which usually involve selling some kind of service or product. The more people you get to subscribe (and provide credit-card details so that they can be debited every month or whenever), the more you will earn. Typical e-products are diet plans, newsletters or other self-help/health material. Most of these schemes do not require any initial outlay, but they will undoubtedly involve some hard-selling techniques and, possibly, expenditure on sending emails or faxes. (See Chapter 4 for more information.)

CASE HISTORY: Natalie

Natalie is at home with a small baby and she has another child at primary school. One day, while browsing on the Internet, she came across several websites that were offering Internet marketing schemes. One, which particularly attracted her, was a slimming club package which she felt she could easily sell to other mothers at her son's primary school. For every person who subscribes, Natalie receives 30 per cent of their subscription fee. However, she is rapidly running out of prospects in her immediate circle and she has been advised to start marketing more aggressively, which will involve putting up posters in the town and selling on the telephone.

Turn your house or land into a money earner

There are endless ways in which you can make your house or land earn you some money and these are covered in detail in Chapter 13. Almost all the options outlined in Chapter 13, ranging from operating a modest bed and breakfast to running a caravan site, require a thorough knowledge of a variety of legislation and may involve planning permission, payment of business rates, fire certificates, food hygiene regulations, and licensing laws among other considerations.

CASE HISTORY: Caroline

Caroline and her husband bought a large, very run-down Georgian house in Derbyshire because they loved it. They discovered that there was a lot of interesting history attached to the house and the surrounding land, so they set about making the house pay for itself. They took out a loan to renovate it and turned it into a corporate hospitality and conference venue. By advertising in the right business magazines and mailing suitable companies they have now built up a regular clientele of large firms that use the house and land for PR functions, training and survival courses and private meetings. Caroline supplies food and drink and the local hotel provides accommodation if necessary, although most of the companies stage one-day events.

Buy an existing one-man/-woman business

This can be an excellent way to start self-employment because it saves a great deal of initial research into customer demand, provided the business is healthy, the individual who is selling has a loyal client list and there is plenty of goodwill.

Often, someone who has run a successful small business as, say, a dressmaker, a mobile hairdresser or a window-cleaner has to retire, or to give up because of ill health or family commitments. Usually the clients are very happy for someone else to take over and continue to run the business.

You could advertise in the local paper or in shop windows that you are looking for such a business. Someone who is thinking about retiring but has not yet got around to doing anything about it may see it and act upon it. Also you can often hear of such openings through the grapevine.

The ideal scenario is that you work in tandem with the existing owner for several months before the final takeover so that the customers get to know you and you can be sure of retaining the goodwill and the healthy customer base. Accountants working for each party can calculate the price of the business based on projected turnover, any assets (such as machinery or vehicles) and the goodwill element. From such a base you can expand if you wish when the time is right.

Buy a totally new business

'New' does not necessarily mean unproven. It is possible to buy the franchise to operate a business that has a good track record elsewhere in the country or even abroad and then develop your own customer base.

CASE HISTORY: Aidan

Aidan was an unemployed bricklayer who was considering becoming self-employed when his father-in-law suggested that they buy a franchise. This was a mechanised repointing service for brick and stone properties, which was within both their areas of work experience. The company offered complete back-up in the form of training and marketing. Aidan and his father-in-law put some of their savings towards the cost of the franchise and got a bank loan for the rest. The bank investigated the franchise thoroughly and found it to be satisfactory.

Many successful one man/-woman franchises are mobile – you take a service to the customer but you are based, for administration purposes, at home. Examples are carpet and upholstery steam cleaning, car valeting, baked potato stands and doughnut stands. Others are based mainly in the home, with some travel to make deliveries, such as T-shirt or business-card printing. All of these services could, of course, be set up from scratch, if your research showed that the market demand was there. The equipment for most of these services can be bought separately and the manufacturers of the equipment will give the necessary training. Some franchises can be very expensive (although many require only a minimum investment of £3,000) and it is worth investigating whether you could assemble the whole package cheaper yourself. After all, many of the small franchises on offer are not common household names so it is doubtful whether having their label would generate more sales.

Set up a new service from scratch

This route requires the most market research, the most preparation and the most faith. If you are convinced that in your area, or your field of knowledge, there is a genuine need for the service you propose to offer – and it requires very little capital to start it up, thereby minimising the risk – then go for it.

There are many shining examples of how such acts of faith have paid off. Specialist mail-order services offering such products as top-quality cookware, patchwork quilt sets, hand-made wooden toys and early music cassettes, for example, have all been started by one person who believed that there was a section of the community that shared his or her interest, did some mailshots and saw things blossom from there. Many are now thriving businesses that employ dozens of people. Sometimes a glaring gap in the market and a sense of frustration prompt someone to set up a service. The lack of a good local clock and watch repair service, fancy dress hire, children's entertainer or driving school – it could be anything that is not easily available, but in demand.

Re-inventing a product or service

This can mean taking ideas or products from the past and recreating them for the future. Several retail and mail-order companies have successfully done this by capitalising on the modern trend of nostalgia for the past. For example, replicas of Georgian and Victorian house and garden ornaments have proved very popular. Reproductions of old nursery equipment, cookware, bed-linen and personal items have also enjoyed a revival in recent years.

It is possible to get ideas for businesses by looking at services that were provided in the past and are no longer available – a dolls' hospital, for example, where toys of all kinds are repaired. This was a commonly available service before the Second World War.

CASE HISTORY: Paul

Paul makes pottery and has worked from home for several years. His business was in the doldrums until one day he saw a gardening programme on television which showed Victorian terracotta domes that could be put over any plants that needed forcing or blanching, such as rhubarb. Paul made some reproductions successfully, so he decided to try to market them. The demand was extraordinary, and he only just managed to keep up with it. He has now taken on two more potters, who both work in their own homes. He intends to copy some other pieces of antique garden pottery and market them to his existing customers.

Sell goods made by other people

One example of this would be distributing foreign goods in Britain. The US Department of Trade publishes a regular magazine listing companies looking for facilities and distributors, and the British Chambers of Commerce* has a regular listing of businesses seeking partners willing to manufacture under licence or to act as sole distributors.

On a more modest level, if selling is your forte – in other words you enjoy meeting people, talking to them, can be persuasive, have the courage to test new ground and can handle rejection – perhaps you can come to an arrangement with a friend who manufactures or produces marketable items but does not actually have the time to sell them. You could agree on a commission on each item sold and then discuss realistic production targets. Don't persuade a shop to order thousands of items that your friend cannot possibly manufacture on his or her own!

Many people make a good living out of being agents for mail-order companies – the large catalogues that offer everything for the home and family. They earn commission on each item ordered (or, rather, paid for) by the customers they get on to their books. One of the most successful international mail-order companies is Avon, the

45

cosmetics manufacturer. It has hundreds of thousands of agents working for it all over the world.

Some children's publishers now sell to homes and schools rather than through bookshops, as the percentage of the cover price taken by the wholesalers and the retail shops is far greater than the commission paid to agents.

Other people sell successfully through 'party' schemes, selling well-known brands of clothing, jewellery, toys and even sex aids and underwear. This involves getting as many customers as possible together at a friend's house for a 'party' with wine and snacks, and persuading them to place orders for the wares. The person hosting the 'party' usually gets a payment or free gift from the salesman or woman. The aim is to hold parties in as many different areas as possible so that you tap into as many social groups as you can.

CASE HISTORY: Tricia

Tricia sells high-class costume jewellery as an agent. She usually sells through the party system, going to someone's house to demonstrate the jewellery to their friends, but sometimes she rents some space in a hospital or factory canteen and takes orders from the workers. She makes a good commission from the agency, but she does have to work at least four evenings a week and several mornings or lunch periods. She had to pay for her sample case and has to purchase any new additions to the range, but does not have to buy and resell to the customers – she just takes the orders and deducts her commission from the money she collects before processing the orders.

Network marketing comes under the category of selling products made by other people. The difference between being involved in network marketing and the other schemes outlined above is that most of the other sales schemes should not require the agent to part with any money at all at the outset, except perhaps in the case of the 'party' schemes where a modest sum is paid for a pack of samples, or a returnable deposit is given to the manufacturers to safeguard against theft. Some network marketing schemes, on the other hand, require the participants to buy the goods or services and then sell them on. Participants also receive bonuses for recruiting other sales staff and take commissions on the new recruit's sales.

Sometimes the parent companies demand payment for providing training to the sales force. Some companies will ask for a modest registration fee (between £20 and £50) in order to eliminate time-wasters, but should provide training, whether face-to-face or in the form of manuals and videos, for nothing. Many people join these schemes because they are impressed by the success stories of other participants. Be warned that any company which expects you to buy vast quantities of its products and sell them on, rather than asking you to buy a few samples and then re-order when you have sold them, is not operating in a reputable way. Companies that are more concerned about the number of agents you recruit rather than the number of products you sell should also be viewed with suspicion. Successful and stable companies go for slow growth of their marketing networks so that they can keep up with manufacturing demand. A successful and reputable company will have regular contact with its sales agents to discuss tactics, sales opportunities and public feedback about products.

Run your own mail-order business

Mail order is one of the most popular businesses to run from home. As a form of selling it is attractive to people who have no aptitude or desire to sell face-to-face or to those who are tied to the home through disability or small children. Those who run a mail-order operation also find that they can make more profit on items if they do not sell them through shops.

Selling goods or services by mail order is regulated by The Consumer Protection (Distance Selling) Regulations 2000, which are covered in greater detail in Chapters 9 and 11. You may choose to use the Internet as your sole marketing tool. Setting up an effective website is covered in Chapter 10.

A mail-order enterprise does not have to be about selling your own manufactured products. It can be a collection of other people's products that, together, represent a new idea. For example, a woman in Yorkshire found it impossible to get pure cotton clothing for her children, who both suffered badly from eczema. So she put together a collection of basic cotton clothes for babies, toddlers and children, some of which came from overseas manufacturers, and marketed them through the Eczema Society and direct mailshots to doctors' surgeries and health centres.

Marketing is another important area of successful mail order. Research your market thoroughly beforehand to ensure there will be a demand for your product. Many people start off with just one product or service. They advertise this in the relevant publications and start slowly. It is important that customers are protected from unscrupulous or incompetent mail-order operations, but it is equally important that any mail-order operation does not run into financial trouble early on because of extending credit to customers. Most small mail-order companies ask for payment with each order. Only some companies are likely to be able to invoice for payment after delivery of goods – for example, business-to-business mail-order set-ups that can offer reputable company clients an account.

Chapter 3

Working for someone else at home

Working for someone else can take several forms, as was briefly discussed in Chapter 1.

Firstly, there are employees, who work at home full-time or part-time, for a company, large or small, and interact with their employer via a PC or other piece of equipment. They should have the same rights as an employee of that company who works in the head office.

Then there are employees of subcontracted companies (such as those companies that provide telephone services to other organisations). These employees should also have standard employee rights and benefits, but they could be on a modest basic rate of pay with bonuses for volume or quantity of work undertaken.

Freelancers are self-employed and they may work for one company, under contract, or several companies. These people usually have skills which are needed by their clients, such as IT skills, creative skills or some other speciality. These workers are responsible for their own tax and National Insurance and invoice their clients for their fees.

The last category is made up of the people with little or no specialist skills who work at home for an employer who requires them to do menial, and often repetitive, tasks such as packing or assembling products, sewing and envelope addressing. These people are called homeworkers or outworkers and can be employees, but are more likely to be self-employed. Although the pay for such work is likely to be low, it should be subject to the Minimum Wage Agreement of £3.60 an hour for workers aged 18–21 and £4.20 an hour for workers over the age of 22. However, in reality, there are still many companies that manage to sidestep the regulations.

Types of work available

All the above types of working from home have changed during the last few years and will continue to evolve as the marketplace changes and new legislation is created.

The employee

Confusion arises when employees of companies who choose or are encouraged to work from home are called, variously, teleworkers, remote workers or flexible workers. All the labels are, technically, correct, but the marketplace has been refined somewhat and the descriptions do seem to mean different things now. **Teleworker** is a term which seems to be applied to employees whose work is specifically to do with technology – i.e. is computer-based – and therefore requires them to work at a terminal at home or in a telecentre. **Remote workers** are employees who could undertake any type of work, for example, marketing or consultancy. They use their home as an office base but they travel around seeing the companies' clients or customers. **Flexible workers** are employees who may have a flexible location (on the move, at home, a telecentre or satellite office), flexible working hours (for example, they may work at home some of the week, job-share or have compressed working weeks etc.) or flexible contracts.

The term **e-worker** (electronic) or **m-worker** (mobile) could be applied to all of the above, since it describes the hardware used to communicate with the employer and not the type of work undertaken. Whatever employers choose to call their home-based employees, this section of the homeworking market is predicted to expand because of the various factors outlined in Chapter 1.

CASE HISTORY: Morris

Morris used to work in a factory assembling computer leads. When he retired at the age of 65, the company asked him if he would like to do the same work at home as an outworker. The rates of pay being offered were the same and Morris decided that he would do it part-time to give himself a bit of extra money. He works every morning and earns about £120 from the comfort of his living room, doing a job that he finds very easy.

This predicted surge has caused concern among the white collar unions that home-based employees should have the same rights as their conventional office-based colleagues. This concern culminated in a large number of employers and trade unions signing an EU agreement in July 2002 guaranteeing equal rights in employment, training, and health and safety for all home-based employees. It is an EU-wide Collective Agreement, not EU legislation, however, and there is some doubt as to whether it affords home-based employees legal protection. The Department of Trade and Industry (DTI)★ states that the Agreement will be enforced in the UK and the CBI and TUC insist that it will be given the same respect as other employment legislation.

The basic framework of the Agreement is as follows.

- Home-based work should be voluntary.
- A full job description and written information about lines of communication and responsibilities should be given to the employee, as well as a properly negotiated contract of employment.
- Home-based employees should have the same rights and benefits as office-based colleagues.
- The employer is responsible for the protection of any data used and processed.
- The home-based worker's privacy has to be respected and any monitoring system must be 'proportionate to the objective'.
- All questions concerning work, equipment, liability and costs should be defined in advance.
- The employer remains responsible for occupational health and safety.
- Workload and performance standards should be equivalent to those of comparable workers at the employer's premises.
- Home-based workers should be given the same opportunities as other workers in terms of training, career development and appraisal.

The freelancer

Freelancers can effectively do what they like, since they find their own work and organise their own hours. However, a freelancer is not to be confused with someone who is running his or her own business from home. Freelancers usually work for other people

---

CASE HISTORY: Rani

Rani started her working life as a teleworker when her employer, a major national bank, decided to offer some of its computer staff the chance to work from home, processing data. She jumped at the opportunity. Her salary was very slightly reduced but she was provided with all the necessary hardware to enable her to work from home. However, after a while the bank became involved in a merger and decided to abandon the experiment of using teleworkers. Although Rani was offered her old job back at the head office in London, she had become used to not commuting and wanted to stay at home. She joined the Telework Assocation and answered an advertisement in its magazine for a bank in America that wanted someone to process cheque payments in sterling in the UK. Rani got the job. She now receives a weekly download of data from the USA, which she processes, printing out cheques, orders and statements, which are then collected by bike for the manager of the London branch to check and sign.

---

under contract. Their work may keep them at home all the time (as in the case of writers, cartoonists and software designers) or they may just use their home as a base and travel around a great deal.

The freelance market has expanded recently in tandem with the development of the Internet. There are many agencies specialising in freelance contracts (admittedly a lot of these are IT-related jobs) which operate through the Internet, offering free subscription, that is, emailing subscribers with the latest contract opportunities.

Freelancers should ensure that all their work is supported by written contracts which detail the following:

- the nature of the job (details of what the client expects the freelancer to provide)
- the length of the job or the deadline by which the job should be completed
- the rate of pay/fee for the job, and when and how it will be paid
- the responsibilities of both parties, that is, who is responsible for equipment/travel expenses/any other expenses incurred

- whether the client is insuring the freelancer for the period of the contract. For example, a freelance consultant engineer who is engaged to manage a project for a few months might reasonably expect to be covered by the client's company insurance in the event of death or injury on site
- any other conditions/penalties/benefits that are relevant.

The homeworker

Sometimes called outworking, this is the low or unskilled end of the homeworking marketplace and the one which causes the most concern. The National Group on Homeworking (NGH)* estimates that there are approximately one million industrial homeworkers in the UK, and publish the following facts.

- Pay is sometimes as low as 15 pence per hour.
- Most homeworkers have few automatic employment rights, such as the right to redundancy pay, sick pay or unfair dismissal rights.
- Health and safety information and provision is often inadequate.
- Homeworkers are entitled to be paid the National Minimum Wage.
- Many of these workers are incorrectly classified as self-employed which restricts their entitlement to state benefits, such as JobSeeker's Allowance, maternity and sickness benefits, and redundancy payments if the work ceases.
- Even if their employers are considered to be reputable, many homeworkers are subject to hidden costs (such as use of their own power supply) for which they are not compensated by the employer.

However, it is possible to find decent unskilled or semi-skilled work to do at home if you are prepared to search for a reasonable employer who is prepared to negotiate fair terms (see below).

Looking for work

You may be one of those people who has been given the opportunity by their employer to do the same job at home and have the same salary, pensions rights and other benefits. Or you may be able to carve out a decent freelance career for yourself, using your skills in a marketplace that is crying out for them.

If you have skills, then you can register with some of the many employment agencies on the Internet. The traditional agencies all have home-based work opportunity listings now and, as mentioned earlier, there are agencies specifically geared up for the freelance and IT markets.

For those with IT skills, a good first step in the search for an employed job or freelance work would be to join the Telework Association* and get a copy of their *Teleworking Handbook*, which is filled with a great deal of useful and practical advice. Members of the Association who subscribe to their online service get job information emailed to them on a regular basis.

There are also several agencies on the Internet which deal specifically with IT jobs. In certain rural areas in the UK there are telework job agencies or skills registers which put skilled teleworkers together with employers or clients – local examples include ICT Marketing* in Wales, Shetland Enterprise* and Work Global* (in the Western Isles).

Starting from scratch

If you are looking for work to do from home but are unsure what you could do, your first port of call could be your local library. A good reference library should stock various business directories which will give details about companies and what they manufacture. Some research should pinpoint those companies who assemble small items and, possibly, use homeworkers. You could then approach these companies by telephone, mail or by personal visit to see whether they do employ homeworkers and whether they have any vacancies. If they do employ homeworkers but have no vacancies, leave your details and check back with them every month or so.

Be careful

Most of the Low Pay Units (LPUs) and Homeworking projects in the UK have spent the last few years working in tandem with local Trading Standards Departments to protect people against misleading homeworking adverts and schemes.

The National Group on Homeworking★ and its colleague groups, which deal with the unskilled end of the job market, have highlighted three main kinds of fraudulent homeworking operation. There are many others, however, so beware. Chapter 4 deals with these in detail and how to protect yourself against them.

All the LPU and Homeworking groups contacted during the writing of this book had produced an information leaflet or pack for the general public, warning against fraudulent schemes and giving advice on how to avoid becoming one of the victims. Trading Standards Departments at your local council offices should also have advice packs available.

Looking for genuine work

If you have specialist skills then you should have some knowledge of the marketplace in which you can make use of your skills. You will need to market yourself fairly aggressively, either by networking with people or by sending mailshots, emails or faxes. If you have IT skills, we have discussed opposite where you can look for work.

Local or national firms

If you have no particular skills, but some work experience, you could contact local companies to see if they have any homeworking opportunities. If you have any previous relevant work experience, tell them about it, and also whether you have any equipment of your own at home, for example a sewing or knitting machine, and what hours you may be able to work. Also tell them about any outside interests that you have; running social groups and serving on committees can demonstrate organisational and managerial skills as much as any work experience. Even if you know that the company does not employ homeworkers at present, you may be lucky enough to catch them at the moment they are considering doing so or else inspire them to do it.

Other routes

You can ask your local trade unions if they know of any opportunities. They may also be able to warn you against some ventures. The local JobCentre may have some homeworking on its books. Your local Business Link★, Chamber of Commerce, or other trade organisations may have details of companies that have just started up or are expanding and are employing homeworkers as a result. It is worth making enquiries in all sorts of places – you never know whether you could suddenly stumble across a useful contact who can offer you a job.

Please note that the LPUs and Homeworking Groups are *not* able to tell you where you can find a job; they are primarily there to offer advice on employment rights and to undertake work that protects homeworkers from exploitation of any kind. However, they can send you advice packs which point you in the right direction when you start to look for homework.

Disabled workers

People with disabilities can contact the following:

- Disability Alliance★ – deals specifically with benefit issues but publishes two useful publications, *Self-Employment – Why Not* and *Moving into Work*
- Royal Association for Disability and Rehabilitation (RADAR)★ – an organisation that represents disabled people and leads campaigns to influence society and government for greater inclusion of the disabled
- Disability Rights Commission★ – provides advice about the Disability Discrimination Act
- Employment Opportunities for People with Disabilities★ – helps people with disabilities to find and retain work
- JobCentres – where Disability Employment Advisers are based (see your local phone book for details)
- AbilityNet★ – for disabled people with IT skills
- National Bureau for Students with Disabilities★ – advice for undergraduates on graduate careers
- Association of Disabled Professionals★ – helps create conditions for disabled people to realise their career and workplace ambitions
- Disabled Entrepreneurs Network★ – a government online resource to help disabled people develop and grow their own businesses
- Shaw Trust★ – provides assistance in job preparation, job finding, job support, job retention and job creation

- If you are a student or graduate, your college Careers Advisory Network may be able to provide advice on employment/career issues.

Disability Employment Advisers (DEAs) may cover several JobCentres over the course of a week, but if you are unable to go to a JobCentre, the DEA will visit your home. A DEA will help you plan a strategy for getting back to work, in the form of a Back to Work plan. He or she may call in a Placement, Assessment and Counselling Team (PACT) first. There are around 60 PACTs in the UK, operating out of local JobCentres, who provide an advice and assessment service for employers.

Never waste an opportunity

Ask friends and neighbours if they know of anything, particularly if you are a mother with children – some of the best homeworking jobs can come from knowing someone at a mother and toddler club or playgroup who has a good homeworking job. Leads on jobs can come from the most surprising quarters. It is always worth mentioning that you would like to work from home when you go to parties or other functions. You might be sitting next to a businessman or woman who is thinking of farming out some work to homeworkers.

When you find work

You need to ask yourself, and the company offering the work, some questions before accepting.

Considerations before starting work

Have you done this type of work before? If not, can you cope with it? Is any training given? Does it involve assembling materials and do you have the room at home to spread the work out? Can you meet the delivery dates? Is it close work and is your eyesight up to it? What quality of work will you be expected to deliver and how will that quality be measured? If your work is substandard, will someone help you to achieve the necessary standard? Think about the following questions in particular.

Is there a minimum quantity required?

Find out how much work you have to do to make a living wage or how many pieces have to be completed each week for the company to continue giving you work. It may be the case that if you cannot complete a minimum requirement of, say, 1,000 cards of hooks and eyes a week, they will give the work to someone else. Companies cannot afford to have stock tied up with workers who cannot meet their quotas.

Is there a co-ordinator or group leader to turn to for advice?

It is not enough to have contact once a week or less with the person who delivers your work, or from whom you pick it up. You need to have access over the telephone to someone who can answer your day-to-day queries.

Is there a manual to help you?

You need a manual that explains your equipment so that you can diagnose any faults or cope with any problems. Some companies, particularly in the clothing industry, have specification manuals because they are producing items of clothing for big chain stores which have very strict requirements. These manuals will explain the exact size of buttonholes required, how the buttons are to be sewn on a shirt and so on.

What quantity of material will be delivered each week?

Can you store it? Twelve thousand buttons to be carded may not take up much room but 12 dozen teddy bears that need eyes sewn on will. Be realistic about your storage capacity.

Is the company properly insured?

The company should be fully insured for loss, theft and fire risk while the goods are in your home. This should not be your responsibility. It should also be insured for goods in transit, even if you are fetching and carrying the goods yourself. If the company does not insure them, maybe you should look elsewhere for work.

Does your tenancy/mortgage/insurance allow this sort of work?

If you are a council tenant you should be aware that certain local authorities require homeworkers to have written permission from them to do work at home. Most tenancy agreements prohibit the use or storage in the home of any inflammable materials, liquids, gases or chemicals, other than those normally required for household jobs. Consequently, you must be wary of any homework which requires you to glue, paint or spray. If any fire broke out in your home and such materials were found to be present it would invalidate your contents and building insurance.

Will your neighbours object?

Council tenants are usually prohibited in their lease from undertaking any activity which might cause a nuisance or inconvenience to neighbours. Neighbours may object to your receiving frequent deliveries of materials by lorry. They may also object to any noise caused by machinery: some industrial sewing machines can be very noisy. The West Yorkshire Homeworking Group recommends the following:

- moving the machine away from a shared wall and from a hollow floor to a solid floor
- using a heavy rubber mat (or pieces of carpet underlay) under the machine to reduce vibration
- having your machine serviced
- changing to a quieter machine – some employers may swap the machine if you point out that complaints about noise from neighbours might mean you have to stop doing the homework.

How will you be paid?

Will you be paid cash in hand, by cheque or by direct debit? Weekly, monthly or at the end of a period of seasonal work? You need to know from the start. You also need to check who will be paying tax and National Insurance – you or the company providing you with work.

Is the work seasonal?

Certain work is obviously seasonal – making Christmas decorations, packing Christmas cards or filling Christmas crackers, for example – but there can also be seasonal highs and lows in other industries. Some firms may only take on outworkers to meet the demand of the pre-season period.

Can the company offer you other work?

Ask if the company can offer you work all year round, even if it is of a different nature. If not, try to get a precise idea of when the seasonal work will start and stop so that you can look for other work to fill in the gaps.

Can you visit the factory?

A company with nothing to hide should be pleased to allow factory visits. You can then see the processes which lead up to your work. It should also give you an opportunity to talk to some full-time workers and gauge whether the company is an employer with a good track record.

Does the type of work allow you to be flexible?

If you have children and you need to work around them, you will require work that can be done at any time of the day, as long as you are able to fill your quota for the week. Some jobs may not offer that flexibility, if they involve daily deliveries or fax transmissions that need to be dealt with immediately. Make sure you fully understand the time schedule of any work that is on offer before you take it on.

Does the employer/company provide you with equipment?

There are various scenarios here.

- You are provided with the necessary equipment and servicing back-up. This is the ideal situation to be in.
- You are provided with the equipment and asked to pay a deposit against it, which is refunded after a trial period. This is not ideal but understandable from the employer's point of view, particularly if you are a new outworker. For all they know you could disappear tomorrow, taking the equipment with you.
- You are asked to buy the equipment by having a small amount deducted from your wages each week. This is only suitable if the company wishes you to be self-employed and agrees that you can then use that equipment to do work for other companies – in the case of computer equipment, for example, or an industrial sewing machine. Check that the price they are asking for their equipment is comparable to that of equipment available on the open market.

- You are expected to provide your own equipment. In the case of small items, such as tools, paintbrushes, hand-sewing or knitting equipment, this is fair enough, but do not agree to buy major items outright.

CASE HISTORY: Priya

Priya found work machining canvas bags for a sports and leisure wear company which employs outworkers all over the north of England. The company supplied Priya with her machine but she pays a weekly rental for the use of it. A company employee came to her home and spent a couple of hours showing her how to operate the machine and put the bags together. She has a telephone number she can ring if she has any problems. The canvas parts are delivered on Monday mornings and the completed bags are collected on Thursdays. Priya is paid by the piece and earns roughly £4.20 an hour, which is quite good compared with the hourly rate that some of her friends get. She manages to amass about £120 a week but it is very hard work: six hours' machining a day makes her shoulders and neck ache.

Do you have to buy anything else from the company?

Some sales schemes expect participants to buy a case of samples. This is common practice and a reasonable safeguard against losing thousands of pounds' worth of valuable stock.

CASE HISTORY: Sean

Sean was made redundant and was unable to get another job for a variety of reasons. Finally, the local JobCentre offered him some outwork, stuffing envelopes for a mail-order company. Although the work is boring and repetitive, it is very easy and he can fit it in whenever he feels like it. Sometimes his wife helps him in the evenings and he has found that he can earn about £80 in a good week.

Can you plan ahead?

You need to know whether or not you can take holidays or take a break for personal reasons, or pack up work for the children's school holidays without losing your chance to work for that company again. Check the position before you start work.

Health and safety

You must not undertake any work which would be prejudicial to your own health and safety and, as you are working from home, that of your family.

Some Homeworking Groups report that employers have given their homeworkers chemicals and glues in unmarked tins and jars. This is against the law. The company should inform you exactly what substances you will be working with, how to handle them and what action to take to avoid illness or injury. For example, fumes from solvents and glues can be very dangerous, or even lethal. They can cause headaches, dizziness, various allergies and heart and lung disease. Some are known to be carcinogenic.

Similarly, working with fibres – cloth, furs, wool – can cause health problems such as skin rashes, allergies and sore throats. The dust created when machine knitting wool passes at speed through the circles of wax into the needles can cause breathing problems for sensitive people.

Continual hunching over a sewing machine can cause back, shoulder, neck and eye problems, while long hours in front of a VDU screen can cause eye strain, headaches, dizziness, nausea and muscle fatigue. Your local Environmental Health Department or relevant trade union will be able to supply you with information on how to avoid a range of work-related accidents or health problems, from asthma to repetitive strain injury (RSI).

Under the Management of Health and Safety at Work Regulations 1999 employers are required to do a risk assessment of the work activities carried out by homeworkers. This may involve your employer assessing your home. You are entitled to see the completed assessment and should ask for a copy. Special arrangements may be needed for new and expectant mothers. For more information see *Homeworking – Guidance for employers and employees on health and safety* from the Health and Safety Executive★ (HSE).

Take sensible precautions

Good lighting, ventilation and seating, as well as frequent rest breaks, are very important for all types of repetitive work. Machinery and electrical equipment must have safety guards to minimise the risk of accident. You should confirm that your power supply is correctly protected and adequate for the task; also, that the company providing the machine has checked that it is both mechanically and electrically safe to use.

It cannot be stressed too often that you need a separate, preferably lockable room in which to do your work, particularly if you have children in the house. If possible, keep all flammable materials locked up outside the house, or in a lockable metal filing cabinet, and keep only the minimum necessary for immediate use. Never smoke when dealing with flammable materials. Do not have your work room next to children's bedrooms, and ensure that the work room is properly ventilated to avoid and evacuate concentrations of fumes and dust. Do not store any flammable materials in a room that gets very warm, such as a loft in summer, or near a source of heat, such as a radiator. Keep plastic packaging materials away from small children and babies. If you are dealing with materials that increase the risk of fire, seek advice from the Fire Prevention Officer at your local fire station on measures you can take to keep you and your family safe.

If you are engaged in sewing work, check that you are not scattering needles or pins around the house that could injure people or pets.

If you are worried about the physical side-effects that your work may be having on you or your family, discuss it with your provider of work. If you get no help there, contact one of the Low Pay Units, your local Environmental Health Department or a local trade union.

The National Group on Homeworking★ gives the following health and safety tips for working at home:

Substances and materials

If your work involves using substances and chemicals, such as solvents or paints, they should be clearly labelled. The company you are doing the work for must supply you with information about the substances and chemicals you are working with, such as:

- Are they flammable or toxic?
- Do they give off fumes? (Is the room where you work well ventilated? Can you open the windows?)
- How should they be stored?
- Do you need protective clothing, for example, gloves or masks?
- Does the work produce a lot of mess or waste materials?
- If so, is the waste a fire hazard? (The company that supplies you with work should collect it regularly.)

Equipment and tools

- Does your work require certain equipment and tools to do the job properly?
- Does the equipment need to be regularly serviced and maintained?
- Does the work involve a lot of close-up detailed work? Do you need extra lighting?
- Do you need protective equipment, for example, a machine guard?
- Do you ever suffer from neck/backache or general aches and muscle fatigue? You may need an adjustable chair with good back support or an adjustable but stable desk to do your work. You may also need a footrest.
- Does the equipment need a power supply? If so, is it safe? You may need a circuit breaker.

What are your rights?

If you are a full- or part-time employee you are entitled to the following:

- A contract of employment or Statement of Particulars, stating the terms and conditions under which you are employed. This should be given to you within one month of starting employment.
- An itemised payslip, whether you receive wages by cash, cheque or direct debit. This payslip should show gross wages and any deductions for tax, National Insurance, pensions scheme etc. and final net pay.
- Irrespective of length of service or hours of work, all women are entitled to 26 weeks' paid maternity leave and the right to return

to the same, or similar, job. Women who have completed 26 weeks' continuous service with their employer by the 15th week before their expected week of childbirth, will be able to take an additional 26 weeks' unpaid maternity leave which must immediately follow their ordinary maternity leave. Intention to take this extra maternity leave has to be given to the employer by the 15th week before the expected date of childbirth.

- From April 2003 the standard rates of Statutory Maternity Pay payable by the employer increased to £100 per week for 26 weeks or 90 per cent of the woman's average weekly earnings if this is less than £100.
- From April 2003, fathers became entitled to take up to two weeks' paid paternity leave when their new baby is born.
- Also in April 2003, a new right to adoption pay and leave was introduced. To qualify, an employee must have worked for an employer for more than 26 continuous weeks and have been newly matched with a child by an approved adoption agency. Adopters will be entitled to 26 weeks' paid ordinary adoption leave, which can start on the day of the child's placement or up to 14 days before, and a further 26 weeks' unpaid adoption leave if needed. Only one period of leave will be given, irrespective of the number of children being adopted at the same time. Statutory Adoption Pay, at the same rate as Statutory Maternity Pay, will be paid by employers for the first 26 weeks. An employee who is an adopter's spouse or partner and has responsibility for the upbringing of the child/children can claim paternity leave and pay.
- Employees who have one year's continuous service with an employer are entitled to 13 weeks' unpaid parental leave per year to care for their children. Parents of disabled children are entitled to 18 weeks.
- Statutory Sick Pay (SSP) is paid to all qualifying employees, irrespective of length of employment. It is not payable for the first three days of a period of illness. It is payable only to employees who earn over £75 per week. In the tax year 2002/3 the SSP rate is £63.25 per week.
- Redundancy payments are made to employees over the age of 18 if they have worked for the same employer for more than two years.

- Compensation for unfair dismissal is paid, provided you can prove your claim, if you have worked for the same employer for more than one year.
- A period of notice must be given if you have worked for an employer for more than one month, unless you are working for a specific short-term contract period.
- You are allowed to join a trade union, if you wish, without being penalised by your employer.
- You are entitled to equal pay, regardless of your sex or race, whether you work from home or in the office or factory.
- From April 2003, parents of young (under six) or disabled children (under 18) have had the right to apply to work flexibly. The employers will have a duty to consider such requests seriously.

Working Time regulations

The Working Time regulations came into effect on 10 October 1998. Since then, all employees (full- and part-time) have the right to paid annual leave. This right comes into effect on the first day of employment and builds up over the year. Other provisions of the Regulations relate to the average hours of work, night shifts and daily and weekly rest periods.

National Minimum Wage (NMW)

A large variety of work is available to semi-skilled and unskilled homeworkers, but the work is mostly irregular and low-paid. However, the National Minimum Wage Act 1999 imposed a minimum wage level which was raised in 2002 to between £3.60 and £4.20 per hour, depending upon status. Usually, workers aged between 18 and 21 years of age are paid £3.60 and workers aged 22 and over are paid £4.20. The only exception to this is when a worker is undertaking a modern apprenticeship or accredited training and is under the age of 26. In such circumstances, an employer can pay the lower rate of £3.60 for the first 12 months. Apprenticeships and training courses are rarely offered to homeworkers.

How does this affect homeworkers?
Many companies using homeworkers prefer them to be self-employed because it is cheaper (no overheads) and they do not

have as much responsibility for self-employed workers as they would for employees. The National Minimum Wage Act expressly applies to all workers as defined by the Act and to homeworkers who do not otherwise fall under this category. Even if the homeworkers are self-employed, generally speaking they will for the most part be deemed to be workers and will benefit from protection under the Act.

The Act requires all employers to keep records of pay and hours worked. Workers should be able to require their employer to produce these records for inspection and take copies of them. The Low Pay Units (LPUs) are still advising all homeworkers also to keep their own strict records of hours worked, whether the work is regular, whether you have any sort of contract or agreement, what you are paid and whether any deductions are made. This information may be useful at a later date if there is some dispute about status and any entitlement to National Minimum Wage. If an employer fails to produce the relevant records, a worker will have the right to take action through an employment tribunal and any records that worker has kept will be very valuable. Under the new law, employers can be heavily penalised for failing to be fair. For example, just failing to produce employment records at the worker's request can result in a tribunal making the employer pay the worker in question 80 times the hourly NMW as compensation.

Even if you are genuinely self-employed – you may proof-read for several publishing houses, or do assembly work for several manufacturers – you should expect to get at least NMW rates.

There has been some difficulty in getting employers to apply the NMW to pieceworkers (that is, workers who get paid per number of units or pieces that they complete, rather than by the hour). However, the law states that pieceworkers should be included in the NMW provisions and the Low Pay Unit (the body established to investigate low pay problems) has recommended that employers use a 'pay reference period' system, whereby piecework and work that has seasonal fluctuations can be worked out to produce an average output per hour and thus a reasonable rate of pay. The pay reference period over which the output can be averaged may not exceed the period of one month.

Employers also have to provide each homeworker with a detailed statement to enable each worker to ensure that they are being paid the NMW. Any worker being paid less than the NMW will be able to recover the difference through a tribunal or county court.

National Insurance and tax

Chapter 7 deals fully with the subjects of National Insurance (NI) and tax. If you are a self-employed freelancer or outworker, you will be responsible for your own National Insurance contributions and tax payments. The system of self-assessment is also explained in Chapter 7.

If you are an employee, NI and tax should be deducted from your wages by your employer if you earn over a certain amount each week (currently £75). If you earn less than that you are exempt from NI. Some employees receive tax forms from the Inland Revenue and are expected to do a self-assessment. Whether or not you receive such a form seems to be triggered by whether or not you receive taxable benefits from your employers, or the State, in addition to your salary.

Be careful

If you are hoping, at the end of the day, to work at home for someone else, either as an employee or as a self-employed free-lancer, it is important to get work that is genuine, reliable and pays a decent amount of money. Spending your first year of homeworking being miserable and insecure, struggling to make ends meet or doing a job that you find tedious and unpleasant, only defeats the object of achieving a decent lifestyle that allows you to combine home, family and work. It is important that you read the next chapter, which contains some cautionary tales about the pitfalls that exist for homeworkers.

Chapter 4

Scams and shams

Unfortunately, there will always be unscrupulous people who seek to part the innocent and gullible from their money. These con artists particularly target desperate people – in this case, those who urgently need to find some way of generating an income and are either unable to work outside the home or cannot find a job because they have no skills or are past retirement age.

Many adverts, mailshots or Internet sites that offer simple, well-paid homework, or offer a way to generate a substantial amount of income without actually doing any work, are confidence tricks. Never forget that there is no such thing as 'easy money'.

Sadly, the Internet has opened up a whole new world of scams and shams, so much so that various Internet fraud watchdog organisations have been set up. In the USA, where use of the Internet has been widespread for several years, the National Consumer's League set up an Internet Fraud Watch department in 1999. In its first year of operation it reported that consumers lost over $3.2 million to Internet fraud and roughly 25 per cent of that was to 'work at home plans'.

We will deal with Internet scams later in the chapter but first we need to address the problem of the scams directed at those people without access to a PC. But basically, the same rules apply whether the scam is on the Internet, through the mail or in the window of your local shop:

- don't part with money
- don't give out personal information
- do ask questions
- do some research
- don't commit yourself if you are not 100 per cent sure.

What to avoid

The National Group for Homeworking* (NGH) offers a great deal of advice on the subject of bogus homeworking schemes. Callers to the NGH Homeworkers Helpline regularly report that they have lost money to these bogus schemes. Annual losses from those people who have admitted to being ripped-off are estimated at around the £50,000 mark. This, of course, does not take into account all those people who have been duped by bogus schemes but are too embarrassed to report it.

Recruitment schemes

Advertisements for recruitment schemes are often found in newsagents and post offices. The advertisement will ask you to send a stamped addressed envelope for more details. In return you will receive a request for a registration fee. This is justified by the sender by saying it deters time-wasters or it is an administration fee. This fee can be anything but it is typically between £10 and £20. Once you have sent the fee, you will receive instructions to place adverts, like the one you replied to, in other shop windows, often using your own address for replies. You will then have to mail out the SAEs sent in response to your adverts. You will be told to insert a letter from the scheme organiser which requests 'registration' fees from other potential homeworkers. The scheme organiser will pay you about 30 pence per enquiry that you forward on to them. This means that at least 50 people would have to send a £15 registration fee to the scheme organiser before you even earn back your initial fee. Aside from the likely financial loss, having given your home address in the adverts you are at real risk of being visited by angry and dissatisfied people who realise that the scheme is a con.

Envelope addressing

Like the recruitment scam you will be asked to send a fee and then your task will be to address envelopes, by hand, using an address list provided or by copying out your local telephone directory. This work is often rejected for failing quality standards, so you never get paid or receive a refund of your initial fee.

CASE HISTORY: Manjit

A dotcom company stated on its website that workers could earn up to £100 per week stuffing envelopes. They would need to send a £25 deposit and, in return, they would receive 2,000 envelopes and the literature to stuff into them. Manjit, stuck at home with two children under five, applied but, needless to say, never received the materials and, after about three weeks, the website disappeared.

Directory schemes

Again, these usually ask you to send a fee in return for a list of companies offering work to homeworkers. What you are likely to receive is a photocopied list of names of companies that don't actually offer homework; or a booklet of addresses or adverts for homework, all of which ask for a registration fee. The NGH states emphatically that, to their knowledge, there is no such thing as a directory of companies offering genuine homeworking opportunities.

Kit schemes

These are usually craft-based schemes which purport to offer homework making craft items, painting, sewing or cutting out stencils, etc. Anyone responding to such an advertisement is asked to send money for an initial kit which is supposed to contain the materials necessary for you to make the items. Often the fee for this kit can be quite substantial. For example, one organisation claiming to offer work cutting stencils charges £35 for a kit which is basically a few sheets of acetate and a template. When the kit arrives it may contain very poor-quality materials or inadequate instructions. In order for you to complete the item, you have to buy further equipment yourself, such as glue, cottons, a scalpel and so on. When you have completed the item or items in question, they will be rejected as below standard, and you will not get a refund because you have used the materials supplied.

CASE HISTORY: Ryan

Ryan is paraplegic but has always been good with his hands. He saw an advertisement in a craft magazine which was advertising for workers to cut stencils for a firm that supplied stencils to 'a major DIY retail chain'. He answered the advert and was asked to pay £35 for the initial kit. When he received the kit, it consisted of twelve sheets of acetate and a very complicated template. The enclosed literature told him that he would have to cut out the design with a scalpel and then return the cut stencils to the company which would 'assess the quality of the finished work'. He found it extremely difficult and even got his mother to go and buy some more sheets of acetate. He managed to return six to the company, which sent him a letter of rejection. He complained but no refund has been forthcoming.

The chain letter

These appear to be sent indiscriminately through the post and, at first glance, they seem to offer a really easy way of making money. The letter will start by saying that the individual sending the letter has made over £50,000 in the last year. Part one of the letter tells you that all you have to do is send £1 to the ten people listed in the letter. You then redo the letter, taking off the top name on the list and adding your name on the bottom. You are then supposed to mail the redone letter out to at least 250 other people, some of whom will, supposedly, send you £1. Your name will remain on that letter for a long time, moving up the list, and the letter will usually include some enticing sums to show how much you could, in theory, make over the course of a year. Part two of the letter suggests that you buy a mailing list from one of the companies listed in the letter. This will cost, roughly, £25 for 250 names but you are encouraged to buy more.

Here we have the point of the letter. It is set up so that the only people who really make money from the whole thing are the companies providing you with the mailing lists. You have no way of knowing whether all of the names and addresses on the mailing list are genuine and, before you speculate, perhaps, £100 on mailing lists and even more on postage, just reflect that your chances of getting back that money from other people who receive the chain letter are very slim indeed.

CASE HISTORY: Moshood

Moshood, a student from the Congo currently studying in England, received a chain letter which told him he could make large amounts of money if he sent £1 to each of the people on the list, added his own name to the letter and sent at least 250 letters out to new people. He purchased a mailing list from one of the companies recommended in the letter for £25, spent £65 on postage and £35 on photocopying. After three months he had received a total of £31 through the post from other gullible people.

Agency opportunities

This scam encourages people to part with frightening amounts of money to purchase a so-called agency to market and distribute the 'parent company's' products via organised parties in other people's homes. There have been tales of people parting with upwards of £5,000 to purchase the rights to sell particular products in particular areas, only to find out afterwards that someone else had purchased the rights to the same area. Sometimes the start-up merchandise never materialises or the company closes down its operation and cannot be contacted. Some homeworkers have found that their initial £5,000 or more bought them a suitcase full of shoddy products they could have bought for £20 in total from a street market and yet others found that, after they had struggled for a while to make a go of the 'agency', the parent company said that they were not selling enough and sold their territory to someone else. They did not get their money back because, apparently, there was a clause in the small print of the contract which gave the parent company the right to do this after three months without giving any refund.

How to protect yourself

It is possible to take steps to protect yourself against traditional scams. We will look at the Internet later in the chapter. But first, arising from the scams outlined above, here is some general advice.

73

Never send money

A legitimate company charging a registration fee or a fee for an initial pack of products should deduct it from your first commission/sales/wages and not ask for the money upfront. A genuine network marketing scheme or agency scheme should only ask you to pay for a small set of samples and then only after a fair amount of personal contact with the company and some training. Any business opportunity offered to you should be thoroughly investigated first and any contract offered should be passed in front of a solicitor before you hand over any money. Always check a company name with your local Trading Standards Department to see if it is on any blacklist.

Read the literature carefully

Does the offer seem too good to be true? Is the company offering suspiciously high rates of pay? For example, mail-order companies can address and fill their own envelopes for less than 2 pence per unit so why would they offer to pay 50 pence? Is the quantity/type of work/level of skill required realistic? You may not know the answer if you have never tried to cut a stencil or engrave a metal disc before, but ask yourself whether a reputable company would want inexperienced people creating products which they are going to sell to discerning consumers.

Some of the literature can be very glamorous and very persuasive. Chain letters that offer an easy way to make lots of money often give testimonials – for example: 'June of Southport says, "In the first two months I earned £41,352 – more than I've ever earnt in my life!"' But they never give you June's telephone number so that you can ring her, or set up a training seminar where you can meet others who have participated in the scheme. Do not let momentary greed or desperation persuade you that this is real.

Beware of companies without a full address or telephone number

It is illegal now under The Consumer Protection (Distance Selling) Regulations 2000 for a company to operate under cover of a PO Box number. Companies have to provide a full name and address and telephone number.

You should be able to visit the company and speak to someone face to face, if necessary, and even be able to see the product that you would be assembling at home or selling from home. If you turn up at an address and it is an accommodation address (an office that earns money by taking in mail for people who do not have proper offices), the company may be a dubious enterprise. However, the company may have deliberately distributed its literature at the other end of the country so that it is impossible for people to visit them. If a telephone number is given, you have no way of knowing if the person who answers represents a *bona fide* company. One check you can make is to phone directory enquiries, give them the number and find out what area the company is actually located in. Then call the Trading Standards Department in that area and ask them if they have heard of the company or know of a scam being operated.

Find out more

If the company seems reputable, ask for written details, no obligation, of what work is involved, payment terms, procedures of delivery and collection of work, company liability for tax, NI, equipment etc. If the company is reluctant to do this, you have to ask yourself why. A good company that employs homeworkers or agents should offer some sort of training and appoint a co-ordinator who deals with the day-to-day interaction between company and outworkers.

Ask to speak to some of the company's other homeworkers

A serious and committed company should offer this sort of contact as a matter of course. Good companies use their experienced homeworkers or agents to train up new ones or at least to provide guidance and advice during the learning process.

The Internet

How deep is the ocean? The Internet has opened up the world to criminals and made it so much cheaper for them to target the unwary and unsuspecting – and to defraud a much bigger network of people. Even if you are very careful and streetwise when you surf the Net, they will come and find you by sending spam (junk-mail) to your email box. Every time you contact a newsgroup site, or a chat room, or leave your email address on a site, con artists will add it to their bulk email list. It is possible to install spam-filtering software which traps the junk-mail before it hits your email box but these are not fool-proof. Most of them operate by looking for specific words in the junk-mail texts and eliminating anything that contains them. Needless to say, inventive criminals will find a way round these if they want to.

You may come across the scams unwittingly, of course, when you are surfing the Net looking for homeworking or business opportunities. Their attractive and appealing websites will be there, waiting to lure you in.

The top ten Internet frauds reported to the National Consumers League of America in 2001 were:

- Bogus online auctions, where the items purchased are never delivered. These are commonly targeted at small businesses and offer bulk items cheaply such as paper, stationery and so on.
- Deliberate misrepresentation or non-delivery of general merchandise purchased online.
- Nigerian money offers. This is an absolute beauty of a scam. It takes the form of an email from someone in Nigeria. This person is usually someone of importance who is under house arrest, fearing imprisonment or trying to get out of the country. Emails have been reported from the mistress of the late President of Nigeria, the son of the former military head of state, vice-chairman of the Petroleum Task Force and so on. Whoever they are, they say that they need the assistance of an honest and trustworthy foreigner to help them move the money they have salted away, namely, nearly $25 million. Because of the laws in Nigeria, they cannot move the money out of the country but, as a foreigner, you can. If you will send them the details of your bank account, they will transfer the money into it and they will give you 25 per cent of the money as a reward for helping them. Needless to say, the moment you give them your bank account details, it is *your* money that is moved, not theirs. Would you be taken in by this? A book-keeper for a leading US law firm was, and in 2002 she

borrowed $2.1 million from her employers to help her new Nigerian friends move their life savings.

- Deliberate misrepresentation or non-delivery of computer equipment or software purchased online.
- Internet access scams, where bogus Internet service providers fraudulently charge for services that were never ordered or received.
- Credit-card or telephone charges for services that were never ordered or misrepresented as free.
- Work-at-home schemes promising wildly exaggerated sales and profits.
- Advance fee loans – upfront charges for loans which never materialise.
- Phoney offers of cheap-rate credit-card deals on payment of upfront fees.
- Business opportunities or franchises sold on the basis of exaggerated profit estimates.

CASE HISTORY: Kathryn

Kathryn runs a one-woman mail-order business from home, making unusual knitwear. She parted with £180 to a bogus Internet company which promised to list her company in a great many search engines in Europe so that she could tap into the fashion clothing marketplace. After she had 'signed up' she tried to find her company in the areas on the Web that had been promised but could not. She called in a local consultant and paid him a fee to do a search of the Web, but he informed her that the company that had taken her money was bogus and her business was not listed anywhere.

Other Internet scams

- **Pyramid schemes** These are illegal but still in circulation. This covers any plan where you are supposed to make money by recruiting others into the plan. Usually, on the Internet, it does not involve selling products but rather something like an e-magazine subscription. If you are selling products you may be asked to purchase a great deal of upfront stock at high prices.

- **Investment opportunities** These promise big returns on little investment with no risk. Common sense should tell you that there is no such thing. If the website is trying to persuade you to invest in a business, the business will usually be bogus and you will lose your money.
- **Pump and dump stock** You may be enticed to buy stock which, in reality, has no prospects. The promoter pumps up the value of the stock with heavy promotions and entices lots of people to buy it. Then he dumps the stock at a huge profit and the stock price falls before you have a chance to offload it.
- **Chain letters** An email version of the snail-mail chain letter (see page 72). You will be asked to send money to each person on the list, add your own name and purchase an email list to send out amended chain letters.
- **Health and diet scams** These promise new ways to lose weight effortlessly. You are either asked to part with lots of money to find out what it is or you are recruited to recruit others.
- **Earn money at home scam** These schemes promise a plan whereby you can earn lots of money at home. What you pay for are some worthless brochures and, perhaps, a video, which tell you to feel good about yourself and go out and hug a tree.
- **Online credit repair scams** A company promises to remove negative information on your credit report if you pay them a fee. It is illegal and impossible to remove negative information from a credit report if the information is true. If it is false you can call the credit company yourself and have the information removed for free.
- **International telephone frauds** This usually takes the form of an email stating that a large number of expensive goods has been billed to your credit card and you must call an international number to cancel the order. Once you call the number you are later billed for the international long-distance call.

How to avoid the Internet traps

The US Department of Justice, Fraud Section, offers the following tips:

Don't judge by initial appearances It may seem obvious, but consumers need to remember that just because something appears on the Internet – no matter how professional or impressive the website looks – it doesn't mean it's true. The ready availability of software allows anyone, at minimal cost, to set up a professional-looking website. So criminals can make their websites look as impressive as those of legitimate e-commerce merchants.

Be careful about giving out valuable personal data online If you see an email message from someone that you don't know, that asks you for personal data – such as your National Insurance number, credit-card number or password – don't just send the data without knowing more about the person who's asking. Criminals have been known to send messages in which they pretend to be, for example, a systems administrator or Internet service provider representative in order to persuade people online that they should disclose valuable personal data. While secure transactions with known e-commerce sites are fairly safe, especially if you use a credit card, non-secure messages to unknown recipients are not.

Be especially careful about online communications with people who conceal their true identity If someone sends you an email header that has no useful identifying data (for example, WT661Z@provider.com), that may be an indication that the person doesn't want to leave any information that could allow you to contact them later if you have a dispute over undelivered goods for which you have paid. As a result, you should be highly wary about relying on advice that such people give you if they are trying to persuade you to entrust your money to them. A reputable Internet site should always contain traditional contact information (address/telephone number/fax). If it doesn't, then the chances are that it is bogus.

Watch out for advance fee demands In general, you need to look carefully at any online seller of goods or services, or one who offers homework, who wants you to send cheques or money orders immediately to a PO Box, before you receive the goods or services you've been promised.

Take your time in making investment decisions Remember that in any 'get rich quick' scheme, there is only one person who is guaranteed to get rich quick and that is the promoter. There are several websites run by agencies and self-regulatory organisations that can give you substantial information on any company or investment opportunity promoting on the Web. The SEC, The Federal Trade Commission, the Commodity Futures Trading Commission, The National Association of Securities Dealers, and The Stock Exchange are just a few examples.

Don't be pressured If the investment, business or homework opportunity being offered is 'for a limited time only', or states that deals have to be made 'within 24 hours', or that a registration fee has to be sent 'within seven days to secure a place' – there is every probability that this is a scam. Any legitimate company does not have to pressure people into responding immediately.

Chapter 5

The importance of market research

If you are intending to take the self-employment/small business route, and particularly if you are still in the process of choosing an occupation or business idea to pursue at home, market research is an essential part of your decision-making process. Its value cannot be underestimated. It will help you identify market gaps that you may be able to exploit. It will also help you to invest wisely if you decide to purchase an existing business or a franchise, and, later, it will enable you to keep ahead of the game by expanding, diversifying or contracting. Most importantly, if you are intending to manufacture products in a small way or provide a service, it will help you to price your products or services competitively.

Market research is so vital to most British companies that they spend over £200 million a year commissioning special research by professionals.

'Market Research is the voice of the consumer. It is vital to industry, commerce and government. It is the means by which ordinary people can influence the development and marketing of goods and services and the formulation of social policy,' says the Market Research Society*, which is the incorporated professional body for those individuals who use survey techniques for market, social and economic research.

Don't fall into the trap of thinking that this has nothing to do with you: the techniques for researching potential markets can be used by everyone and, in this information age where huge amounts of data are readily available in all forms, the lone individual can easily reap the benefits of some very expensive corporate research without going further than a regional library.

Market research isn't only valuable to the self-employed or the entrepreneur. It is of great value to those looking to find employed work as well, as we will demonstrate later in the chapter.

Where will my customers come from?

This is the burning question. You intend to make a product, perhaps several products, or supply a service – but where will you sell this product or service?

- the general public
- specialist markets
- other businesses
- retail outlets.

Will your market be:

- local
- regional
- national
- global?

Making the decision about the market sector at which to aim your product or service is inextricably linked to how, eventually, you will market it – that is to say, how you will reach the market you have targeted. You may say, 'Well, I thought I would sell to the local general public by just putting an ad in the local newspaper.' That may work if you are a jobbing gardener or a hairdresser but, even then, you might get work faster if you found out which people were most likely to want your product or service and addressed your sales pitch directly to them.

CASE HISTORY: Stephen

Stephen's home-made fishing flies were often admired by fellow anglers. He decided to research the market to see whether he could set up in business making these flies. He went to the library and was advised by the librarian to look at several press directories which contained details of all the fishing publications in the country and their circulations. He discovered that the combined circulations of the magazines represented a large market. He then looked through several *Yellow Pages* directories for different areas and photocopied the pages of fishing shops. He rang many of the shops at random and asked them where they bought their flies and whether they would be interested in a new source of supply.

After a lot more research into his marketplace Stephen set up his business, starting by selling to shops. Eventually he progressed to mail order.

Sources of information

Libraries

The best libraries in which to start your search are either good reference libraries or what are known as business libraries, which are usually found in large towns or regional centres. These are ordinary libraries but the reference section specialises in information, in many forms, about commerce and industry and related matters. The librarians are trained to help you wade productively through the available information or, if they have not got it, to tell you what you need and where to get it. Hospitals, colleges and universities also have libraries that may hold the relevant information you require.

You may be saying, 'I just make patchwork bags; how is a visit to the library going to help me?' If all you have been doing is taking your wares, week after week, to craft fairs and hoping to sell one or two, a visit to an appropriate library could help you find a better, bigger and more reliable market for your goods.

CASE HISTORY: Amrit

Amrit invented a gadget which stored computer disks safely, but he did not know whether it was marketable and whether he should go to the expense of taking out a patent. He went to a large business library and spent a whole week reading all the past year's reports and surveys on computer equipment that had appeared in newspapers and business magazines. He then obtained lists of manufacturers of computer accessories from a manufacturers' directory and rang them to ask if they manufactured something similar to his invention. None of them did and many of them were very interested. He went ahead and applied for a patent, then sold the rights to manufacture to a Scottish company.

Directories

Good reference libraries stock all kinds of directories. You can find out, for example, the titles of all the craft/needlework magazines published in the UK by consulting, for example, *Benn's Media* or *BRAD*. You may then consider advertising in some or all of these magazines, thereby reaching a specialist audience that would be interested in your products. A reference library should have all the *Yellow Pages* directories for the UK. You could photocopy the pages which contain the gift/craft shops and send them all a mailshot (selling your products on a regular basis through shops would give you some security). Most reference libraries stock the *Directory of British Associations*, which gives details of associations, societies, institutes, regional and local organisations, chambers of commerce and national federations. Say, for example, you decided that your product would appeal to the members of women's organisations. The *Directory* would give you the addresses of the national body of the Women's Institute, Townswomen's Guild, Mothers' Union and so on. You could then write to them to buy advertising in their magazines or pay to insert leaflets in their mailshots.

So, just a couple of hours' research can open up some positive markets for the woman who makes patchwork bags. It is also worth pointing out that by exploring these markets you may find out that the product/service you are offering is not as marketable as you thought and this will influence you to adapt or abandon your scheme.

If you have no experience of doing research, arm yourself with a list of questions and ask the librarian (try to pick a quiet period). For example, you may be considering setting up a sandwich delivery service for local industries, so you ask, 'How do I find out how many industrial estates are in the area?' (The librarian may point you towards the local authority planning department.) Or, you may be considering marketing your house as a film location and you ask, 'Is there a directory of television and film production companies?' (There is more than one. If your library does not stock them the librarian can tell you the names of the publishers if you want to buy copies, or which library in your region does stock them.) You may manufacture a product which would interest the head teachers of primary schools and you ask, 'Is there a list of primary schools for the whole country?' (The librarian will say yes; he or she may have to point you to a government source for the information, but first will arm you with the necessary information to ask for the right publication.)

CASE HISTORY: Gloria

Gloria wrote and published her own book about jam-making, but not before she had thoroughly researched the market for her book. When it was still in the manuscript stage, she went through the *Directory of British Associations* and noted down all the women's groups in the country that would have an interest in domestic arts. She had a book jacket designed and used it as the basis of a leaflet and order form which she mailed to the secretaries of all the women's groups for them to distribute. During the process of market research which Gloria undertook while putting the book together, she discovered a printing company which was able to print books on demand – even just one copy when required – by utilising the latest CD technology. The price of her book had been very carefully worked out before she advertised. The book was a modest success and she now plans another cookery book using the same marketing route.

And so on – the possibilities are endless. Libraries not only stock information in book form but on microfiche and often CD-ROM as well. They may stock a whole year's back issues of trade or business magazines or national newspapers. You can look through them to see whether a particular topic of interest that is relevant to your product or service has been covered in depth. Most libraries now, even the smallest ones, offer access to the Internet, where you can find all sorts of useful data and information. Don't forget that any statistics published can be used in the marketing of your product. For example, if you run a carpet and upholstery cleaning service, it would be useful to quote in your sales literature from any relevant research published by, say, the British Carpet Manufacturers Association. You could find out about this by reading through back issues of the appropriate trade magazine.

Other professional sources

Alternative sources of information are local Chambers of Commerce, Local Enterprise Agencies, regional branches of the Department of Trade and Industry (DTI)*, and Learning and Skills

Councils (LSCs)★. They can also help you with further advice, give you literature, point you in the direction of companies that sell mailing lists for particular market sectors, introduce you to people with whom you may possibly enter a productive business relationship and so on.

CASE HISTORY: Sasha

Sasha has a degree in textile design and wanted to work from home as a freelancer. Her Local Enterprise Agency was able to provide her with lists of textile manufacturers in the UK to whom she could offer her services. The Enterprise Agency was also able to point her in the direction of information about arts and crafts grants and other financial information to help her through her first year.

If you make a product or provide a service which you feel would be successful abroad, contact your Business Link Office★ in the first instance if you live in England. If you are resident in Scotland, contact Scottish Enterprise★, in Wales contact Business Connect★. (See also Chapter 9.)

Chambers of Commerce deserve a second mention here because they have often built up productive relationships with overseas business groups and can also provide contacts and information.

The commercial sections of embassies in the UK are a valuable source of information – for example, the US Embassy in London has a huge reference library and can offer all kinds of help.

The Internet

The Internet is the world's largest library, available at your fingertips. If you do not have personal access to the Internet then, as mentioned earlier, there may be a library nearby that does. Some colleges and universities offer an access service for a fee. Many towns now have cybercafés where you can get online for a small fee, and you pay for the time you use.

For more on the Internet and other technology see Chapter 10.

Conducting your own survey

British businesses spend millions of pounds each year getting professional researchers to conduct surveys on their behalf and, as discussed in the first part of this chapter, you can reap the benefit of some of that research if it is published. You can also take a leaf out of the big companies' book and conduct a modest survey of your own. It is not difficult and it can pay surprising dividends.

It can mean pounding the streets, knocking on doors or stopping passers-by. A significant proportion of people will not co-operate, but in the end it will be worth your while, provided the questions are framed properly to give you accurate information.

First, be clear in your mind *exactly* what you want to find out. If you are searching for an occupation and have not yet decided what it should be, perhaps you need to canvass house-to-house in the area to find out what services people want. You need concise questions that prompt simple answers. For example:

1 Do you employ a gardener?   Yes/No
2 Would you like to employ a gardener?   Yes/No
3 (If the answer to question 2 is yes) What jobs would you most want a gardener to do? Weeding/mowing the lawn/digging/repairing the fences/taking all the garden rubbish away/designing a new garden.

From that simple questionnaire you might be able to ascertain that most people already employ a gardener – so no work there for you. Alternatively, you may discover that most people would like to employ a gardener (but have not done so far) and that the job they most want done is mowing the lawn.

Your next piece of market research is to find out what the competition is charging by telephoning a few jobbing gardeners and asking their prices. If you can undercut them and still make a living, the next step is to print some leaflets offering lawnmowing services at so much per hour and stick them through the doors of the people you have surveyed.

Surveys don't have to be conducted door-to-door, of course. They can be carried out by post but, unless you are prepared to offer stamped self-addressed envelopes, the chances are you will get very few replies. You might be able to come to an arrangement with a magazine to distribute surveys on your behalf. For example, perhaps the church magazine would, for a fee (and provided they felt the subject matter was in keeping), insert your survey in its pages and ask members to drop the completed survey into a box (which you would provide) when they next attend church. This was the route by which one entrepreneur arrived at a local pet-sitting service.

You may be considering setting up a baby-sitting service, in which case you could ask the local mother and toddler groups, play-groups and nursery schools if they would distribute your survey to the parents and, again, you would provide a box in which the completed surveys were collected.

Perhaps you are planning to offer a car-valeting service. You could approach local offices and factories which have large numbers of personnel who commute to work by car and ask if you could survey them to see whether they would be interested in having their car valeted while they work.

There are lots of 'captive' markets that could be explored in this fashion and then targeted.

Using professional routes

It is possible to buy into what are called Omnibus Surveys. These are surveys that are continuously conducted by professional market research companies among specific markets. You can, for a relatively modest fee, buy some space on these surveys and insert some questions of your own. For example, you may be considering producing a self-help book for people with a specific medical problem. You could buy some questions on a regular survey which is sent out to GPs all over the UK. You could ask those GPs if they would find such a book valuable; whether there is a book that they recommend to patients; and how many patients they have on their register suffering from this condition. The research company would then collate the answers and present you with the results.

Some market research companies regularly produce in-depth market reports about certain industries, markets or social groups. Mintel, for example, publishes regular business and industry reports. You can buy these reports (although they are usually quite expensive because of the man-hours put into the research), or access them via the Internet. Many government departments also produce regular surveys about certain social groups. If the sort of information you need is contained in any of these, then reading them can be immensely valuable.

CASE HISTORY: Angela

Angela had often thought that commuters from her two local stations would be interested in buying sandwiches, tea and coffee before they boarded the morning trains to London. There were no existing facilities, as the stations were fairly remote. She was offered the chance to buy a mobile shop van which would be ideal as a sandwich bar. Before she took the plunge, she conducted her own survey among all the commuters who took trains every day between 6.30a.m. and 8.30a.m. Most of the replies were positive, particularly from one station's commuters, so she selected that one as a starting point. She contacted Railtrack, who owned the station and car park, to ask if, for a fee, she could park outside their stations in the morning. They agreed, provided she did not obstruct car parking, and her business was born. She now has three mobile vans, servicing other suburban stations in the area.

Other ways of gathering information

Using your eyes and ears is important. You can glean lots of useful information by talking to people and learning from the mistakes of others.

Many craftworkers, unfortunately, take a 'scatter gun' approach to marketing their wares, mainly by renting stalls at the many craft fairs held all over the country every week. This can often be a total waste of time and money. Try to attend as many fairs as you can, purely as an onlooker, before choosing the venues at which you will rent a stall. Spend a day at a fair and watch the various stalls. You will probably notice that the very beautiful and expensive items do not sell at all but the stallholders dispense leaflets and business cards in the hope that a percentage of the public who are browsing will come back to them at a later date and commission something special. This is not a cost-effective use of time. You may note that certain items always sell quickly – preserves, herbal products, cushions, small pictures of local views, for example. Take note of the price ranges and what most people are prepared to pay for items. Listen to the public as they walk out of the fair or while they are having a cup of tea, and note their comments. They may indicate preferences or discuss prices or compare one craft fair with another. Look at the locations of the stalls. Does the stall nearest to the tea stand attract the most customers, or the one nearest the door? What display equipment do the busiest stalls have? Is there a steady flow of customers through the doors? Has the weather affected the attendance? Is there enough parking for everyone? All these factors have a bearing on whether a particular craft fair is a good marketplace for you to invest the time and money to display your wares.

Reading local newspapers is important. You can pick up some very useful information about perceived gaps in the market from comments in the features or from the wanted ads. Perhaps a local councillor gives an interview in which he or she says that the council has decided to give financial and practical aid to local tourism projects, in which case your plan to turn your front room into a tea shop would be a suitable project for them to consider. Perhaps a local conservation group is offering a grant for any undertaking that involves beautifying the local villages. This might just fit in with your proposed business of establishing and maintaining hanging baskets on lamp posts.

You will find sections in local newspapers that describe the activities of special interest groups in the area. These may be some of the captive markets which you are looking for. Perhaps someone may complain in an article about the lack of a certain service or facility in the area and you can think of a way of filling the gap, or you may read about the imminent closure of a business and move in to take over its customers.

Information is a valuable asset when you are aiming for success. Compile as much of it as you can to help you make the right decisions at the beginning of your career and continue to keep your 'market intelligence' up to date to help you make the right decisions in the future.

Researching working for someone else

One area of employment is working as an agent, or subcontractor, for someone else. It is in fact self-employment, but in the case of subcontractors, someone else finds the work, and in the case of agents someone else manufactures the products which they sell.

Subcontracting

Subcontracting used to be most common in the building trade; however, it has become an increasingly common practice in other trades as well. Gardening is a case in point. Many successful gardening businesses start off as one-man-/-woman bands and, as they grow, require extra staff. Because the ability to carry out the work is dependent on the weather, it is risky to employ others full-time and pay them to do nothing on rainy days, so subcontracting is the answer.

CASE HISTORY: Paolo

Paolo did a very simple piece of market research. He was an unemployed builder whose speciality was building patios. He therefore rang all the jobbing gardeners in the area and the garden centres that offered gardening services and asked if they provided a patio-building service. If they did not, he asked why, and they usually replied that it was too specialised for them. He then wrote to all those people offering his services as a subcontractor. Many of them took up his offer and began to look for patio work from their regular clients. Business was a little slow at first but now Paolo has a steady amount of work.

If you are fit and able to turn your hand to any labouring job, whether it is digging a garden, mixing concrete, carrying bricks or cleaning windows, then you should do some research and find out which firms in your area employ subcontractors. You can then make yourself known to a variety of companies and get yourself put on their books for casual work.

If you have a special skill, try to find others with similar skills who have been in operation longer than you and may be in a position to give you some of their overflow work. Alternatively, you might suggest to people with an allied skill that they offer their customers an extra service or product which you can provide when required. This will add an extra dimension to their business without their having to employ another person.

Some examples of this might be:

- you possess binding and laminating machines and you suggest to a word processing agency that they offer to bind and laminate their clients' reports. You charge them a price for doing it and they add a bit extra on that price to their clients
- you are a skilled embroiderer and you suggest to someone who manufactures or sells children's clothes that they could offer a service to their customers whereby clothes are embroidered with the children's names
- you design and plant up container displays for gardens. You could suggest to local gardening businesses that they purchase ready-made tubs of plants, hanging baskets and so on from you.

Agencies

An agent is a commission-only salesperson who sells products for one or more manufacturers. There are untold numbers of people involved in this type of work, from the women who sell cosmetics, clothing and jewellery through catalogues among friends to the thousands involved in network marketing schemes (see page 18) selling household products.

At the top end of the market are manufacturers' agents, represented by the Manufacturers' Agents' Association (MAA)★. They have a large membership in the UK selling products for both UK and overseas manufacturers. Members are mainly people with a professional sales background and a great many contacts which they have built up over the years. This is why the manufacturers are interested in their representation. However, no matter how good their contacts are, they still have to do the kind of research described in this chapter in order to add to their sales and to develop new sales lines.

Anyone wishing to become a manufacturer's agent can contact the MAA, which publishes a newsletter in which manufacturers from all over the world advertise for agents. Also, the various commercial sections of foreign embassies have lists of manufacturers seeking agents. There is also a British Agents Register★ which puts agents in touch with manufacturers.

General home-based work

Finding home-based work of the general kind is not quite so easy. As stated in Chapter 3, there is no list of reputable companies offering homework, according to the National Group on Homeworking★. However, a 'blacklist' has been compiled of companies that have been involved in cheating workers, operating scams or paying dreadful wages. Check with the NGH, a local Homeworking Group or Officer, a Low Pay Unit or your local Trading Standards Department. None of these organisations mentioned can find you homework or provide you with a list of potential employers: finding the work is up to you. However, when you think you have found some work you can check with them to reassure yourself that the employer is reputable. All of the research methods required to find reputable homework are detailed in full in Chapter 3.

Researching business opportunities

If you are thinking of setting up a business from scratch in England or are trying to research business opportunities generally, contact your nearest Business Link★ facility for information, counselling and advice. Most Business Links offer a mix of free and chargeable services – before arranging counselling services or requesting information about grants from any source, check whether or not a fee is payable. If you live in Scotland, contact Scottish Enterprise★; in Wales, contact Business Connect★.

Regional Arts and Crafts Councils may know whether local artists and craftspeople are looking for partners or investors – you may have a skill that perfectly complements another person's and adds to your business potential, or you may have the money and marketing know-how to invest in the right project.

The British Franchise Association (BFA)★ and banks will have information on franchises but, often, the best place to go is to one of the major franchise exhibitions in the UK and have a thorough look at the variety of options on offer. Contact the BFA for details of forthcoming exhibitions.

Whether you are taking over an existing small business, buying a new one, or investing in a franchise, researching its potential and its solidity can really only be done by an accountant and/or your bank. (Most of the high-street banks now have a franchise department which will investigate and assess a franchise before you buy it, whether the bank is lending you money to purchase or not.)

No one should ever buy a business – even a newspaper delivery round – without having a qualified person look at the books and without doing some of the research outlined in this chapter regarding existing and potential markets.

Chapter 6
Money – how to raise it

If you decide to go down the route of self-employment you will need some money behind you, if only to cushion you against the bad weeks when your income is low. You may not need much of an initial investment in stock, materials or equipment but it helps your confidence if you know that you are not completely without money. Of course, you may be in receipt of a state benefit or have some redundancy money or some savings, in which case you will not feel totally penniless. But, for the purposes of this chapter, we will suppose that you need to raise some money in order to get yourself started. This might take the form of:

- money to cover start-up expenses (for example, equipment)
- finance for the ups and downs of cash-flow (for example, if your cash-flow forecast suggests that you may need to borrow in some months)
- money to buy stock.

Loans and grants are available in certain circumstances, from government and other sources, and we outline some of these later in this chapter, but it should be appreciated from the outset that these are not quick ways of obtaining start up money. Bank loans take some time to be approved, loans from government sources and allied bodies take much longer and grants can take forever to come through. So you either have to be prepared to hang on to your full-time job while everything is processed, or you have to borrow the money from a friend or relative on the strength of the grant coming through.

Do not, however difficult it is proving to raise money, borrow money from a money lender who charges horrendous rates of interest: you will cripple your business venture before it even gets off the ground. Similarly, a finance house which charges between 25 and 30 per cent interest per year could prove just too expensive for your fledgling business to sustain. Also, unless you have an interest-free loan or grant confirmed on paper and therefore can definitely pay someone back, do not borrow from friends or relatives if you can help it. Borrowing money is the quickest way to damage a relationship.

The first step

Until you have worked out how much your product or service will cost to make or provide, what you are going to sell it for and what your estimated outgoings and income will be, you cannot answer the question about whether you need to raise finance. Costing your work is covered in some depth in Chapter 8.

In order to present your fledgling business to a lender, you will need to put together certain documents that give a picture of how you are going to conduct your business and your expected income. Two important documents you need are a cash-flow forecast and a business plan.

Cash-flow forecast

A cash-flow forecast is a complete breakdown of sources of income as well as expenses. The crucial point about a cash-flow statement is that it shows the timing of receipts and outgoings. It is perfectly possible for a business to look profitable but then fail because of adverse cash flow. Working from home means that you may put down a proportion of your rent/mortgage/Council Tax, and bills for light, heat, phone and so forth. You must also consider petrol and car maintenance, if relevant, so that you can sell and deliver your goods. If you are planning to pay any wages during the year, these must be included in your projections. You should also include any upfront investment that needs to be made in equipment or publicity, in order to get you started, as well as any money that will need to be spent later in the year to continue to publicise your business.

This exercise should be done in conjunction with costing your work (see Chapter 8). After you have made these calculations you should be able to see whether or not your planned venture will be able to make a profit. If not, you can either abandon the idea or see whether you can adapt it.

Cash-flow forecast

	Jan	Feb	Mar	Apr	May	June	July	Aug	Sep	Oct	Nov	Dec
Mortgage/rent	*	*	*	*	*	*	*	*	*	*	*	*
Council Tax	*		*	*	*	*	*	*	*	*	*	*
Water rates				*						*		
Gas		*			*			*			*	
Electricity	*	*			*			*			*	
Telephone	*			*			*			*		
HP repayments	*	*	*	*	*	*	*	*	*	*	*	*
Equipment rental	*	*	*	*	*	*	*	*	*	*	*	*
All insurances			*					*				
Loan repayments	*	*	*	*	*	*	*	*	*	*	*	*
Car expenses		*(tax)		*(service)	*(insurance)			*(tax)		*(service & MOT)		
Car running costs	*	*	*	*	*	*	*	*	*	*	*	*
Purchase of supplies	*	*	*	*	*	*	*	*	*	*	*	*
Credit-card repayments												
Miscellaneous												
Projected income	*	*	*	*	*	*	*	*	*	*	*	*
Income over expenditure	–	–	+	–	–	+	+	–	+	–	+	–

A cash-flow forecast not only gives a forecast of expenditure but, as you fill in the amounts, it will also give you a historical record of expenditure. The purpose of the cash-flow forecast is to identify heavy months of expenditure so that you can be prepared. The categories will obviously differ according to your particular business circumstances and, also, the starting month can be at any time of the year. You should fill in the table with actual amounts or estimates. Be generous with the estimates. It is better to find yourself paying less when the time comes than to have budgeted for too little and find yourself short.

You should include your projected income in the calculations. Bear in mind that this may be variable. The plus signs in the bottom row indicate the months where you have may an excess of income over expenditure, and the minus signs show where expenditure could be greater than income. This can help you plan whether you are likely to need an overdraft or loan facility in certain months.

The forecast of income will obviously have a large element of hope involved. You must show if your sales are likely to be seasonal, for example, if you make greetings cards and the bulk of your sales are at Christmas. A Christmas card manufacturer may have a lot of cash going out during the first year and not much coming in until the first quarter of the following year.

A business plan

A business plan is a concise report which explains your business – what it is and how it will make money – and gives a financial forecast. Local Enterprise Agencies, Business Links★ and banks may be able to help you formulate a business plan but they may charge you for this. Check first. (Business Links are business-led partnerships of all key providers of business support in a locality. They aim to provide help through teams of commercially experienced, independent business advisers and specialist counsellors. In Scotland, contact Scottish Enterprise★, in Wales Business Connect★.)

The first part of the plan should be easy. By now you should have worked through in your mind what you are going to do and how you are going to go about it. You will have decided what product or service you are going to offer, done your research, identified your market and how you are going to sell to that market. This all has to be explained clearly and fully and, preferably, briefly. No one wants to wade through a 20-page report on a small business you are running from your back bedroom; two pages should suffice. In these two pages you need to explain the points below. Work through these questions to help you formulate your business plan concisely as you compile the report.

Before you start, it is important to check whether the organisation to which you hope to present your business plan has a standard format that they prefer. Some banks, for example, have forms that they expect you to fill in, rather than presenting your own report.

What is your business?

Explain exactly what your product or service is. Do not try to blind anyone with science or use fancy management consultancy jargon. If you are selling cosmetics door-to-door do not call it a health and beauty consultancy. If you are using an umbrella term – for example, you are a teleworker who is running a data management service – explain in the report that this covers creating and amending mailing lists, and keeping personnel records, etc., on computer.

Why have you chosen this business?

If it is relevant, outline your past experience in this field, your training and qualifications. If this does not apply, and you have just decided on a business because the potential is good and you need no training to be able to operate, explain that too.

What is the market for your product or service?

Explain what your market research has uncovered. If you can throw in a few statistics and name the sources, all the better; it will show that you have done your homework. If you have done a house-to-house survey yourself in your local area, translate that into percentages for the report – for example, out of 54 households interviewed 47 per cent said that they were looking for a window cleaner, 23 per cent already had one, and the rest cleaned their own windows.

Have you identified the competition?

Do you know who else is offering the same product or service and is likely to affect your market? Or have you found a genuine market gap with no competition in sight? Are you sure it is a market gap? Has anyone tried to fill it before and come unstuck? Perhaps the only competition is 100 miles away and will not affect your sales area. Perhaps there is healthy competition but the market is continually growing – for example, you want to set up as a childminder; plenty of other childminders are operating in your area but you have ascertained that the demand is so great that it outstrips the supply.

Why is your product or service better?
Take the example of a children's day nursery. Maybe you want to be better than the others and charge more, so you need to borrow money to put better play equipment in the nursery garden. In order for you to arrive at this decision you need to understand what the market wants and to identify what the competition is offering.

How will you reach your customers?
List all the ways in which you want to market your work and how often you would wish to run marketing exercises in the first year. (Marketing your work is covered in detail in Chapter 9.) You need to be able to quote the costs of advertising, leaflet printing, distribution and so on and then add this into your cash-flow forecast.

How much can you achieve on your own?
You have to be realistic about your capacity for work and exactly how much revenue you can generate on your own. If you are doing the selling and the paperwork as well you will have only so much time to make your products or provide your service. If you are a craftworker who makes a variety of products, list them and explain how much time it takes to make each one and what the profit margin is.

Someone who is considering giving you a loan (such as your bank manager or Enterprise Agency) may then call in a marketing expert, who could advise you that some items are too time-consuming and not cost-effective and that you should concentrate your business efforts on certain products only. (Chapter 8 discusses how to cost your work.)

When will you need to expand?
You may need to use outworkers or take on someone part-time right at the outset or you may be planning to employ someone else, if all goes well, in about a year's time. This needs to be explained in your

business plan so that a potential lender can assess your financial needs in the future.

What equipment do you have or need?

You may not have any equipment as such, or you may have old equipment that needs replacing. Perhaps you need to invest in another piece of equipment to allow you to diversify.

Who are or will be your suppliers?

Where do you buy or intend to buy your raw materials? Have you investigated the best prices? Can you get special deals? Anyone considering lending you money will be impressed if you can show that you have investigated all the possibilities.

What type of finance do you need?

A grant would be ideal, but you may not be able to get one. Perhaps you could get a bank loan or, if you can do without that, an overdraft facility to cover you for those periods when money is going out faster than it comes in.

A bank or an Enterprise Agency will go through the finished business plan with you and discuss any weak points before you present it to the ultimate source of finance. It is an important part of your preparation and you must get it right. It is also a document you can build upon and re-present at a later date if you should require further finance to expand or diversify.

Ideally, you should have planned your work-at-home career sufficiently to be able to have saved some money to start yourself off. It is important that you keep all the money for and relating to your fledgling business in a separate account from your personal money. This does not have to be a business account to start off with, as the charges on such accounts are steep. However, if you are starting an ambitious enterprise which will require applying for loans or overdraft facilities you will, undoubtedly, have to open a business account with your lender.

Raising some money quickly

Earning money at home is all about careful planning and exercising caution. There can be occasions, however, when a business opportunity, vehicle or piece of equipment becomes available and you cannot wait for lengthy financial procedures to be completed. Below are some suggestions for how to raise money quickly:

- **Sell something** – you could sell your car and get a cheaper one. You could sell all your unwanted items at a car boot sale: this will not raise a lot of money, of course, but it might be enough to help you on your way.
- **Hire purchase** – this is a good way of getting some essential equipment for your enterprise, if such an arrangement is available. Only opt for *bona fide* hire-purchase agreements, after thoroughly investigating the true cost involved. Can you afford the monthly repayments? It is vital to establish this first.
- **Interest-free credit** – this may be available on certain items such as sewing machines, knitting machines or computers. In the current competitive climate, you can get some good bargains, provided you are able to pay the initial deposit and either keep up the monthly payments or pay the outstanding money at the end of the credit period. In particular look for bargains in the annual sales, when you can get equipment at a reduced price but also take advantage of the interest-free credit offer. Computers and other electronic equipment are often greatly reduced after the Christmas rush.
- **Credit-card borrowing** – buying items of equipment on a credit card will give you up to 56 days interest free before the bill must be paid; after that you can, if you wish, pay in instalments. It is an expensive way to buy as the interest rates are high if you do not settle the whole sum when you get the bill. But in the short term this form of credit can still be cheaper than a bank overdraft.

In the longer term, you could consider taking on a business partner – this may be a way of borrowing from close relatives or friends, though you should put proper safeguards in place and take legal advice – or taking out a second mortgage on your home. Note that this is a risky option as you could lose your house. Consult an independent financial adviser for detailed guidance appropriate to your circumstances.

Private sector finance

Most business start-ups approach the high-street banks and building societies first. Remember that these institutions do not lend money without some sort of guarantee that they will get it back in one way or another. This usually means some form of security against the loan (unless you are able to get on the government's Loan Guarantee Scheme). Whether this is necessary will depend on the size and type of the loan – for example, security would not normally be required for a small overdraft facility. The security demanded is usually one of the following.

A mortgage on your home

If you default on the loan the lender has a right to sell your home to get its money back. However, it is unlikely that the bank will want your home as security unless you are borrowing a very large amount of money. The size of the loan allowed will depend upon how much your house is worth when any outstanding mortgage is subtracted. Before putting your house forward as security against the loan, discuss it thoroughly with your spouse/partner/family. It is not recommended for those of a nervous disposition.

A life insurance policy

A life insurance policy with a substantial surrender value of more than the value of the loan is signed over to the bank for the period of the loan. In the event of the borrower's death the bank will be automatically repaid and any balance will be handed over to the family. In the event of default, the bank will surrender the policy and reclaim its money. You have to keep up the premiums on the policy, of course. This is a good way to secure a loan and does not threaten your home at all. Make sure you have enough life insurance cover so that your family will not be penniless if you die. Term life insurance is the cheapest and, as it has no investment value, it cannot be used as security for a loan.

Stocks and shares

A block of shares worth considerably more than the value of the loan (because of the fluctuating nature of the market) can be signed over to the bank for the period of the loan. As with the life insurance policy, should you default on the loan or die, the bank sells the stocks and shares. This is also a popular way of securing a loan because it does not risk your home and you do get the stocks and shares back after you have paid off the loan.

A personal guarantee

This is a written guarantee from a third party stating that he or she will pay off the loan if the borrower cannot. Banks will rarely accept this as total security (unless your guarantor is a multi-millionaire) and will probably ask for one of the other securities listed above to be given by the guarantor as a back-up. The guarantor should be fully aware of the risks involved in acting as guarantor for someone.

What the banks can offer

Most lending institutions will expect you to bank with them if you want financial help. However, if your existing bank will not give you a loan or is not offering an attractive package, there is no reason why you cannot apply to other institutions and offer to move your account if they will help.

Overdrafts

An overdraft is an agreement with the bank that the bank will let you overdraw your account up to a set sum. It is a useful way of borrowing money in the short term to finance the difficult cash-flow periods. It is, however, not the best way of borrowing money as there will probably be several charges incurred – to set up the facility, a monthly administration charge and, of course, high charges should you exceed the overdraft limit or not repay on time. The interest charged will be linked to the bank base rate and so it will vary and overdrafts are usually reviewed every 12 months unless the customer is causing problems and the bank feels obliged to review the situation before the end of the agreed term.

Short-term loans

The banks usually classify 'short term' as up to two years. Rates of interest vary from bank to bank and can be fixed or can fluctuate with the base rate. Fixed-rate loans are where the interest is fixed, that is, does not fluctuate, for an agreed period (it is rarely for the whole term of the loan). It is worth shopping around to see which lender offers the best deal. For financing the purchase of equipment a short-term loan usually works out cheaper than hire purchase or leasing, but investigate thoroughly because you may be able to get a cheaper deal on hire purchase through an arrangement made by your local trade association or other body of which you are a member.

One vital difference between a loan and hire purchase is that once you have bought a piece of equipment with a loan it is yours completely, whereas when you obtain a piece of equipment through hire purchase it is not yours until the last payment has been made and, therefore, could be repossessed if you do not keep up the payments.

Medium-term loans

These may span up to ten years and repayments are usually flexible in that they can be scheduled to suit the demands of your business. If, for example, you are in a seasonal business where you receive the bulk of your income at a particular point in the year you can schedule repayments for that time each year. To attract customers, many lenders offer incentives such as 'repayment holidays', meaning that no repayments are made for the first two years of the life of the loan. These are especially useful for business start-ups, but the banks do not lose out and the higher repayments later on have to be built into your financial forecasts.

Long-term loans

These are of over ten years' duration. They are unlikely to be of interest to the home-based business as they are commonly used to buy fixed assets with a long lifespan, such as buildings or large pieces of machinery. If you need to buy a bigger house in order to work from home, a conventional mortgage is much cheaper than a long-term loan.

Commercial mortgages

If you want to buy a property that will become your business as well as your home – a nursing home or shop, for example – you can take out a commercial mortgage. They are usually for a shorter period than domestic mortgages, requiring, say, a 10–15-year repayment rather than 20 or 25 years. Lending institutions say that they currently take each application on its merits and it is possible to negotiate deals similar to domestic mortgages, with low initial repayments, endowments attached and so on. It all depends on the size of the loan, whether the business is new or existing and several other factors.

There is tax relief on this form of mortgage and no upper limit on the size of the loan. Many lenders offer incentives in the form of 'repayment holidays' for the first year or so. Payments can be made monthly or quarterly and interest can be fixed or variable; you can usually opt to review your choice of interest status every year. Security for the finance is given by signing over the deeds of the property to the lenders so that in the event of default they can sell the property and reclaim their money. They will probably also require insurances to be taken out.

Special loans, grants and bursaries

If you have planned ahead, you may be able to apply for one of the grants or loans that are currently available. Finding out what is available requires a little research. Librarians should be able to access up-to-date grant information via their online databases. There are publications that give information about funding and, if you know what you are looking for, you can get plenty of information on the Internet: the Department of Trade and Industry (DTI)★ or European Social Fund★ websites are a good place to start. Also, the Small Business Service★, your Local Enterprise Agency, Learning and Skills Council (LSC)★ or Local Enterprise Council (LEC)★ in Scotland, or Business Link★ will be able to tell you what, if anything, your venture might be able to gain.

It is not possible to list in this book all the grants and loans available in the UK and EU. Below are the ones most likely to be of interest to the individual just starting out.

Bear in mind that the availability and size of grants change all the time because they are controlled by government policy regarding public sector largesse.

Government help

Loan Guarantee Scheme
The Department of Trade and Industry (DTI)★'s Small Firms Loan Guarantee Scheme provides a government guarantee for loans by

approved lenders. Loans are to firms or individuals unable to obtain conventional finance because of a lack of security. Changes were announced in November 2002 and these took effect on 1 April 2003. The scheme now operates as follows.

- There will be a single guaranteed interest rate of 7.5 per cent for all new loans.
- The scheme has been expanded and no longer excludes retailing, catering, coal industry and by-products, hairdressing and beauty parlours, house and estate agents, libraries, museums and cultural activities, motor vehicle and repair and servicing, steel, travel agents.
- The maximum turnover for an eligible non-manufacturing business has been increased from £1.5 million to £3 million.
- The premium (this is in addition to the interest) paid by the borrower has been raised from 1.5 per cent to 2 per cent per year on the outstanding balance for all new loans.
- Loans made prior to 1 April 1993 no longer count towards the maximum loan amount.
- The Small Business Service★ is to look at adding to the list of approved scheme lenders after 1 April 2003. At the time of writing 23 financial organisations participate.

Investors in small businesses
There are various schemes which match up investors and small businesses seeking start-up or growth capital. They are: Business Angels, found through the National Business Angels Network★; Corporate Venturing UK Ltd★; EquityLinkTM, which operates in the south and east of England and is contacted through Business Link Hertfordshire★, and LINC Scotland★.

Enterprise Investment Scheme
The Enterprise Investment Scheme (EIS) has been introduced to help small, unquoted trading companies raise equity finance and to encourage 'business angels' (outside investors who contribute both capital and management expertise) to invest in these companies. The advantage to these 'angels' is that they get income tax relief at 20 per cent on their investments (up to £150,000 a year) and capital gains tax exemption or deferral, depending upon

the amount of shares disposed of. Businesses that are excluded from the EIS are financial activities; dealing in land, commodities, futures, shares, securities or other financial instruments; dealing in goods other than an ordinary trade of retail or wholesale distribution; leasing or letting assets on hire; recurring royalties or licence fees (a special case may be made for film production or research and development); legal or accountancy services; property development; farming or market gardening; holding, managing or occupying woodlands; operating or managing hotels, guest houses or hostels; operating or managing nursing homes or residential care homes.

Venture Capital Trusts
Venture Capital Trusts (VCTs) are quoted limited companies whose purpose is to invest shareholders' funds in smaller unquoted trading companies. VCTs will provide a new source of finance for both new and expanding businesses.

Regional Selective Assistance (RSA) and Enterprise Grants
Discretionary RSA grants are available to assist projects that either create new jobs or protect existing jobs in those parts of the UK designated as Assisted Areas, where unemployment is high or major industries have closed. Unlike a loan, grant money does not have to be repaid. It is, in effect, a gift. Assistance can be provided to

- establish a new business
- expand/rationalise/modernise an existing business
- set up R & D (research and development) facilities
- enable businesses to take the next step from development to production.

The grants are normally paid in annual instalments and they are usually for 5 to 15 per cent of fixed project costs. All projects must last for at least five years.

Rural areas
Most of the grants or loans available for rural areas are concerned with diversification of land or turning a redundant building into a business enterprise and are covered fully in Chapter 13.

Career Development Loans (CDLs)

These deferred payment loans help individuals, including business owners, pay for vocational training courses lasting no longer than two years, plus, if relevant, a maximum of one year's practical experience, where it is part of the course. The government pays the interest on the loan for the duration of the course, which is administered through certain high-street banks, and for up to one month afterwards. The borrower then repays the loan and any further interest over a period agreed by the bank. Loans start at £300 and can go up to £8,000. At the moment CDLs are available through Barclays, The Co-operative Bank and The Royal Bank of Scotland.

New Deal Packages

At the time of writing, this initiative by the government has replaced all of the previous schemes that existed to encourage people to go back to work who have been unemployed and/or claiming benefits for at least six months. The New Deal packages offer different levels of support to different sections of the community:

- 18–24 year olds
- 25+ year olds
- 50+ year olds
- disabled
- lone parents.

The 18–24, 25+ and disabled groups are offered subsidised work (a guaranteed wage each week for a specific period), help with housing costs, and a range of benefits such as Working Families Tax Credit and Disabled Persons Tax Credit. The support applies also to those who wish to be self-employed.

Lone parents can receive help with expenses to attend meetings/interviews, fares and training plus childcare costs of up to £100 per week for one child or £150 for two or more.

The 50+ package pays Employment Credit – £60 a week, tax-free, on top of a wage if a full-time job is taken, or £40 if a part-time job is taken. Or the money can be used to become self-employed or start up a small business.

A Training Grant of up to £1,500 may be available. Further information on New Deal Packages can be obtained through local JobCentres.

Help with skills and technology

Listed below are some grant schemes geared towards research and development. A lone inventor, or a very small hi-tech company working from home, may be eligible for these schemes.

The Teaching Company Scheme (TCS)

The TCS★ is run by the Teaching Company Directorate and helps businesses of all sizes, but especially small firms with potential for growth, to access the knowledge, skills and technology in UK universities through partnerships between academia and business. A TCS programme involves one or more graduates each working for two years on key technology transfer projects identified by the company. For small firms, 70 per cent of the cost of using a graduate's skills can be awarded in grant form, and the remaining 30 per cent has to be found by the firm itself.

SMART

The SMART scheme is an initiative of The Small Business Service. It provides financial help, in the form of grants, to individuals and small- and medium-sized enterprises (SMEs) to review their use of technology and to develop new products and processes. It offers the following.

- Grants of up to £2,500 to individuals and SMEs (fewer than 250 employees) towards the cost of expert reviews of technology.
- Grants of up to £5,000 to help identify technical opportunities.
- Grants of 50 per cent of project costs (maximum £10,000) to individuals and micro-firms (fewer than ten employees) to develop prototypes of products or processes.
- Grants of 75 per cent of commercial feasibility studies costing a minimum of £30,000 and lasting 6–18 months.
- Development project grants of 30 per cent for larger projects costing more than £60,000 and lasting six months to three years.

Contact the website *www.business-adviceonline.org* for further information.

Export support

Advice on exporting is available from Business Link★ in England to any lone entrepreneur or small company wishing to export goods or services. In Scotland contact Scottish Enterprise★, in Wales contact Business Connect★.

Special funding is available for companies that want to operate in Central and Eastern Europe. The European Investment Bank also finances loans to small and medium enterprises. The European Investment Fund★ underwrites loans to small firms. Information is available from Euro Info Centres★. There is also The Export Award for Smaller Businesses. Any small firm that exports goods or services can apply. For further information, contact the Department of Trade and Industry (DTI)★ on their website *www.dti.gov.uk*.

Other sources of grants and loans

The Prince's Youth Business Trust* and the Prince's Scottish Youth Business Trust*

These two organisations help unemployed young people aged between 18 and 30 to start their own businesses by providing financial help, business monitoring and marketing opportunities. Applicants must have a viable business idea and be able to demonstrate the necessary initiative and commitment to make it succeed and they must have been unable to obtain funding from other sources.

The Trusts will award a loan of up to a maximum of £5,000 at a low fixed interest rate, without security, to a person starting a business. Special awards can be made to disadvantaged applicants. The Trusts will also suggest additional sources of support and finance and help people make applications.

Highlands & Islands Enterprise (HIE)*

This organisation is interested in assisting the social and economic development, training and environmental renewal in the Highlands and Islands, which covers half of Scotland. Grant provision varies but is quite generous, and the HIE is particularly interested in emerging businesses in the areas of food and drink, manufacturing and production, tourism, and IT and telecoms.

Livewire*

Sponsored by Shell UK Ltd, Livewire offers advice and assistance on business start-up and planning. This is for young entrepreneurs aged between 16 and 25. Livewire also holds an annual competition to reward the achievements of young people new to business. Winners receive cash awards.

The Crafts Council of England*

Established in 1973, The Crafts Council Development Award (CCDA)has helped over 1,200 craftspeople to set up a creative practice. The Award provides financial and business support for those at the start of their creative career (at any age), over the course of one year. It has no limits to the number of awards but applicants need to have practised their craft for more than three years.

The CCDA comprises a maintenance grant of £2,500 that is divided into four payments of £625 over one year and is intended to assist with the cost of funding the practice and with general subsistence. Applicants may not receive this grant if they are in receipt of other government funding. The CCDA also offers an equipment grant of up to £5,000, of which the Crafts Council contributes 50 per cent of all eligible purchases. A third of the money may be used towards purchasing marketing equipment such as cameras or computers.

Similar awards are run by the Arts Council of Wales★ and the Scottish Arts Council★.

The Arts Councils* (National and Regional)

Grants are available for both individuals and organisations. The Arts Councils of England, Scotland and Wales tend to reserve their grant aid for projects of national or international significance. Regional and local councils have a budget and they decide on their own local priorities. If you think you might stand a chance, put in an application. Remember, too, that Arts Councils cover all the visual and performing arts.

NESTA*

NESTA is the National Endowment for Science, Technology and the Arts, and was established under the National Lottery Act. It aims to fill a funding gap by investing in outstanding ideas and the people who have them. If you have an idea for a new product or service in the above categories, then it is worth applying.

English Tourism Council (ETC) and Regional Tourist Boards*

Many of the grants and loans available for tourist projects are discussed in Chapter 13. However, not everyone wants to start up a tourist business using their own home and land. In certain areas, such as Wales and Scotland, there is a general policy to encourage tourism as much as possible and therefore new or potential businesses are more likely to get financial support, particularly if they will employ others.

The ETC and Profunding*, a specialist provider of advice on funding sources, have joined forces to highlight sources of funding for tourism. The website *www.fundinginformation.org/tourism* is a subscription-only website. Contact the ETC for free information first.

Chapter 7

Organising yourself

Organising yourself covers many things, so this chapter looks at your workplace, as well as getting to grips with your accounts; tax, expenses and VAT; the various insurances you may require; and that pension for your retirement.

The place where you work

It is important that your home does not turn into a complete tip, with explosions of paperwork or manufacturing-in-progress everywhere. Try to make one particular place your work base. This does not mean that you cannot sit in front of the television during the day or in the evening doing your envelope stuffing/embroidery/dried flower arrangements and so on, but it does mean that you should have a room or a cupboard where everything is put away when you are not doing it. And, if you have small children, that place should preferably have a lock on it for their safety and your sanity – you do not want to find the kids tinkering with your computer when your back is turned and wiping out all your records! However, try not to make one part of your house exclusively for work, as you may find yourself liable to pay business rates. (Storing away dangerous or valuable equipment in a lockable room is different.)

The place you set aside for most of your work should be comfortable, the temperature should be adjustable, there should be some natural light and good ventilation. In your enthusiasm at starting your own venture you may think that you can happily work in a damp cellar, a draughty attic or a cold shed, but after a few weeks the reality will begin to get you down.

If you intend to do a lot of office work, you will require a proper office set-up. You will need space to lay out all your papers; a suitable desk and a comfortable, adjustable chair that offers lumbar support for the small of your back (you don't want to get backache or stiff shoulders and neck); somewhere to file all your documents; a telephone near at hand (you cannot keep running up and down stairs every time it rings – perhaps it is time to think about a mobile or a cordless phone); and peace and quiet if the job at hand requires concentration.

When planning your workstation, consider how many power sources your equipment needs and keep electrical cables out of the way with cord clips or inbuilt channels in work surfaces or desk legs. To minimise distractions, a screen, curtain or bookcase can give you privacy and separate your work station from high-activity areas. Store material according to how often you use it – you shouldn't have to keep stretching to reach things you need. Papers and files you don't use regularly can be archived somewhere else in your house.

To stay healthy at your workstation:

- avoid working with your head, upper body or legs twisted when at your desk. This can restrict blood flow and cause muscles and tendons to overwork
- don't cross your legs or hug your chair with your legs while using the computer, as this may result in lower limb circulation problems and fatigue
- ensure that you can reach your mouse without having to stretch for it, and that the desk surface supports your forearm. Move your mouse with your arm, not just your wrist, and don't grip it tightly
- use a footrest if your feet don't touch the floor. This will ensure there is no undue pressure from the edge of your seat on the backs of your thighs
- make sure that neither you nor your computer screen are directly facing windows or bright lights, to avoid glare and reflections on screen
- when working at your computer, keep the lighting lower than you would for reading paper documents, and look away often and blink to avoid eyestrain
- take short, frequent breaks from the screen. Stand up and stretch regularly, roughly every 20 minutes.

If you are manufacturing, repairing, renovating, or raising plants in your outbuildings, you need some space and a source of power for your tools and to provide warmth and light. Someone in the house may answer the phone for you but it might be useful to have an extension in the shed or a cordless telephone. The outbuilding should be waterproof and easily heated.

You may be able to do work such as hand-knitting anywhere, but you need a place to store all your materials. This should be dry, animal/insect/children-proof and easy to get at – you do not want to have to bring out a ladder and climb up into the roof every time you want a box of wool.

Organising yourself for work is basically common sense but sometimes the enthusiasm of starting this new career prevents a calm assessment of the true picture. You can work successfully only if you have the space and you have prepared your working conditions properly.

The structure of your business

Preferably before you start up, you should decide on the structure of your business (though you can change the structure later on). Will you trade as a self-employed person (and perhaps in partnership with others) or as a company?

If you decide to operate as a **company**, you can form a new company or buy one off the shelf and register it yourself – free booklets from Companies House★ and self-help books from libraries or bookshops explain the steps you need to take. But it is much easier to get an accountant to do the work for you. Either way, there are various fees to pay.

If you opt for **self-employment**, you simply start trading with no formalities to go through first. But, within three months of the end of the month you started up, you must register with the Inland Revenue★; there is usually a £100 penalty if you fail to do so. You don't have to wait for the three months to be up – it's best to register straight away. Do this by calling the Inland Revenue helpline 08459 154515 or filling in the form in booklet P/SE/1: *Thinking of working for yourself?* from tax offices or the Inland Revenue website *www.inlandrevenue.gov.uk*. The Inland Revenue arranges for you to start paying Class 2 National Insurance contributions, ensures you are in the income tax system and, if applicable, passes on a request to become VAT-registered.

When making your choice, you need to consider the following factors.

- A company is much more formal. It has a separate legal identity from you and there are strict legal rules it must follow, for example, on preparing its report and accounts and filing returns with Companies House within strict time limits.
- You are more likely to need the services of an accountant if you operate as a company, so expect to pay more in professional fees than you would as a self-employed person.
- You need to involve at least one other person if you form a company. Although you can be a sole director, you'll need a separate person to act as company secretary.
- Paying yourself is much more formal if you have a company. You can receive a salary and/or dividends. Your company must operate Pay-As-You-Earn (PAYE) if you receive a salary or benefits. The board of the company must meet to declare a dividend. If you are self-employed, you can draw money from your business at any time with the minimum of fuss and you work out any tax due later.
- At the time of writing, most small businesses could save a lot of tax by operating as a company rather than through self-employment, provided dividends formed part of the pay.
- A company may have more credibility, which could help you win contracts and obtain credit from suppliers and lenders.
- A company has limited liability: this means, in theory at least, you cannot personally be held liable for the debts of the company. (In practice, a bank might well insist that a business loan is secured against personal assets such as your home, and you will be liable for the company's debts if you trade knowing that the company is insolvent.) If you are self-employed (or in partnership), your business does not have a separate legal identity from you, so the business debts are also your personal debts.

Keeping accounts

It is important to keep a careful record of all financial transactions concerned with your work, not only to check whether you are making a profit or loss but also because the record forms the basis of your dealings with the Inland Revenue and, if you register for VAT, Customs and Excise. These bodies can ask at any time to see past accounts from roughly six years previously, or longer if they suspect fraud. You can be fined up to £3,000 if you fail to keep your records for this time.

Keeping records means having a piece of paper for every transaction. File all your invoices, bills, receipts you give or are given, cheque stubs, letters and anything else at all relating to your takings and expenditure. If you do not have a receipt for small items, make out a petty cash slip to put in your records describing the item bought, the place you bought it, the amount spent and the date the transaction occurred.

Always make a note of any item that might possibly be allowable for tax purposes (see page 124): it is difficult to get a claim allowed for any items if they have not been recorded in the business books. Be especially careful to record all expenses that relate to your work where part of your business expenses come out of the household account, such as electricity or telephone bills. You will need some record of all such expenses when compiling a claim for tax allowances.

File your records in date order and give every document a consecutive number which can be cross-referenced to your accounts. If there are not many, they can be put into a folder or box file or on a spike; alternatively, keep them in a ring binder. If you transfer money between your personal finances and your business – for example, because you pay for a business item with your personal credit card or use the business account to pay a domestic bill – keep the relevant personal records too.

The records are the evidence of your business transactions, but don't make a lot of sense until you compile them into a set of accounts. The first stage is to keep a set of books. In a simple business, you may just need separate books for receipts, payments you make, your bank account and petty cash. Every business transaction must be entered in the books – for example, if you pay the phone bill by cheque, this needs to be recorded in the payments book and also in the bank book.

Your volume of work will dictate what records need to be kept. For instance, a writer whose year's work produces, say, one book may just have a single receipt of payment from the publisher with few expenses – perhaps paper, floppy disks, postage, fares – and you may be able to create accounts by simply using one book in which to record your income and expenditure. On the other hand, someone offering hairdressing will have numerous small receipts of cash and expenses for stock, equipment and telephone, a car if he or she travels to clients and so on – such a business will probably require more than one accounts book.

If you are registered for VAT, you are usually required to keep a separate VAT account, so that you can work out how much to pay to or claim back from Customs and Excise, though you may be able to avoid this if you opt for the flat-rate VAT scheme (see page 132).

Depending on the volume of business you do, you should make up the books daily or weekly. You can either do this yourself or hire the services of a bookkeeper (look in the small ads of a local newspaper or directory). If you opt for the DIY route, consider joining an evening class on bookkeeping or buying a simplified accounting process. Many accountants recommend using something like a Simplex D account book. Or, if you have a computer, you could choose one of the many accounting software packages. Remember to keep a copy of all computer accounts in a separate place, in case of theft or fire.

The books are used at the end of the year to draw up your accounts. If you operate as a company, the accounts must be drawn up using standard accounting practices and presented in a standard format with various prescribed statements. Unless you are very confident that you understand the rules and can keep up to date with changes to them, use an accountant – he or she will have computer software that automatically churns out the accounts in the required format. A company must produce a balance sheet as well as a profit and loss account.

If you are self-employed (or in partnership), you are also required by law to follow standard accounting practices but, for now at least, there seems to be some leniency provided your accounts present a true and fair view of your business. You need to produce a profit and loss account but are not required to produce a balance sheet (though it is good practice to do so and will help you to spot any errors in your accounts).

Business bank accounts

It is advisable to keep all your business money in a separate bank or building society account so that you can keep track of your income and expenditure and do not get them mixed up with your domestic finances. If you set up your business as a company, you must by law have a separate company bank account.

If you are self-employed and don't have a separate business account, the money that comes in and goes out for your work should still be kept strictly separate from your personal and household finances. You could have two cheque books and paying-in books, using one for business and one for private payments. Where you have a separate business account, remember to mark all personal transactions drawn from the account as 'drawings'. Having both a personal and a business account need not be expensive. Most personal accounts do not levy any bank charges provided your account is in credit. Business accounts used to carry a charge for each transaction but, following a government review, in 2003 banks started to be required to offer business customers either free banking while in credit or interest on the balance in their account. Some banks already do this, so shop around.

You need to keep track of your business finances, so ask to be sent monthly statements. Even if you are just a personal account holder you are entitled to ask for regular monthly statements, or more frequent ones if you wish, although you might be charged for any service that is not standard. Check at regular intervals that the balance of your account agrees with your account books.

It is essential to set aside, in an account which earns interest preferably, the money required to meet tax and VAT liabilities when these fall due. You do not want to be faced with a staggering tax bill with no money available to pay it.

Employing an accountant

You might use an accountant for various reasons: to draw up your annual accounts from your books and records, prepare your VAT returns, complete your tax return or give you tax advice. One way to find an accountant is by personal recommendation. It is important to check that you are using someone who is properly trained and qualified and has insurance to protect you if things go wrong. Check that an accountant belongs to one of the following professional bodies, who can give you a list of their members in your area: Association of Chartered Certified Accountants★, Institute of Chartered Accountants in England and Wales★, Institute of Chartered Accountants in Ireland★ or the Institute of Chartered Accountants of Scotland★.

Alternatively, look in *Yellow Pages*. If you are looking simply for help with your tax return and/or tax advice, choose a firm which belongs to the Association of Taxation Technicians★ or, for more highly qualified advisers, the Chartered Institute of Taxation★.

When first contacting a firm of accountants, make it clear that you need somebody who knows about the financial aspects of a small company, self-employed or freelance person, as appropriate. An accountant knowledgeable about the hazards and complexities of self-employment can save you a lot of money as well as time; one who specialises in a different area may be unaware of all the pitfalls and possibilities.

Professional accountants charge on an hourly basis, according to seniority and type of work, plus expenses. There is no fixed scale, but allow for at least £70 an hour, plus VAT. Some accountants offer special rates for small businesses, depending upon the type of business and the work involved. Specify (preferably in writing) what work you want an accountant to do for you and ask what his or her charge is likely to be. The bill should be itemised according to the work you have agreed between you – for example, giving advice, preparing a tax return, dealing with VAT and any other bookkeeping matters. Obviously, the more thorough you are in your method of bookkeeping, the less work an accountant has to do and the more money it will save you.

The accounting year

With the possible exception of the first year, your accounts should run for a 12-month period which begins and ends on the same dates each year. Your accounting year need not necessarily be the calendar year 1 January to 31 December, nor need it coincide with the tax year 6 April to 5 April or the financial year 1 April to 31 March.

If you operate as a company, your tax bill is worked out for each financial year. If your accounting year is different, the tax bill is based on a proportion of the profits from each of the accounting years that straddle the financial year.

Self-employed people (and partners) are taxed on the basis of tax years. But, apart from the first year or two in business and the year you close down, your tax bill is worked out using the profits for the accounting year which ended during the relevant tax year. This means substantial tax advantages or disadvantages can result from the selection of the annual accounting date.

If you choose your accounting year carefully, that is, end it a little after the start of the tax year, you will maximise the period of time between making the profits and paying the final instalment of tax due on them. As long as your profits are rising, this is an advantage, as you will be paying tax on lower profits than you are currently making. Take advice from your accountant and/or refer to *Which? Way to Save Tax* (a book published annually by Which? Books) or *The Which? Tax-Saving Guide* (issued with *Which?* magazine in March every year).

Tax

The Inland Revenue★ has a wide range of publications that cover many aspects of tax. They can be obtained from the Inland Revenue orderline (0845) 9000 404, any tax office or downloaded from the Inland Revenue website. A free catalogue of leaflets and booklets is available.

Submitting accounts

Companies pay corporation tax under the 'pay and file' system: within nine months of the end of an accounting period, they must estimate and pay their tax bill. The tax return, accounts and tax computation must be filed within 12 months of the end of the accounting period and further tax payments or rebates may then be due. (In addition, you personally may need to complete an income tax return on which you declare any salary, benefits or dividends you receive from the company along with any other income or gains that you have. For information on this, see *Which? Way to Save Tax* published by Which? Books.) Under separate rules, the company must also file its accounts each year with Companies House★. Since you are most likely to leave all of this to an accountant if you operate as a company, the rest of this chapter looks at the position if you are self-employed.

Individuals and **partnerships** pay income tax on their profits under the self-assessment system. They must normally deliver a tax return by 31 January following the end of the relevant tax year. The tax return itself is made up of a basic section that everyone who gets a return fills in, and one or more supplements – there is a supplement for people who are self-employed and a separate supplement for people who work in a partnership. The supplements are very similar and ask for details of your business income, expenses and reliefs for the relevant accounting period.

Individuals and partnerships who have an annual turnover of less than a certain amount (at the time of writing it is £15,000 per year) may submit a simple three-line summary to the tax office, if they wish. The turnover is the gross or full amount your business earns before deducting any expenses.

For example:

Turnover	£13,847
Less business expenses	3,017
Net profits	10,830

The Inland Revenue reserves the right to ask for more details if, for example, your turnover has suddenly done a nosedive to a low figure when previously you were earning far more. However, the simple tax account is usually acceptable, particularly in the case of people just starting up.

If you are genuinely self-employed, you will be taxed under Schedule D. This may allow you to claim tax relief on more expenses than if you were an employee and taxed by PAYE under Schedule E and also means that you pay less National Insurance. It is important that the Inland Revenue has accepted your self-employed status, because if it has not some of your clients might make you pay employer's contributions.

To be considered self-employed, you have to prove to the Inland Revenue's satisfaction that you meet most or all of the criteria in the box on page 126. This may be especially hard to do if one person has the sole rights to your working time: therefore, try to get work from several sources.

Whether you are employed or self-employed depends on the terms of the particular engagement you have entered into. If you supply a service to only one, or predominantly one, customer, a

Tax checklist

Record all business receipts and earnings. These must include:

- all money earned, but not necessarily received, by the main activity of the business, that is the provision of goods and services
- all tips, commissions, discounts or rebates
- the normal selling price of any goods or materials you took out of the business for your own use or for your family and friends, or donated to charity or competitions
- the value of any goods or services you received in exchange for work done or goods sold
- any grant, allowance, subsidy or bursary you receive.

Record all day-to-day expenditure. This includes:

- purchases of stock
- rent, heat, light, phone
- insurances
- running costs of a car, van or other vehicle
- printing, photocopying, faxes, stationery, delivery costs and postage, computer software with a limited useful life (say no more than two years)
- staff, outworker or subcontractor wages or payments.

Record all capital expenditure. This includes:

- any plant or machinery you have purchased for your work

formal letter or contract might clarify your position as an independent self-employed contractor.

Allowable expenses

The Inland Revenue defines an allowable expense as 'any expense which is wholly and exclusively incurred for the purpose of the trade' but some items are allowed if a 'proportion' of their use is for your business, for example, premises, cars or a telephone. The following are usually allowable:

- **Stock and services** – things or people's services (as in the case of an agency) that you buy and then resell.

- vans, cars, motor bikes and so on
- furniture and fittings
- computer hardware, computer software where it has an expected useful life of several years, fax machines, telephones, word processors and so on
- other equipment, for example scaffolding, ladders, buckets, wheelbarrows.

Record the details of the purchase and sale of capital equipment. If you are buying equipment, the Inland Revenue will want to know the following:

- what did you buy?
- when did you buy it?
- how much did it cost? (If you are VAT-registered, record the amount of VAT included in the price)
- what proportion is used for business purposes? (A telephone, for example, may have a domestic use as well.)

If you sell equipment the Inland Revenue will want to know:

- what you sold
- when did you sell it?
- how much did you receive in cash or part-exchange?

- **Accommodation costs** – a proportion of your rent, business rates (note that it is the whole amount of business rates and a proportion of domestic rates or Council Tax), heating, lighting, telephone and repairs carried out to the 'business' part of your home.
- **Employee costs** – wages/salaries, pensions, insurances and employers' NI contributions.
- **Marketing** – anything under the headings of advertising, sales promotions or public relations. This also includes any 'free' gifts to clients/customers, provided they are not in the form of alcohol, tobacco or food, that they advertise your company (for example calendars or diaries with your company name on) and

125

Employed or self-employed?

The Inland Revenue leaflet (IR56/NI39) *Employed or Self-Employed? A Guide for tax and National Insurance* offers the following checklist.

If you can answer 'yes' to the following questions, you are probably an employee:

- Do you yourself have to do the work rather than hire someone else to do it for you?
- Can someone tell you at any time what to do or when and how to do it?
- Are you paid by the hour, week or month? Can you get overtime pay?
- Do you work set hours, or a given number of hours a week or month?
- Do you work at the premises of the person you work for, or at a place or places he or she decides?

---

that they do not exceed £15 each in cost. Also included are the materials you may purchase in respect of market research, such as publications or surveys.

- **Bad debts** – monies that you cannot recover from customers, that is, specific bad debts.
- **Finance** – interest on any bank loans, bank charges, the interest element of hire purchase or leasing contracts.
- **VAT** – if you are not registered for VAT, the VAT you pay on the goods and services that you buy is treated as an allowable expense.
- **Pre-trading expenses** – any money spent on research, setting-up costs and so on.
- **Other** – transport, travel, hotels, training costs (if incurred after business start-up), stationery, postage, professional services such as accountants and solicitors, insurances.

Non-allowable expenses

- **Entertaining** – taking customers for a meal; hospitality of any kind (although entertaining staff is allowed within limits).
- **Excluded professional fees** – architect's fees or the costs of drawing up a lease, for example.

If you can answer 'yes' to the following questions, you are probably self-employed:

- Do you have the final say in how the business is run?
- Do you risk your own money in the business?
- Are you responsible for meeting the losses as well as taking the profits?
- Do you provide the main items of equipment you need to do your job, not just the small tools many employees provide for themselves?
- Are you free to hire other people on your own terms to do the work you have taken on? And do you pay them out of your own pocket?
- Do you have to correct unsatisfactory work in your own time and at your own expense?

If you are in any doubt, the Inland Revenue will advise you over the telephone.

- **Clothing** – unless your occupation demands special protective clothing or uniforms.
- **Depreciation or cost of capital items** – you can usually claim capital allowances instead in respect of the purchase of plant, machinery, equipment but not usually premises unless they are industrial or agricultural buildings.
- **Fines** – any fines incurred through the legal process, including parking tickets.

Non-taxable income

In your first year of business you may be relying on income from redundancy payments or state benefits until you are able to generate other income.

- **Redundancy payments** – anything below £30,000 might be tax free – your previous employer should be able to tell you if this applies.
- **State benefits** – this is of particular relevance to disabled and retired people. See Chapter 3, which contains details of non-taxable benefits.

National Insurance

The principal National Insurance rates for 2003/4 are detailed in the table below:

Main National Insurance rates in 2003–4

Class 1 contributions

On weekly earnings:	Employee pays this rate:	Employer pays this rate:
£0–£77 (lower earnings limit)	0%	0%
£77.01–£89	0%	0%
£89.01–£595 (upper earnings limit)	11%	12.8%
£595.01 and above	1%	12.8%

Class 2 contributions

Flat weekly rate	£2
Small earnings exception	£4,095

Class 4 contributions

On annual profits of:	
£0 – £4,615 (lower profits limit)	0%
£4,616 – £30,940 (upper profits limit)	8%
£30,941 and above	1%

If you are self-employed, you normally pay flat-rate Class 2 contributions: these are optional if your income is below the small earnings exception. However, Class 2 contributions are very cheap and can entitle you to state benefits if you are ill or when you retire, so they are usually worth paying. If your profits are above the lower profits limit, you also have to pay Class 4 contributions.

Directors count as employees. So, if you run your business as a company, you have to pay employee's Class 1 contributions on any salary that you pay yourself above the primary threshold. (Provided you pay yourself at least the lower earnings limit, you will be building up entitlement to state benefits even if you are paying no contributions.) In addition, the company, as your employer, has to pay employer's Class 1 contributions on the salary it pays you and also contributions on most fringe benefits that it provides you with (such as a company car). There are no National Insurance contributions on dividends, so that can be a particularly tax-efficient way to pay yourself.

However, a company or partnership that provides personal services (broadly, labour only) to its clients may fall foul of the 'IR35 rules'.

The IR35 rules were created to stop consultants and contractors avoiding National Insurance by calling themselves companies or partnerships although they were working full time and long term for one employer. Rather than being paid as employees, they would invoice the 'client' and then pay themselves in dividends, upon which, of course, there are no National Insurance contributions. In order to stop this practice, the company or partnership is treated by the Inland Revenue as if it has paid you a deemed salary at the end of the year (whether or not you really did get any salary) on which income tax and Class 1 National Insurance are charged. The IR35 rules do not apply to sole traders who would in any case be taxed as employees if they did not appear to be genuinely self-employed.

If you employ anyone in your business, both you and your employee are liable for Class 1 contributions on their pay.

It is possible for a person to be in the situation of being both employed and self-employed, for example as an employed tele-worker but doing some freelance work on the side, in which case Class 1 and 2 contributions together will be limited to no more than the maximum contributions an employee would pay. And special rules limit the total of Classes 1, 2 and 4 contributions you can be liable for. Instead of claiming back excess contributions later, you may be able to apply to defer them. Get advice on National Insurance from the Inland Revenue★.

Exemptions

You are exempt from paying National Insurance contributions if:

- you are in receipt of maternity allowance
- you are sick for a prolonged period
- you have reached pensionable age (though employer's contributions continue)

- your earnings are below the limits shown in the table, and
- in some other circumstances.

It is worth noting that Class 4 contributions are related to profits and if you should make a loss in any taxable year you will not pay income tax or Class 4 contributions. Also you can claim relief for losses so that they reduce income tax and National Insurance payable in other years.

It is always advisable to check with the Inland Revenue if you are in any doubt about the contributions you should be making and to read their literature before starting your venture or seeking work.

VAT

Registration for VAT is compulsory if your sales for the preceding 12 months or your anticipated sales for the next 12 months are over the current VAT threshold of £55,000.

Some traders register voluntarily for VAT, even though their sales do not come above the threshold, because it is advantageous for them to be able to reclaim the VAT they pay out on purchases; for example, you will be able to claim back the VAT on all your business expenses on which VAT is charged. Working from home, you can claim back a proportion of VAT on such items as the telephone bill and petrol for your vehicle. This is especially advantageous if you do not have to charge your customers VAT because you are making zero-rated supplies, or they can claim back any VAT because they are themselves VAT-registered. If you register before you start trading you can reclaim VAT on pre-trading business expenses (but see 'Cash Accounting', below).

The VAT that you pay on your purchases is called 'input tax' and the VAT you charge on goods or services you sell is called 'output tax'. The difference between the two is what is paid to the Customs and Excise (unless you have opted into the flat-rate scheme – see below). In other words, you buy an item from a company which costs £1 plus 18p VAT. You then sell that item on to your customer for £2 plus 35p VAT. The VAT that you then pay to Customs and Excise is 35p – 18p = 17p, the difference between the two.

Most goods and services are classed as standard rate VAT, which is currently 17.5 per cent in the UK. Some goods and services are exempt, for example, finance, education, insurance and postage; and some are zero-rated, for example, books, public transport and children's clothing. (Check with Customs and Excise* for a detailed list.)

If you register for VAT you must issue a tax invoice to every customer who is VAT-registered or who asks you for such an invoice. The tax invoice gives a complete breakdown of the transaction. By law, it must show the following:

- your business name and address
- your VAT registration number
- your invoice number
- either the date of invoice, date of supply or date of receipt of payment (this is called the 'tax point')
- customer's name and address
- manner of supply, that is, rent, sale, lease
- description of goods or services supplied
- quantity or period of supply, for example, six lawnmowers or one temporary typist for three days
- cost of those goods or that service before adding VAT
- the amount of VAT on each item
- the rate of VAT on each item, that is, 17.5 per cent
- any cash discounts given
- the separate total VAT
- the grand total.

Note: no tax invoice is necessary for sales direct to the public, for example in a shop or market, unless the customer insists.

If you are registered for VAT, to reclaim VAT on your purchases, you have to keep all the relevant invoices of purchases made. They should, preferably, be tax invoices showing the complete breakdown of how the VAT was arrived at.

Usually you pay or reclaim VAT by making a quarterly return to Customs and Excise. You can ask for the pattern of quarters that fits best with your accounting year. Except where you have registered voluntarily, you can ask to make monthly returns if you normally expect to reclaim VAT: this means you will be reimbursed more speedily but you will have more paperwork. To reduce paperwork, small businesses can opt for annual accounting or the flat-rate scheme (see below). With annual accounting, you send in just one VAT return a year, and in the meantime make nine monthly payments on account. But on the minus side you have a long wait for repayment if you have overpaid VAT through the monthly payments. Discuss the options with your accountant.

If you go for quarterly returns it is very important that they are submitted within one month of the end of the quarter. Failure to do so can result in, at the least, interest being charged on the late payment and, at the worst, a heavy fine. There are also severe penalties for any 'misdeclarations' or attempts to falsify VAT returns.

On the other hand, you receive interest on delayed repayments of VAT from Customs and Excise.

Cash accounting
Normally, VAT is due on the invoices you send out, even if you have to wait some time for payment. So, if you send out an invoice towards the end of your VAT quarter, you will probably have to hand over the VAT on it to Customs and Excise before your customer pays you, causing you a possible cash-flow problem.

However, most small businesses opt for the cash accounting system by which to pay VAT: this means that the tax point is the date when money is received from customers, not the date when you asked them for the money. This greatly assists the cash-flow problems of small businesses because it means that you do not have to pay Customs and Excise the VAT you have charged until you receive that money from your customers (but businesses who opt for it are not able to claim back pre-start-up VAT on business expenses). Accountants often advise registering for VAT and then changing to the cash accounting system later, particularly if pre-start-up expenses are considerable.

Flat-rate scheme
Since April 2002, small businesses can opt to use this scheme which is designed to reduce the amount of paperwork involved in being VAT-registered. The idea is that, instead of keeping full records of all the VAT you charge on your supplies and pay on your purchases and working out the difference, you simply hand over to Customs and Excise an amount worked out as a flat percentage of your turnover including VAT. The percentage you must use is set according to the type of business you do – for example, 5 per cent if

132

you're a food retailer, 10 per cent for photography and 14.5 per cent for IT consultants. But you still give your customers tax invoices as normal and still charge them the normal rate of VAT.

The percentages reflect the net rate of VAT that different types of business tend to pay on average but, if you're not average, using the flat-rate scheme could mean you pay either more or less VAT than you would by accounting for VAT in the normal way.

Using the flat-rate scheme means that, in theory at least, you need only keep a record of your sales including VAT and can forget about the rest of the usual VAT record-keeping. However, when you come to draw up your accounts and prepare your tax return, depending on the accounting approach you use, you may need to know the actual VAT on your sales and purchases as well as the amount you have paid under the flat-rate scheme. In that case, you will not have saved yourself paperwork after all.

To find out more, get VAT Notice 733 *VAT flat rate scheme for small businesses* from your VAT (Customs and Excise★) office or the Customs and Excise website *www.hmce.gov.uk*.

Developing a good relationship with the VAT inspectorate

Despite the fact that most businesses hate VAT, mainly because it adds to their paperwork, it can be a very useful tool for disciplining the small businessman or -woman to keep accurate records. Also, the VAT system is fairly flexible and VAT inspectors are there to help and advise. You can, as discussed, change from the traditional to the cash-accounting system, or the flat-rate scheme, if you wish. You can do monthly or quarterly or even annual returns, depending upon which is more convenient for you. The VAT inspectorate will advise on how to deal with VAT on bad debts. De-registration, if you expect your sales to be below the VAT threshold of £55,000, is a simple procedure.

The main thing is to have a good relationship with the inspectorate: get the most out of the staff, who will advise you willingly, from start-up to de-registration.

Insurance

Most people go through life with some life insurance, a household contents policy, mortgage insurance, buildings insurance and perhaps some health insurance.

You should inform your insurers if you become self-employed or start up a business from home. Some household contents policies may cover home computers, as these come into the sphere of home entertainment, but nothing more. You should in any case talk to your insurer about this. You will certainly need a special insurance – or an extension to your household policy – to cover any business equipment, machinery, tools and other items necessary to your trade. You will not only need to insure them against theft, fire and any other hazard but you might also want to insure them against breakdown and the consequential loss of business while they are being repaired or replaced. Currently, the high-street banks offer home contents policies which cover those conducting clerical or teleworking-type businesses from home – so do some other insurers. There are also office equipment policies which cover certain items such as computers, faxes and answerphones. The average amount of cover would seem to be around £35,000. Some policies also cover business money (up to around £3,000) and stock and trade samples, up to a certain value, kept at home.

What you pay for your insurance depends very much upon what business you are engaged in. For example, furniture restoration involves the use and storage of flammable products, as does photography, if you develop your own photographs. Catering from home may be deemed by the insurer to be an increased risk of fire and so on. If you sell your wares in markets and fairs this will mean carrying large quantities of cash around and transporting your goods from location to location. You may be involved in mail order and need to insure your goods while in transit. You may rear animals or market garden crops and need a special veterinary or farming insurance.

Some off-the-shelf packages are available which cover particular trades – but read the small print *very carefully* to make sure that every aspect of your operation is covered. Computer insurance, for example, is only of value if it covers the data (which may be your most valuable asset) as well as the hardware and software. If your house or workshop should burn down or be destroyed in a storm, you need to be able to rent somewhere else to work while repairs are being done, so this should be an integral part of your cover.

Some professional bodies and national associations have negotiated special insurance packages on behalf of their members: for example, a driving instructor may be able to get insurance cover that combines all his or her needs through the appropriate organisation.

It is worth mentioning here that recent national disasters in the UK such as localised flooding and foot and mouth outbreaks among livestock have radically altered the insurance scene in some industries. It is not just farmers who have problems. Any business that manages or cares for animals could be affected and businesses/properties that have been damaged by flooding more than once are now having difficulty getting insurance cover.

What insurances do you need?

To find out what is available, most trade, business and professional bodies will tell you what insurances you need for your enterprise; trade magazines will probably carry articles about them. Alternatively, contact the Association of British Insurers★ or a reputable broker for comprehensive information. To find a broker contact the British Insurance Brokers Association★.

Business insurances

A variety of business insurances can be purchased, depending upon the needs of your business or venture. They can be bought separately or put together in one package.

Engineering This insurance provides cover against electrical or mechanical breakdown for most machinery, including computers. By law, most items of plant such as boilers, lifts and lifting machinery must be inspected regularly by a qualified person but an insurer would probably require any pieces of machinery that you wished to insure to be inspected as well.

Money Money insurance is on an 'all risk' basis and covers cash, cheques, postage stamps and certain other negotiable documents. This type of insurance cover is particularly important if you have to move money around all the time, say from your home to craft fair to bank. Also, if your work, say in network marketing or collecting catalogue payments, means that you are going to be walking the streets carrying money, many policies include a compensation clause for you or your employee being assaulted during a theft of money.

Goods in transit This covers goods against loss or damage while in your vehicle or when sent by carrier. The sum insured may be a limit for each vehicle or for any one consignment. Very useful if you are trying to run a modest mail-order company.

Business interruption This compensates you financially for any loss or interruption to your business because of damage to your property.

Credit insurance Gives cover against the risk of debtors becoming insolvent and being unable to pay.

Book debts Cover against loss of money arising from accidental damage to or theft of books of account.

Frozen food Cover against loss of frozen food in deep-freeze units caused by breakdown or damage to the unit or failure of the electricity supply. An absolutely essential policy if you are running a catering business from home.

Glass Cover for the replacement of glass following malicious or accidental damage.

Legal expenses Policy that covers most business-related legal expenses, from employment tribunal hearings to High Court actions.

Key personnel This type of insurance cover can be particularly important for small businesses where each member of the organisation performs a vital function. If a member of staff becomes seriously ill or dies, then the cost of a temporary replacement to stop the business grinding to a halt can be high.

Mobile phone cover Increasingly important as the mobile phone has now become the essential business tool and the object most targeted by thieves. Packages offered by mobile phone retailers and the networks cost £20 to £30 a year. Some operators also include cover for up to £100 of unauthorised calls made after the phone has been stolen.

Liability cover

The following areas of insurance cover are very important.

Employer's liability insurance This is required by law if you employ anyone. It covers you if an employee should make a claim for injury, sickness or disability arising from their employment.

Public liability insurance This is not compulsory but advisable. It covers you if a member of the public should suffer injury to him- or herself or his or her premises through your business and sues you – for example, you are a plumber and you flood someone's house or a member of the public visits your weaving studio, trips over an item left carelessly on the floor and breaks a leg. If you employ sub-contractors you need to extend the cover to third-party public liability.

Product liability insurance If you manufacture a product, even in a small way, you need to insure yourself against a lawsuit should a customer be injured by your product. If you think that what you manu-facture could not possibly harm anyone, beware – there have been two cases in recent years that should be noted. One was of a handmade quilt manufacturer being sued because the wadding she bought in good faith, believing it to conform to the fire safety regulations, was in fact flammable and burst into flames, badly injuring a woman. The other case was of a woman who raised herbs from seed and sold the plants at craft fairs. However, she was either not aware of or neglected to mark those plants which had a poisonous or irritant effect and she was subse-quently sued by a customer who developed painful skin rashes.

Professional indemnity insurance This is of most interest to any business people such as freelance consultants or those running agencies, whose main job is to give advice or provide services. This insurance covers claims made against you if a client has incurred some financial loss due to your alleged negligence, error or omission.

Motor vehicle liability By law you must insure your legal liability for injury to others and damage to their property arising from the use of vehicles on the road – this is third-party insurance. Most business policies are either for third party, fire and theft or comprehensive. Comprehensive cover includes damage to your vehicle. The third-party section of a commercial vehicle policy is usually limited up to £1 million. If you own more than five vehicles a fleet policy may be arranged.

Fidelity Guarantee or Bonding This is insurance cover against loss of money or stock arising from dishonesty by your employees and is an insurance policy usually taken out by any company whose employees have to handle money on the company's behalf – for example, a salesman who takes payments from clients when he delivers stock for you.

Tax and investigation insurance Covers you against the extra costs and disruption of an investigation by the Inland Revenue or Customs and Excise. Even if your accounts are impeccable, you might be selected at random for enquiry under the self assessment tax system.

Other insurances

Income protection insurance (formerly known as permanent health insurance) This is an insurance that provides you with some level of income if you are ill or have an accident. These policies pay out after you have been ill and off work for a specified period which is usually from four weeks up to 52 weeks depending on the option you choose. Most policies set a maximum payout, for example, three-quarters of the insured's gross earnings for the previous 12 months.

Private medical insurance is going to be of benefit if you cannot afford to be off work for a long time while waiting for treatment under the National Health Service. Private medical insurance premiums are generally lower in group schemes, so it is worth checking with any relevant business, professional and trade associations to see if they have a scheme for members which works out cheaper.

Don't forget that pension

Once you become self-employed, your own retirement savings become crucial if you want to have more than just a state pension to exist on in your old age. The government is anxious for everyone to make private provision for their old age, but the problem is that the pensions marketplace is in a mess. Values of pension funds have halved since September 1996 as the UK stock market has declined. However, let us run through the options available at the present time. A good place to start to gather information is the government's advice website, www.pensionguide.gov.uk. Try, also, the *Which? Guide to Planning your Pension*.

State Second Pension (S2P)
This replaced SERPS from April 2002 and is designed to give a better pension than SERPS to employees on low earnings. However, you do not build up any S2P at all if you earn less than the

lower earnings limit (£4,004 in 2003-4). Provided you earn at least that much, you will be treated for the purposes of S2P as if you have earnings equal to the low earnings threshold (which was £10,800 in 2002–3). Bear in mind that income tax and National Insurance do not start to become payable until your earnings exceed £4,615 a year in 2003–4. So, if you are a director of your own company, consider paying yourself a salary between £4,004 and £4,615 in 2003–4. That way, you'll be clocking up state pension at an enhanced rate but paying no taxes.

Occupational pensions

Contributions to these may be paid into by both employees and employers. The government allows employees to pay a maximum of 15 per cent of salary per annum into a scheme. There is no limit on the amount your employer can pay in, though there are limits on the benefits that can be taken from the scheme. These generous contribution rules offer tax planning opportunities if you are running your business as a company.

In a money purchase scheme, contributions are invested and then used to buy a pension when you retire. There are special types of these schemes – 'executive pensions' and 'small self-administered scheme' (SSAS) – suitable for small companies, but this is a complicated area so get advice from an independent financial adviser. A major advantage of using the occupational scheme structure is that your company (as employer) can make very large contributions to your pension, which both helps you to save for retirement and gives you the opportunity for tax planning. A further advantage is that these schemes can advance loans to your business.

Most employees and all self-employed can have:

- a stakeholder or personal pension contracted out of the additional state pension
- a stakeholder or personal pension on top of the additional state pension.

Stakeholder pensions were introduced in 2001 as 'better value' alternative pension plans. Life insurance and other authorised financial institutions operate them. You are eligible if you are under 75 years of age. You do not have to be in work or have any earnings to be eligible. If you are an employee and you already belong to an occupational scheme, you can have a stakeholder scheme or personal pension only if you earn less than £30,000, and are not a controlling company director (which you almost certainly will be if you are operating your own business as a company). Everyone who is eligible can contribute up to £3,600 per annum (£2,808 after tax relief). Above this amount, the government has set limits on contributions, based on age and earnings (see table below). Contributions in one year can be based on earnings in the current year or any of the five preceding years.

Personal pension plan contributions allowable 2002–3

Figures may change after publication.

Individual's age on 6 April	Max % of net elevant earnings	Cash limit during 2002–3
35 or under	17.5	£17,010
36–45	20.0	£19,440
46–50	25.0	£24,300
51–55	30.0	£29,160
56–60	35.0	£34,020
61–74	40.0	£38,880
75 and over	You can no longer contribute	

Personal pension plans are individual retirement plans operated by the financial services industry. They have the same eligibility rules as a stakeholder pension. Some employers offer Group Personal Pension Plans that benefit from the buying power of the group.

As well as a pension, you may have the option to take up to 25 per cent of your retirement fund as a tax-free lump sum.

As has been pointed out by many financial advisers, the biggest drawback in the British pension system is that once your pension is cashed in and you have bought an annuity to give you that monthly income in retirement, the funds are lost forever should you and your partner die. There are such things as Estate Protection Plans, which enable you to pass the cash spent on an annuity to your children, but they are thin on the ground and expensive. Some companies, like the Norwich Union, are trying to persuade the government to allow them to sell a 'capital protected pension scheme' but it appears not to be high on the government agenda at the moment.

One good thing is that, in autumn 2002, the Financial Services Authority (FSA)⋆ has ordered all pension companies to explain to their customers that they have the right to shop around to get the best value from their funds for an income in retirement. The FSA maintains that many policyholders do not understand that a personal pension plan is just an investment vehicle that is quite separate from the annuity that is bought at the end of the pension-plan term. Many people were just buying the annuity thrown at them by the pension-plan provider and not realising that they could shop around for the best deal. Annuity rates are currently at their lowest for decades but it is possible to improve an annuity income by about 15 per cent if you shop around.

However, the crisis in the pensions industry has deepened to such an extent that many financial writers are now counselling in favour of other forms of investment to cushion old age, such as property – although the buy-to-rent market in the UK has become saturated and house prices appear set to slump at the time of writing, the overseas holiday property market is still buoyant in many parts of the world – or gold (the price of gold has risen recently).

This is the thinking behind the growing trend of Self-invested Personal Pensions (SIPPS). The SIPP Provider Group⋆ has almost 60 members and many of them are using the Internet to market their investment plans, which cuts down on set-up fees (to start up an account) and dealing fees (to manage an account). With a SIPP you have a much wider range of investments to choose from including, for example, British and international shares, gilts and deposit accounts, and commercial property as well as the collective funds available to ordinary personal pensions (including stakeholder schemes). However, SIPPS do require investment of a large sum of money, in order to get the best value from them, so they may not be a suitable option for some people. Nevertheless, the *Sunday Times* reports that the number of people switching from traditional funds to SIPPs is expected to grow from 15,000 to 50,000 in the next five years.

Chapter 8

Costing your work

This is an area where the experts advise you to go through specific formulae to arrive at the correct price to cover all your costs and make some money in addition. But, realistically, you first have to ask yourself: 'What price does my product or service have to be?' In other words, what you can charge for your product or services very much depends upon: what the customer is prepared to pay; and what the competition is charging for the same product or service. You may have little choice in this matter. For example, if you are a hairdresser, you may know that your clients will only pay, say, £15 for a shampoo and set; if you run a driving school you know that your customers will only pay £30 maximum for a driving lesson.

So you have to start from the point where you know how much you will charge and why. The question is, can you make a profit? You then have to look at all your costs and see whether they are sufficiently low to enable your product/service to make you a profit. If not, can they be lowered? If they cannot, then you should rethink your undertaking.

It may be that you are not restricted in what you can charge for your product or service because it is something new, unique or rare and the customers may be prepared to pay highly for it. This may apply if you have created a totally new service or product to be marketed on the Internet. If the marketplace is wide open for you and there are no competitors to give you price guidelines, it is a case of have a go and see. Just a cautionary word, however. Most of the first, and second, wave of dotcom companies that went spectacularly bust in the last five years, did so because they were greedy and badly managed. Pricing policies were not thought out and, sometimes, discount prices for products were financing the directors' champagne lifestyles. Pricing may be an inexact science but you do have to give it your best shot or the consequences can be disastrous.

Having decided on the price for your product or service, you can then return to the conventional method of assessing your cost structure. It is an exercise which should be done very early on, before you start your venture. You will certainly need to do it if you are going to present a business plan to a lending institution, but it is advisable to do it anyway – you will not only arrive at a cost structure but also at an operating budget, that is, you will know how much you can afford to spend on certain items and whether your business, as you envisage it, will make a satisfactory profit.

The exercise we are going to conduct in this chapter shows 'fixed costs' (the costs that you will always incur, such as business rates, telephone rental, etc.) and 'variable costs' (the costs that can change because you may decide not to advertise by mailshot next year and therefore will not incur large postage costs). For the purpose of this exercise we have taken the example of a one-person second-income earner.

Be aware though that if you are contemplating earning money from home and you are the person who pays all the bills, obviously that must be your starting point in all calculations: you need to earn enough money to pay all the bills. Your fixed costs are your domestic outgoings. If you are unable to cover those, you will not be able to survive, unless you can supplement your earnings with perhaps savings, a grant, interest-free loan or state benefits.

There is no doubt that the businesses that survive those first tricky years are those that manage to keep costs down. Earning money from home is not a good idea if your overheads are so high that they are going to cripple your new business.

If your monthly outgoings are reasonable and you are, say, intending to take up an occupation that is truly home-based – and you are either on your own, with no commitments or, if you have a family, your spouse or partner intends to get a job and contribute some income while you look after the children's needs as well as your work – then perhaps you have a workable proposition.

Factors in pricing

Many external factors can contribute to changes in costs and, therefore, changes in your prices, so the costing/pricing exercise has to be repeated at frequent intervals throughout the life of your business. Here are some of the factors to be aware of at all times.

Interest rates

The interest rates on loans and mortgages can change. You may have negotiated fixed rates for a couple of years and therefore those portions of your fixed costs will stay put for that period, but most people are subject to the rise and fall of interest rates.

Child care

Working at home and looking after your children may not be a workable proposition once you get a large quantity of orders/ contracts/commissions. You may have to build in the extra cost of child care at some point. If you have more than one child, this can be considerable.

Rises in fixed costs

Insurance premiums will rise, as will the cost of the telephone, electricity and gas, postage, petrol and so on. While insurance premiums may rise only once a year, items such as petrol can become more expensive at any time and if your business is a heavy user of petrol this will obviously affect your prices.

Costs of materials

Your suppliers will pass on any of their rising costs to you. You could also be in a position where your main supplier ceases trading and you have to find another source which is more expensive, or your particular materials may come from a part of the world which is suddenly ravaged by war, affecting supplies. You will then have to buy alternatives from other countries, which again may be more costly.

Customer demand

Success does not always mean more profits. You could suddenly get a contract tomorrow to supply large amounts of your products, transforming you from a one-man/-woman band into an employer overnight. Generating more goods means incurring more costs. The bulk-buying customer may also demand a discount which you feel unable to refuse, and this would obviously affect your general cost/price structure.

Customer demand, on the other hand, may peter out so you find that you have to diversify into other products or services, re-market them and incur a whole new set of costs. These would not necessarily be greater but they would certainly be different.

Time constraints

You may manufacture products that have a limited 'shelf-life' – seasonal goods that have to be sold before the relevant holiday (Christmas decorations), commemorative goods that celebrate particular events (sporting fixtures, for example), or goods that cater to a passing fad (remember Cabbage Patch dolls?). Once the marketing opportunity is gone, the merchandise has to be sold at a greatly reduced price. The wastage of stock has to be built into the initial pricing decision if you are going into such a risky market.

Competition may get tougher

If your competitors start slashing their prices you could be in trouble unless you have allowed some margin for discount right from the beginning. This is why it is important before trading to work out in detail the profit you need to make on each unit (product or hour of service) in order to survive should any of the above external factors affect your business.

Fixed costs

First, assess your fixed costs. These are the costs that do not vary with the amount you produce – in other words, you have to pay them even if you produce nothing at all.

Write down a list, for example:

(Per year)	£
Any business rates[1] (say 12 × £50)	600
Electricity[2]	500
Telephone rental	200
Any loans	500
Insurances	500
Any equipment hire	500
Total	**£2,800**

[1] Don't forget that, even working from home, you could be liable to pay business rates.
[2] This should be the amount of extra electricity, on top of your household usage, which your business demands.

Variable costs

Next assess the costs to your business which fluctuate according to the amount you produce. For example, the materials you purchase to make your product, the packaging for your product, and any seasonal labour that you might use.

This is a complex sum. Basically you have to assume a realistic figure that you will hope to produce and sell in your first year. Let us say that you are making soft toys and you plan to work alone for the first year. You buy your materials in a reasonable quantity from a wholesaler. You know that £60-worth of materials enables you to make 100 soft toys in one month, which the marketplace will allow you to sell at £10 each.

Make a list of your variable costs:

(Per year)	£
Materials (12 × £60)	720
Transport (running costs, petrol)	760
Postage (regular mailshots, etc.)	500
Telephone/fax calls	300
Cost of advertising material (leaflets, adverts, etc.)	300
Extras (e.g. sewing machine repair)	100
	£2,680
Add your fixed costs	£2,800
Total	**£5,480**

Now we know that your total costs for one year will be £5,480. Divide that by the number of soft toys that can be made in one year (100 x 12):

$$5,480 \div 1,200 = 4.56$$

So each toy costs £4.56 to make and the resulting sale price of £10 should produce a healthy profit. This difference between the costs of your business and the revenue from sales is called the profit margin.

However, you must bear in mind that these figures are only very basic illustrations. Any accountant would advise you that you must build into your calculations hidden costs such as waste of materials, depreciation of equipment or any periods of illness when you cannot produce toys.

Other factors could influence your profit margin, for example:

- rise in petrol costs
- rise in postage costs
- rise in costs of materials
- competition forces down the market prices for your goods
- regular sales outlets lose interest in your product
- you need to make a large investment in equipment
- you need to expand and employ staff
- your customers force you to offer credit-card facilities
- you acquire some bad debts
- you are forced to find money for legal fees.

Some of these can be built in at the planning stage. If you know, from the above calculations, what your basic profit margin will be, then you will have to allocate some of that hoped-for profit towards a contingency fund for those unexpected expenses.

The factors listed above may cause you to raise your prices or cut your overheads. For example, if you know that the marketplace will not tolerate a rise in the price of your goods and services, then you will have to cut costs, in order to achieve the same profit margin. You will also have to engage in some costing exercises for possible future scenarios, such as diversification or expansion.

Diversification

Going back to our soft toy manufacturing operation, let us assume that you have your finger on the pulse of the marketplace and you feel confident that you can produce soft toys that meet current trends, for example, all the kids are mad about trolls, so you decide to manufacture trolls for a few months, in addition to your regular line. First you have to investigate the costs of the materials required to make the new product. Let us say that for six months you will allocate half your workload to the manufacture of trolls. Therefore your materials costs will be as follows:

6 × £60 (for your usual range)	£360
6 × £90 (for the new range)	£540
Total	**£900**

This alters your variable costs total by £180, bringing your total to £5,660. Divide this by your output of toys (1,200) and your new basic product cost is £4.71. So your profit margin has been eroded by approximately 15p.

Whether to diversify or not is a 'Catch 22' situation. If you are still going it alone, then, on paper, all you are succeeding in doing is shaving 15p off your profit. But you may be in the position of not having any choice. If you do not offer what the market wants, it is eventually going to get tired of your limited range of soft toys and you will lose sales anyway. Often, diversification forces a business into the next phase of new calculations, which is expansion.

As mentioned in Chapter 6, you have to be realistic about how much you can achieve on your own. You also have to be realistic about the number of hours you are spending on manufacturing each item. If you are at the 'luxury' or 'original piece of art' end of the marketplace, where the price reflects the labour and originality of the item, then it doesn't matter. However, if you are aiming to mass-produce, albeit on a modest scale, you will have to review your manufacturing methods and, perhaps, the suitability of the items you produce. See the table below.

Product	Time to make	Cost of materials	Price
1 Patchwork cot quilts	3 hours	£5	£20
2 Patchwork bags	2 hours	£4	£15
3 Patchwork bed quilts	20 hours	£35	£200

Formula: price – cost of materials + number of hours = gross hourly rate

Item 1 = £5 per hour to make

Item 2 = £5.50 per hour to make

Item 3 = £8.25 per hour to make

Do you want (or is it easier) to make more of the lower-profit items, or would you prefer to take longer and make fewer, larger-profit items? No amount of calculations can really sum up the factors of market demand versus job satisfaction.

Expansion

If you employed someone to make a further 1,200 toys for you at, say, £6,000 per year (including tax and National Insurance), you could market them more aggressively. This in itself would necessitate expanding some of your other variable costs, such as transport and postage, as you would want to sell to more people and would presumably have more deliveries to make.

Let us redo the sums:

Fixed costs (remain the same for the moment) £2,800

Variable costs:

Materials (as above but for two products)

	£
12 × £60	720
12 × £90	1,080
Transport	1,000
Postage	800
Telephone/fax	500
Advertising	500
Extras	200
Wages[1]	6,000
Total	**£10,800**

[1] Wages are regarded as a variable cost for the moment as the long-term situation may not work out.

So now we repeat the earlier sum. Divide the total running costs by the new number of toys (2,400) that can be produced in one year:

$$10,800 \div 2,400 = 4.50$$

As you can see from this exercise, if you can sell all the toys, which now cost £4.50 to make, you have enhanced your original profit margin of £4.56 by 6p.

If the calculations for your business are not as favourable as shown above (your profit margin has been eroded, say), but you have no choice but to expand, then you have several options open to you to get the profit margin up again.

- Trim your fixed costs, if possible. For example, you could: pay off any loans; get a cheaper loan; buy rather than rent telephone equipment (or other equipment). Remember too that telephone equipment and service providers are in competition and that by shopping around you can get some very good deals.
- Trim your variable costs, if possible. For example, you could negotiate discounts with your suppliers for buying in bulk; subcontract or use self-employed workers who pay their own tax

and NI; see if a delivery service would work out cheaper than using your own transport; negotiate special deals with postal services for all your mailshots. It is also worth comparing prices for utilities: by shopping around you could reduce your bills.

- Change your product yet again to one that can be manufactured at a lower cost.
- Find new ways of selling that allow you to sell at a higher price.
- Charge more for your products, if the market will allow. (For more on marketing see Chapter 9.)

As you can see, the whole business of costing is complicated but it has to be done. You have to know whether your product or service can compete in the marketplace and make you money at the same time. If you are providing a service, you have to cost by the hour and estimate how long it takes you to do a particular job. The guidelines are basically the same as given above.

Of course, the figures above are optimistic. You know that you can comfortably make that number of toys in a year but will you be able to sell that number? What you need to work out next is your break-even point. In other words, how many toys will you have to sell in order just to cover your costs?

The answer is simple. If the costs (fixed and variable) of running your business are £5,480 and you are able to sell your toys at £10 each, then £5,480 ÷ 10 = 548. You will have to sell 548 toys a year in order to cover your costs. Producing too much stock is an important reason why many small businesses fail. Tying up too much of your money in materials without guaranteed sales can result in a serious cash-flow problem. It is better to work out a system of stock control whereby, in the early stages of your business, you produce goods to order, and the client clearly understands that there is a waiting period between order and receipt of goods.

Pricing a service

Again, you are probably restricted by the current market rate for your service. Customers will pay no more and you may not be able to afford to undercut it.

Aside from *how much* you should charge there is the question of *how* you should charge. In other words, should you charge by the hour, the day, per project or ask for a retainer for an ongoing job?

Charging by the hour

This can be the best way to charge for quick jobs, such as word-processing, or work where you may be observed, such as gardening. This way the customer can see that a job really has taken a certain number of hours to complete.

Charging a daily rate

If a job is going to occupy one or two days of your time and you know you will not be able to offer a service to any other customers during this time, then charge a daily rate. It is reasonable for a daily rate to be slightly more than the combined hourly rate, to compensate for your time being monopolised by one job.

Charging per project

Hairdressers, masseurs, chiropodists and other such service providers charge per project. The public expect to pay a set fee per hairdo or pedicure rather than per hour. Consultants frequently charge per project, particularly if it is likely to be an unknown period of work, such as investigating a problem and preparing a report.

A retainer

If you are, say, a data processor, and one of your clients wants you to be constantly available to do their work but they cannot say exactly when that work will be ready, you would be in a situation to negotiate a retainer, that is, a monthly fee to keep you on standby. This fee reserves your availability; you would then be able to add your usual rates by the hour or the day. Being on standby does not prevent you from taking on work from other clients, but the client paying you the retainer must get priority when his or her work comes in.

A formal quotation

Sometimes you may be asked to give a formal quote on price before the potential customer will place a definite order, particularly if you supply a service. A quotation is a legally binding document which could be used against you if you fail to keep to its terms, so you have to be absolutely clear in your written quotation exactly what you are offering for the price you are asking.

Make a realistic estimate first of how long the job will take you and what expenses, if any, you will incur in order to do the job.

Let us say you are a dressmaker who has been commissioned to make a wedding dress. You will have discussed with the customer what type of dress she wants. Will it be straightforward or will she want hand embroidery on the bodice? Does she want one of your existing patterns or will you have to design something new just for her? Will she provide the material or will you? Will she come to you for fittings or will you have to go to her, thus incurring travel expenses?

Having sorted out the preliminary details you will then issue a quote stating:

- exactly what service you are offering, for example, designing the dress as well as making it
- who is providing materials – you or the customer. Emphasise that whatever arrangement is agreed, the material is of the customer's choice
- how long you will take to do the job. (Put in the phrase 'unforeseen circumstances excepted': this covers you if you are taken ill or some disaster occurs)
- how many fittings you will require in order to complete the job
- the price you are quoting for the job
- how long that price will stand, that is, how long the customer has to make up her mind before the price goes up
- you reserve the right to alter the price during the course of the job should the cost of the basic materials go up, or the customer demands a change in the planned dress
- whether the price is inclusive or exclusive of VAT, if that pertains to your business
- terms of payment, that is, by when the customer has to pay for the job. In this case, with a custom-made wedding dress, payments should be spread throughout the period of the job, with the first payment covering the complete cost of the materials so that you are not out of pocket should the customer disappear. It would be wise not to purchase the materials until this first payment has been made
- cancellation fee: in order to cover your time and effort you should state in a quotation that once an order is placed by the

customer and the job has started it cannot be cancelled without some charges being incurred

- finally, ask for the customer's acceptance in writing. It may expedite matters if you include in your quotation an acceptance sheet which the customer just has to sign and return. It could simply read as follows:

I have read the enclosed quotation and I
accept the terms and conditions offered.
I enclose the first payment of £XXX

Signature

Date

Tendering

This is just another way of quoting for a job, except that you definitely know that you are competing for a job because several others will have been asked to tender. It is a common practice for, say, consultants or office service bureaux – any business that sells to other businesses.

None of the companies or individuals tendering a price will know what prices they are competing against. It is not always the lowest tender that is accepted, as other factors can have a bearing.

Never tender an impossibly low price for a job, no matter how desperate you are. You have to cover your costs at least. Never undervalue your time or expertise – it will only arouse suspicion in customers.

If, after the tendering process, you find that you did not get the job, ask why. If several companies tell you that your price was too high, then you can review your pricing structure and see whether you can resolve the problem. It may just be that you are competing against people who have a bigger profit margin than you, because of lower overheads, more resources and so on and can afford to quote lower prices. If this is the case, review your own service and see if you can offer a different, higher-value product.

Chapter 9

Marketing your work

The whole idea of marketing (and public relations) is that you should never rest on your laurels. You have to keep plugging away at your markets, carrying out research, anticipating any changes, developing new markets and continuing to impress your customers with your efficiency, enthusiasm and determination. The image that you project, however small your operation, is an important part of the business of attracting custom.

Chapter 5 discussed market research and how to gather information to select the best markets for your work. You should have gained from this some pointers towards the best methods for selling to those markets. If, for example, your product or service is designed to sell to a specialist hobby market you may have discovered that the only way to reach that market is through targeted mailshots and by advertising in specialist publications. The product or service is then sold by mail order.

Alternatively, your research may have determined that your product or service is of most value to retailers and your marketing therefore has to be done on a one-to-one basis, visiting the retailers and persuading them to buy from you. This does not preclude a preliminary mailshot, of course, which can pave the way for you to follow up by telephone and make a sales appointment.

You may be tempted by the glamour of the Internet. You may have read that every modern business should have a website and that doing business on the Internet opens up huge market possibilities. It is true that a website can be a valuable way of disseminating information about your company but you have to ensure that it can be easily accessed by the people you are interested in reaching. It is also true that you can do business virtually anywhere in the world via the Internet – but are you ready to take that step? Later in the chapter we will look in detail at the procedures for marketing and selling via the Internet. We will also look at when you need help and advice on using PR as a way of promoting sales.

Marketing options

First you need to look at all the options to see what will suit your particular situation. Often the simplest methods are the most effective.

Putting a postcard in a shop window

This is a useful way of drawing attention to your service in a small community where shop-window postcards are frequently scanned. It is not recommended as the sole form of selling, however, if you really want to generate a decent volume of business.

Calling door-to-door with the products in hand

This may be suitable for agents or manufacturers of household products – in other words, where you have a small selection of reasonably light-weight products which might instantly appeal to a person at home during the day. (In today's society, unfortunately, many people don't want to answer the door to salespeople at night.) You need to have a car or van close at hand, so that you can keep topping up your hand-carried selection of goods. If someone decides to buy at the door they want to have the product instantly rather than place an order.

Delivering leaflets door-to-door (or car-to-car)

The leaflets advertising your service or product have to be eye-catching, the message has to be punchy and the contact information very clear. Leaflets stuck under windscreen wipers have a tendency to blow away and cause litter problems, or the drivers come back and immediately throw them away. If the local authority pick up several of your leaflets they might take action. Also, many people do not like car-leafleting as it can be an indicator, to a potential thief, of how long a car is left unattended. Sometimes it is better to hand out leaflets at a strategic point – say the exit to a car park. Many local authorities offer very competitive rates to advertise on the back of their pay-and-display parking tickets. This can often be a very effective way of getting your name known, particularly if your business is related to cars, such as a mobile mechanic or valeting service.

Delivering catalogues door-to-door (and returning to collect them)

This is double the work but you will eventually build up a round of regular customers who wish to order from your catalogue every month. However, the products contained in the catalogue have to be of limited life span, such as cosmetics or household cleaners – otherwise you will not generate regular sales.

Delivering leaflets to target markets

Many people successfully generate work and/or orders by asking relevant organisations to distribute leaflets for them. Now this can be local or national. For example, if you are a craftworker who manufactures wrought iron articles for use in the garden, you might persuade local and regional garden and allotments societies to distribute your leaflets to their members for you – particularly if you offer some kind of discount on your goods upon presentation of the leaflet. This acts as a form of payment for the service. Nationally, it is possible to pay a national organisation with a closed membership list to distribute your leaflets with one of their regular mailings, provided they approve of its content.

Selling through agents or bureaux

If you use an agent you have to provide that person with back-up marketing material such as samples, leaflets or brochures, business cards and so on. Using an agent is a relationship of trust: you believe the person when he or she claims to have all the right contacts and can produce a certain volume of sales, while he or she trusts you to pay commission promptly and to meet the order deadlines and quantities. You should make it clear at the outset whether the agent is doing all your sales or whether you or a member of your family is also selling whenever possible. If the latter is the case, you need to earmark an area for yourself and let the agent cover everywhere else. You also need to discuss a pricing structure at the outset. You have to build into your prices the agent's commission and also any delivery costs that may be incurred if the agent sells your product further afield. You also need to be able to give the agent the latitude to offer a discount for bulk orders and so on. All of this has to be built into the pricing structure before marketing starts.

CASE HISTORY: Sally

Sally is a self-employed freelance writer and she gets all her work through an agent. This agent finds Sally work writing magazine articles and books. The agent takes a commission on all Sally's fees. The advantages for Sally are that she does not have to spend time selling her skills as the agent has a large network of contacts to call upon.

You may be offering a service as a subcontractor to various other service organisations, for example you ring-bind reports typed by a secretarial bureau or you hand-polish cars repaired or maintained by a local garage. In this case you will do the initial marketing of your service to the relevant organisations and they will continue to market your service as one of theirs. You may have to agree that you will not perform the same service for local competitors, which is fair enough. However, you must reserve the right to shop around and market your services elsewhere if the organisations do not provide you with enough work.

Selling to retailers

Quite often, craftworkers and artists find that shops will take their work initially on a sale-or-return basis, and then place regular orders. Having several retail outlets can provide a bedrock of regular income which leaves you free to sell in other ways that do not compete with the retail outlets. Again, it is probably a question of area. If you regularly sell paintings of scenes of Bournemouth through a shop in that town, no one is going to mind if you sell scenes of Brighton at a Brighton arts and crafts fair.

Selling through your own retail outlet

Many people take a stall at a craft fair or market as a first exercise in marketing. It has the advantage that you don't have to pay anyone else to sell for you but you probably have to pay for the stall space.

It is of least advantage to a manufacturer because time taken to staff a stall for a few hours, plus the loading and unloading of wares, is time taken away from manufacturing. This type of marketing really works best for those who sell other people's products – for example, they go to wholesale outlets and buy women's clothes to sell on at a profit.

CASE HISTORY: Maria

Maria makes wall tapestries and is particularly fond of including cats in her designs. After visiting a pedigree cat show, Maria decided to rent a stall at one of the shows and display her tapestries. The response from all the assembled cat lovers was so good that she sold more tapestries in one day than she had sold the previous month by other methods. She now concentrates solely on cat shows and has extended her product range to include cushions and bags with cat designs because customers indicated an interest.

Women's Institute (WI) co-operative markets are a good place to sell home-made, home-grown and hand-crafted goods. There are over 530 WI markets in England, Wales and the Channel Islands and they are usually held once a week in certain towns and villages. New producers are welcome and do not have to be WI members. Stallholders are usually charged a small commission to cover the running expenses of the market. You have to become a shareholder, which costs the tiny amount of 5p. WI markets are true co-operatives and everyone is expected to help run their market. The WI Country Markets* can supply a list of the local markets and information on what is deemed to be suitable produce to sell. Usually, the markets sell food, crafts, clothing, flowers and plants. The organisation also runs a Parcel Scheme, where individuals can contact local WI markets to purchase a hamper of selected goods to be delivered to someone as a gift. The minimum order for such a hamper is £5 and, at the time of writing, the service is not available in large urban areas or in Scotland.

Some craftworkers or caterers manufacture products all week and then sell them at fairs or markets at the weekend. This is fine if the sales generated justify you using up some of your free time, and if you have other sales outlets – it is very dispiriting to keep packing and unpacking the same products weekend after weekend and selling just a few items here and there.

If you produce foodstuffs, crafts or clothing, another sales outlet is the regular Farmers Markets held around the UK. Most markets have a rule that the produce has to come from within 25–30 miles of the market; you can only sell your own produce and all the products on offer have to have been grown, reared, caught, brewed, pickled, baked, smoked or processed by the stallholders. For more information, contact the National Association of Farmers Markets*.

Sending mailshots to targeted markets

This can be a good way of selling because you are targeting people you know are interested in your product or service (if you have got your research right, that is). It is not quite the same as enclosing your leaflets in with other people's literature, where it can, possibly, be overlooked easily as the recipient concentrates on the other pieces of paper. The only piece of paper in the envelope will be yours. It is obviously more expensive to do your own mailing, rather than buy into someone else's

If you are operating from home, be wary of inviting people to visit you – not just from the security aspect but also from the nuisance caused to neighbours by parking problems or unwanted traffic in what was previously a peaceful road. If you live on a farm with acres of space and you have made one of the barns into a furniture workshop then that should be fine – but make sure that you don't contravene the local planning laws.

Contact lists need to be carefully checked. There are now systems in place whereby companies and individuals can opt out of receiving unsolicited mail, telephone calls and faxes. Households not wishing to receive unsolicited mail can register with the Mailing Preference Service*. While it is not an offence to continue to mail these people, it would be a waste of your money, as they will probably immediately throw your mailshot away.

The same brokers who sell lists (see Chapter 5) also offer a list-cleaning service, whereby you can download your list to their website and they will remove all the restricted addresses or phone/fax numbers. The Royal Mail* also offers this service for mailshots by cleaning your list against its Royal Mail Postal Address File.

Selling by mail order requires careful planning and control. Timings, stock levels and credit control are crucial. You must also be very clear in any advertising about what your product or service is and what it is capable of doing. Under the various Trade Descriptions Acts and other legislation it is an offence to make a false or misleading statement about the goods or services.

Asking for payment in advance means that you must comply with the Mail Order Transactions (Information) Order 1976, which requires you to show your full name and address in any advertisement or mailshot. You may not use a PO Box number on its own.

The Advertising Standards Authority★ can provide information on what you can or cannot say in a mail-order advertisement and lays down a format for accepted practice regarding times of despatch, refunds, supply of goods on approval and so on. Another source of information is the Direct Marketing Association★.

Direct mail, via the postal system, is still one of the best ways of selling but it has come under some scrutiny in recent years. Apart from the introduction of the various registers which remove people from contact lists, there is also the question of the Data Protection Acts. If you hold personal information about people you must comply with the rules in the Acts. You must register with the Office of the Information Commissioner★. You must make sure that the information you hold is accurate and obtained lawfully. The information must be accessible by the person to whom it relates but you must take steps to make sure that it is secure. You will need to get the consent of the person to whom it relates to hold and process information about them. The legislation applies to all businesses, large and small. Just because you hold information on only a few people, this will not exempt you from registration and having to comply with the rules. Contact the Data Protection Registrar for information.

Royal Mail services to business

If you are contemplating marketing by direct mail then you should investigate the various services on offer by the Royal Mail★ which is an expert in the postal field. Its Address Management Service, for example, offers postage discounts for large-volume mailings and can reduce production and postage costs by eliminating duplicate records, undeliverables and 'gone aways' from your mailing list. It can sell you prepaid envelopes to enclose with your mailings and can deliver stamps to your door in quantities of 100 to 10,000. The Royal Mail's DM Online service can do the whole mailshot for you, from beginning to end, by providing a mailing list, targeting the right customers, creating mailpacks, co-ordinating printing and delivery of the packs and doing the mailings. The charges for these services vary depending upon quantities, weights, return mailings and so on.

Advertising your product in newspapers and magazines

Advertising can be a hit-and-miss affair. It needs to be carefully targeted so that you do not pour money down the drain. A certain amount of experimentation is necessary and you have to analyse the results in order to gauge the return you are getting on your money. If you manufacture a product or provide a service to a specialist market you will have discovered, during your market research, those publications which cover that market. Several media directories (for example, *Benn's Media* and *BRAD*) are published each year which list publications, their circulation and advertising rates. A good reference library should have them.

By comparing circulations and rates, you will be able to assess the ones that you think will give you the best response. You then need to study them and find what you think are the best positions for your advertisements. Perhaps you would like your advertisement to be opposite an article that relates to the sort of product or service you are offering? Perhaps you would like it to be under a special heading

---

CASE HISTORY: John

John strips and renovates pine furniture. He tried various forms of advertising – local papers, parish magazines, posters on noticeboards – none of which was really successful. He thought about his customers and realised that most of them were youngish couples who had just bought their first or second home and were looking for cheap but stylish pine furniture. He then hit upon the idea of advertising in all the estate agents' magazines and newspapers, and also paying for an advertisement to go on the back of all the house detail sheets that were sent out to interested buyers. This worked very well. He had reached the right market and demand for his products soared.

in the classified section? Negotiate with the advertising department of the publication. Take advantage of any special offers they may have. Before you consider advertising in newspapers and magazines, which can be costly, read the section later in this chapter on public relations. You may be able to get free publicity for your product or service by issuing press releases or writing articles.

If you do decide to place advertisements, be aware that just one advertisement will not usually give you a true picture of whether that medium works for you or not. Three consecutive advertisements are considered to be the normal 'try-out' period. By the end of that you will know whether to invest in more advertisements or try something else.

You could take some advice from an advertising agent. A reputable local company will be able to give you a preliminary report on where it thinks you might advertise to best effect and it will suggest a starting budget. Make sure that the company understands from the beginning, however, the modest size of your overall budget, so that it won't waste time on grandiose plans.

However, advertising or enclosing a mailshot in some national publications is not as simple as it seems. Because of past frauds and some companies going bust and leaving the customers without both money and goods, various organisations decided to set up the Mail Order Protection Schemes (MOPS)★, which are insurance plans that reimburse the readers if they should suffer at the hands of a mail-order company.

Each section of the media runs its own scheme. The National Newspapers Mail Order Protection Scheme★ covers national daily and weekend papers and their magazines, the Periodical Publishers Association★ covers most of the magazines in the UK and the Newspaper Society★ covers all the regional and local newspapers.

None of these organisations will allow you to advertise in any of their publications unless you have supplied the following information:

- the type of company you are operating
- your VAT registration number
- the registered address of the business and/or the operating address
- the number of staff employed
- financial information such as the amount of capital invested in the business, any loans outstanding, annual turnover, copy of the last annual accounts, type and extent of insurance cover.

The depth of detail demanded by certain publications can be quite daunting. Generally, the larger the circulation, the more stringent the entry rules for advertisers. The publication has to know if you can cope should you be swamped with orders from their readers. It is not unknown for a single placing of an advert in a national newspaper to attract 30,000 orders.

Delivering samples to an office or factory

Several network marketing book companies have adopted a sales technique of leaving sample books and order forms in offices and factories for the staff there to look at. The agent for the company returns a week later and collects the samples and the orders. The orders are then fulfilled and delivered to the workplace. If you are a small manufacturer, you could approach a local company or factory where the director will agree to your adopting this procedure and find a staff member there who is willing to take responsibility for your samples and order list. It is usual to offer this person some commission on sales or a free item from your range. One disadvantage to this method is that, if you cover several companies and factories, it will tie up a number of your samples.

CASE HISTORY: Sasha

Sasha buys plain T-shirts and appliqués beautiful designs on them to make them suitable for evening wear. She tried selling them to shops but the shops wanted her to cut her prices quite a lot in order for them to make a large profit. A friend suggested that she sell some T-shirts in her office canteen over a lunch period. Sasha did this and sold quite a lot of T-shirts. However, she could not afford the time to man a stall for several hours when she wanted to be making her products, so she approached a few large companies and asked the managing directors if she could set up an unmanned display in the canteen area where customers could fill in order forms and put them in a box, which she would collect later. She then fulfilled the orders, delivered them a week later and collected the monies outstanding. She sold just as many T-shirts but without losing any production time.

Selling through a party scheme

This is a method of selling to an assembled group of customers at a 'party' where light refreshments – cheese and wine, say, or tea and biscuits – are provided. Many party scheme agents begin by asking a friend or relative to host the party in his or her home and to ask a group of friends or acquaintances round. The 'party' scheme works quite simply but relies on the host or hostess being able to gather a sufficiently large group of people; also, you or your agent has to be present to sell the product. Some companies have had success using this sales technique. You need to advertise, perhaps in the local newspaper, for party hosts and you need to vet the applications by visiting the intended party venue. It is not going to be very productive if the person lives in a very small house because you will not be able to display your products properly and there will not be enough people present to make it worthwhile. Also, the person hosting the party should have the sort of friends likely to be interested in and able to afford your wares. It's no good trying to sell hand-made silk quilts that cost £800 each to a group of young mothers on low incomes.

Getting orders by word of mouth

This works for some people, particularly those who produce commissioned work such as sculptures, tapestries or furniture. You may have a business such as upholstery or dressmaking where news of your abilities spreads from friend to friend and, before you know it, you cannot take on any more jobs. However, this is not a marketing strategy upon which anyone should base their future prospects. Even someone who has lots of clients from the start due to word of mouth should aim at some point to glean new clients through a different route.

Advertising in the *Yellow Pages*

This works very effectively for people who offer domestic services such as plumbing, bricklaying, carpet cleaning and so on. Whenever a job needs doing in the home, many people reach for the *Yellow Pages* and ring up a few numbers. You have to be prepared to visit the potential customer and give a free estimate, because that is what everyone else does. This can mean a high proportion of dead-ends but it could teach you something valuable about your marketing – perhaps you are overcharging or your timekeeping is not what it should be?

Joining a professional body

This is a must for consultants of all kinds, because membership of a professional body means that your name and often your details are included in any membership lists or in any directories that are sent out to interested parties. It also means that you have access to the right market through the organisation's mailing list and newsletter or magazine.

Selling by telephone or fax

This could mean selling your skills or your ideas (for example, a consultant, journalist or writer who makes the initial sales pitch to a client or editor over the telephone or fax) or getting an individual or a telesales or fax bureau to sell your product over the phone. People and companies not wishing to receive unsolicited calls or faxes can register with the UK Telephone Preference Service* or the Fax Preference Service*. Once they have done that it is an offence to contact them and you could be liable for a £5,000 fine.

Selling on radio or television

You might think that this is far too expensive for all except the multinational corporations, but that is not necessarily so. Local radio certainly is not out of the small business league and regional television sometimes has community advertising slots where reduced rates are offered to companies who want to reach a purely local audience. You could perhaps band together with, say, several other stand-holders at your forthcoming office services exhibition and purchase some airtime to advertise the event.

Selling at special promotions

Some people sell their products or services only at exhibitions or conferences and find it a very successful way of marketing. If you have a product or service that appeals only to a niche marketplace, where better to sell than at a gathering of people who are there only because of their interest in that very marketplace?

Marketing and selling on the Internet

Small businesses and one-person enterprises can use the World Wide Web facility on the Internet to advertise their services for a negligible amount of money. An advertisement in a national magazine can cost hundreds or even thousands of pounds, whereas a website that can be seen by an equivalent number of people takes about two weeks to design and costs perhaps £50 a month to maintain. If you subscribe to an Internet access provider (IAP) then a free website may be included in your monthly subscription. The other advantages of advertising on the Internet are that, unlike an advertisement in a magazine or newspaper, a website can be updated regularly, even daily, and can maintain a record of the people who have 'visited' the site. You can use this to build up a profile of potential customers. You can also put high-quality images on your website as well as text. You can make your site interactive by publishing a list of frequently asked questions (FAQs) about your product or service that interested parties can access.

CASE HISTORY: Ron

Ron owns a small video production company. He and his brother specialise in copying very old television programmes for the nostalgia market. They bought the video rights to various UK and American programmes from the 1950s and 1960s and they copy them for sale to the general public. The have several websites under the names of the various programmes – for example, one site is *Robin Hood*, another is *The Milton Berle Show*. In the eight years since Ron and his brother have advertised on the Internet they have built up a mailing list of over 67,000 TV nostalgia fans in the UK and North America and are beginning to attract attention from Australasia. Their customers also email them with suggestions for other programmes. Ron then investigates the programme with a view to acquiring the rights.

The international nature of the Web makes it especially valuable if you want to sell a product all over the world to a specialised group.

For example, a company manufacturing and selling daylight spectrum lamps for use by people suffering from Seasonal Affective Disorder would not wish to confine its marketing to the UK. By advertising on the Internet it can access most of the northern hemisphere and answer queries on its website. Some estate agents advertise house-finding services for business around the globe on the Internet.

Be aware that there is a big difference between advertising on a website and actually selling products. A straightforward website simply gives information about you and your products or services, so that customers can contact you by other means. A sales website requires you to set up an ordering system and ways of receiving and processing credit-card transactions (see Chapter 12). You can also purchase advertising space which flags up when people access other websites or use the search engines. There is software that can be purchased which can track the success of online adverts by showing you:

- how many people visited your ads
- which ads generate the most visitors
- which ads generated the most subscribers/sales/downloads etc.
- how much each ad is costing by calculating the cost-per-click, cost-per-sale and click-to-sale ratios
- which ads are the most profitable
- how to group your ads by site, type of ad etc.
- how to organise your ad schedules.

On the next page, we examine some typical website features.

For detailed information on how to cope with doing business via the Internet you can read *The Which? Guide to Computers for Small Business*, plus the various reports that have been published in *Computing Which?* and *Which?* magazines.

The rest of this chapter looks at getting specialist help selling your product, and PR.

Website design basics

Even the simplest site needs certain design basics, which include the following:

- **'Real world' contact details** These include a company's telephone number and postal addresses. If you want to give something more business-like than a home address, you can always use a PO Box number. Your post office can supply you with details of how to set up one of these.
- **Product information** If there is a lot of information in your website, it can be very helpful indeed to include a 'search facility' to make it easier to find specific bits of information. Online support, in the form of frequently asked questions (FAQs) about products, is another extremely helpful option, and can be applied successfully to almost any product or service.
- **Navigation bars ('navbars')** Traditionally these appear in the top left of the page, but should always be visible wherever they are on the page. Navigation bars make it easy to click straight through to a chosen page or facility.
- **A text-only option** This feature is for people who are looking at pages using a palm-top or a very old or slow computer that cannot deal with pictures or audio.
- **A 'Last-modified on' line** This optional feature indicates the date when the site was last updated.
- **A 'hit counter'** Also optional, this feature shows the number of times the page has been viewed.
- **Key selling point** The Internet equivalent of a unique selling point (USP), it may include free information that is useful to visitors, a prize draw, some other free or special offer, or something amusing and entertaining that changes regularly. The point here is to create something that persuades visitors to come back to your site repeatedly, even if it does not close a sale directly.
- **Strong image and branding** You can use graphics and fonts to create a consistent look and feel to your site that mirrors the kind of service that you provide. The stronger the image, the more likely it is that your site will make an impression.

When do you need help?

You can take advantage of marketing advice and help at any time, if you can afford it, but there are certain areas where specialist help is essential.

Selling your reputation

This is for those individuals who initially sell themselves purely on the strength of their CV – for example, consultants who put themselves forward for short- or long-term freelance appointments, either on their own initiative or through an agency. Making one CV stand out from all the others is sometimes the job of an expert, usually a recruitment consultant, who can advise on the arrangement of information and the presentation of a CV in order to achieve maximum effect. These people usually advertise in trade magazines or through the newsletters of the relevant institutes.

Selling your product or services abroad

This critical step requires as much help and advice from experts as you can muster. In the first instance contact your nearest Business Link Office★ if you live in England. In Scotland, contact Scottish Enterprise★, and in Wales, Business Connect★.

CASE HISTORY: Roshni

Roshni makes embroidered silk blouses. A Spanish friend told her that she thought her blouses would be very popular in Spain. Roshni went to a Business Link Export Development Counsellor for advice. The Counsellor provided her with a lot of market information which helped her pinpoint likely buyers and gave her the opportunity to exhibit at a British fashion trade show in Barcelona. From that trade show she got several contracts to supply department stores throughout Spain, which she now does via a distribution agent in Madrid.

Unless you are fluent in another language you will need the services of a translator because you cannot successfully market abroad in English. Even your letters of introduction to potential agents or customers should be translated into the relevant language. It does pay to use a professional such as a translation bureau rather than a friend of a friend who has an A-level in Spanish, say. You need a translator who is skilled in commercial and industrial language; you may even need someone who has a background in engineering, architecture or science. You must communicate effectively or you will only give a bad impression.

It is possible to function on the Internet, when doing business overseas, by using one of the many translation software packages around. These do, however, have their limitations, as the translation process is not as creative as a human translator might be. There are some Internet service providers (ISPs) and websites which offer free computer translation for simple documents but offer a human translation service via email for a fee.

Selling ideas

This covers inventions, books, and film or television scripts – anything that may need the help of a specialist agent (patent agent, author's agent and so on) or a lawyer.

Any invention which you feel is totally new (it could be a household object or a board game) should be patented, in order to prevent exploitation of the same idea by others. The procedure for obtaining a patent is fairly complicated but there are patent agents who will deal with the whole procedure for a fee and advise on all aspects of patenting or other forms of protection of manufactured goods. Patent agents can be found listed in *Yellow Pages*. Also the Chartered Institute of Patent Agents* should be able to advise you on which agents specialise in certain subjects. A patent agent will not help you sell your invention but he or she may be able to point you in the right direction through some useful contacts.

Authors' and scriptwriters' agents are often choosy about whom they take on their books. The *Writers' & Artists' Yearbook* and *The Writer's Market* are two publications which list agents and their specific areas of interest. Agents try to sell the writer's work and, if successful, take a commission on the sale, usually between 10 and 25 per cent. You can but persevere and hope that your track record or new work proves attractive enough for an agent to take you on.

Free or assisted marketing advice

Plenty of free help and advice is on offer but it is best to do some research first so that you can pick the appropriate body that has an interest in your particular line of work. This subject is covered in detail in Chapter 6, where all the organisations mentioned will assist in some way with the marketing process, either financially or by giving free consultancy time.

Anyone considering purchasing a franchise should, of course, find that training in marketing techniques and back-up material is included in the purchase price.

Smallholders, market gardeners, and those engaged in animal husbandry and rural or tourist industry activities, may qualify for free advice and/or financial assistance from the Department for the Environment, Food and Rural Affairs (DEFRA)★, ADAS (The Food, Farming, Land & Leisure Consultancy)★, Food from Britain★, the National Farmers' Union★, and the Regional Tourist Boards★.

Arts and Crafts are supported by their respective Councils in the form of either grants or loans for marketing (particularly in Scotland and Wales and areas of high unemployment) and they also have specialist consultants who will advise on marketing strategies.

Exporters fare particularly well. The Export Market Research Scheme (EMRS) provides professional advice on all aspects of international market research for companies with between 5 and 500 employees. Small companies may be eligible for a grant of up to 50 per cent of the agreed costs of approved marketing research projects. EMRS can be contacted through the Export Team at your local Business Link★. The government offers its main support to exporters through Trade Partners UK, which is administered by the British Chambers of Commerce. Your local Chamber of Commerce should be your first port of call when looking for help with marketing abroad.

For young business owner-managers, the Livewire★ Export Challenge (supported by Shell UK Ltd and Bass plc) provides specialist advice and training and an opportunity to undertake a market research visit to mainland Europe.

Using marketing professionals

This can be very expensive but it may be that you feel you could afford a one-off fee to pay a professional marketing company to look at your business and come up with a plan of action – ways in which you should tackle the whole business of marketing – which you could then use as a blueprint for all your future activities. Professionals may have some suggestions and contacts which you would not otherwise think of or stumble across. Don't be intimidated by the fact that a marketing company probably deals with accounts worth millions of pounds. If they are a good marketing company they will spot your potential as a future customer.

An important marketing tip

If you do a mailshot/leaflet drop or place an advert and you get a healthy response, then you should keep every name and address of the customers who responded as a potential mailing list. They obviously liked your product or service and may be interested in anything else you have to offer. You can then contact them directly in the future. This is called building a target market. A mailing list of previous customers can be a great asset.

Public relations (PR)

Now we come to the area of public relations (PR), which you can conduct yourself very effectively. The aim of PR is to keep your name and product or service in front of the public as much as possible. You do not even have to be self-employed to do this – lots of agents, selling on behalf of others, become involved in self-promotion as part of their marketing strategy. There are various cost-effective ways to do this.

Sending out press releases

Compile a list of all the relevant media: these could be just local radio, newspapers, TV and magazines or might include the trade or hobby press. A press release is just a simple story – no more than one page – about something your business has achieved: a new product or service, an expansion, or some other event in which you are involved. If a photograph is relevant, send that too. You would be surprised to know how often local newspapers print small stories about local business people just to fill space in a 'slow news' week!

Some ideas for press releases might be as follows:

- You make soft toys and you have just sold your thousandth teddy bear.
- You make patchwork quilts and you have just had your first overseas order.
- You run a driving school and you have just taught someone famous to drive.
- You make children's clothes and you are donating some of them to the Romanian orphanages.
- You grow speciality plants and you are going to be featured on a TV gardening programme.

And so on – the ideas are endless. Some happen naturally, others you can create. Once you have trained yourself to think in public relations terms the ideas for continued promotions and the subsequent press releases will come thick and fast.

Writing articles

If you are an expert on a particular subject related to your occupation, write articles about it for the trade or hobby press. Many consultants build their reputations through writing authoritative articles in management and industry magazines. Copies of these articles can be included in any sales literature sent out to potential customers. Insist that you are properly credited at the end of the article, for example 'Mary Johnson runs a company from her home in Leicester called The Flower Tub' or 'David Smith is a freelance consultant engineer based in Harrow'. It is even better if you can get the magazine to include your phone number and/or email address as well – after all, you probably will not be paid much for the article, if at all.

CASE HISTORY: Elizabeth

Elizabeth grows herbs and sells them for culinary and cosmetic purposes and as plants. She advertises in one or two gardening magazines and gets a steady flow of orders for plants and seeds through those. After she started writing articles about the uses of herbs in cookery and catering magazines, she began to get orders from restaurants for fresh herbs. Within just a year she was mailing a modest catalogue and price list to over 1,000 large restaurants in the UK and is now gradually building up a regular clientele.

CASE HISTORY : Maya

Many years ago, Maya was finally diagnosed as having an underactive thyroid. Her annoyance at the length of time it took to diagnose her condition led to her doing some research and writing a book to help other sufferers. She then set up a free newsletter on a website and, at the same time, set up a company to sell products that were of benefit to thyroid disease sufferers. She has since written two more books about diet and exercise and she sells these and other products through her newsletter which now has over 17,000 subscribers worldwide.

Writing articles online

Many small business and sole traders who are experts in particular fields have generated a good reputation and consequent sales by writing article for e-zines (email magazines and newsletters), or by generating their own free email or subscription email newsletters which talk in depth about their subject matter and provide a platform for sales of their books or products. Many health professionals in America use this method to give the latest information and advice to subscribers suffering from certain ailments and, at the same time, they sell their books and medicines/supplements to the interested parties.

Giving talks and lectures

Get yourself on to the lecture circuits. This may be through the Women's Institute (WI), Townswomen's Guild or some other organisation that is always looking for speakers on crafts, leisure pursuits, cookery or similar topics. Sports clubs are another outlet for after-dinner speakers (you must be able to inject a great deal of humour into your presentation!). Professional institutes and business organisations such as chambers of commerce are always looking for interesting speakers on business-related topics, as are Rotary Clubs and Round Tables.

The object is to give your talk and display your wares or sales literature at the same time, or hand round business cards.

Running workshops

This is an effective way to boost sales. If you grow flowers and dry them for sale to flower arrangers and florists, you could also run flower-arranging workshops and convert your pupils into customers at the same time. All you need to do is hire a local hall and charge your pupils a modest fee for the day to cover the hire, provision of refreshments and the advertising of the workshop. It should pay for itself, with the added bonus of extra custom at the end of it.

You could also offer to run workshops during the summer at tourist attractions. Many 'living history' museums like to offer the general public an opportunity to see a craft at work. Local authorities are always on the lookout for people who can run workshops for children as part of their summer holiday activity programme. As long as you get some publicity out of it and it does not take you away from your main business too much, why not?

Giving demonstrations

Giving demonstrations is more or less the same idea as lectures or workshops. You demonstrate your skill – cake-decorating, sweet-making and so on, and promote your services or products at the same time.

CASE HISTORY: Sam

Sam and his family run a skip hire business from his home. The local village hall was desperately in need of funds so Sam conceived the idea of providing an adapted skip, with a thief-proof cover, into which all passers-by could put pennies. The skip, with his company name and phone number, sat in the car park of the village hall for three months, until it was full with pennies. It raised thousands of pounds for the hall and it gave Sam three months of press coverage in all the local media for very little cost.

Donating prizes to local competitions

Most local newspapers like to run competitions and are always looking for companies to donate prizes. You could do this in return for some blurb about your company and perhaps a free advertisement. Insist that you receive all the entries to the competition because then you will have the benefit of the names and addresses of people who, although they did not win your product, might like to buy it if you write them an enticing letter.

You could donate prizes to raffles or draws held at local events, but you get less benefit from that exercise unless the organisers are willing to give you free stand space in return.

Holding open days

If you are a market gardener, a smallholder, keep animals or have a craft workshop on your premises, you could hold regular open days and let members of the public in to see how you work. Give them all some promotional literature as they leave and, depending upon your budget, a small free gift, and with luck they will buy from you in future. You could set up a special 'gift shop' for the day.

Staging publicity stunts

The world is your oyster here. You may specialise in hand-knitting jumpers so perhaps you could, in conjunction with the WI, organise a knitting marathon for charity, making sure that your name is featured prominently in any publicity. You may make sports clothing in a modest way and manage to persuade a sports personality to host an event for charity. You may have a lot of land around your house so could host a dog show and at the same time promote the hand-tooled leather dog collars you make.

CASE HISTORY: Christine

Christine hires out a bouncy castle to children's parties and other events. She dreamt up the idea of a bouncing marathon to raise money for a local hospital. The castle was set up inside a school hall and it was continually bounced upon for three weeks by schoolchildren and their parents, working on a rota system. It set a new record and got Christine lots of publicity.

CASE HISTORY: David

David hand-makes walking shoes and walked from Land's End to John O'Groats to prove the durability of his shoes. It generated publicity all over the country and even made national television.

Sending 'free' gifts

The gifts, of course, are not free to you. It is a common practice in business to send valued customers a gift at Christmas of, say, a calendar or a pen – something that carries your name and phone number on it. It is not a bad public relations ploy to copy, if you can make something small and cheap but charming that will encourage good customers to continue to buy from you.

Chapter 10

Buying equipment, support and skills

Equipment

Whatever occupation you are involved in, it is essential to have equipment that will enable you to function from home as efficiently and professionally as possible. Obviously, if you require specialist equipment for your craft or engineering work, you will know what you need and, probably, the sources of such equipment. Later in the chapter we will talk about purchasing and finance. Initially, we need to look at equipment that may be relevant to any kind of home occupation – recent advances in technology have made it possible for the lone individual working from home, or who is out and about fulfilling work obligations, to be able to communicate at all times. Mobile technology, in particular, has improved in leaps and bounds in the last couple of years.

Telephone services and answering machines

The telephone is often the first point of contact that the outside world has with your home business and, therefore, it is important that you have a facility for taking messages or redirecting any calls to your mobile. You may wish to invest in a telephone answering machine (answerphones) so that you can leave a reassuring message on the system to encourage the leaving of messages or the redialling of an alternative number. Or you may wish to take advantage of the many services offered by the telephone companies – and have your messages taken by the phone system after the phone has rung so many times and not been answered. It is possible to access details of any numbers that have rung you while you have been out or on another call. It is also possible to have calls diverted to your mobile phone while you are out, or for a person who is answering your phone at home to divert a call that they have taken to your mobile. You can invest in a handset that displays the number of the caller before you answer the call. The telephone service can also tell you when a caller is waiting on the line, if you are engaged on another call. It is also possible to arrange conference calls where three or more telephone callers can speak to each other at the same time and have a meeting.

The services that are available through the telephone companies are changing constantly as new technology makes more things possible. You can check with your current telephone service provider to see exactly what is on offer.

It can be helpful to shop around for alternatives, especially for calling abroad. Heavily discounted rates are widely advertised in small business magazines and on the Internet, and you can save a fortune if you regularly call other countries. Similarly, discounted mobile phone schemes can save you money over a typical standard contract from the major service providers.

An alternative to answerphones and telephone services is to use your computer as an answerphone. Up-to-date computer modems allow for voice messaging: you can record a message via a microphone plugged into the computer and play back any messages you receive.

Broadband

Anyone conducting business from their home would benefit greatly from switching their existing telephone line to broadband, if they are able to do so. Ordinary telephone lines are transformed into high-speed digital channels capable of carrying data at a much higher rate; files can be downloaded faster; and email and Internet services operate very much faster than through dial-up modems or ISDN (integrated services digital network, which provides quicker access than standard dial-up rates). A broadband connection allows you to make and receive telephone calls at the same time as using email and the Internet. It also has the advantage of being a permanent connection: email and the Internet can be accessed immediately without having to 'dial-up' first. The costs are fixed in a monthly subscription fee and there are no charges for online work. Although the line rental itself costs more than for standard analogue or ISDN, the savings through not having to have a second phone line just for the Internet and not paying call charges for online work will quickly become apparent. BT★ is the largest supplier of broadband through the telephone lines.

Another way of receiving broadband is by cable, from NTL★ and Telewest★, via the networks used for TV services. This is being heavily promoted to residential users; however, you need to have cable TV in order to get broadband.

Just on the market, through various companies, are wireless broadband services, mainly in towns and cities. Still under development is satellite broadband for remote areas. You could check with a satellite provider to see if this is available for your location; however, note that this is very expensive at present.

BT's own phone-line broadband service remains controversial. In rural areas customers are required to sign up for broadband via their ISP. If enough people sign, BT will convert any rural exchange. If you live outside a large city and don't yet have broadband, it can be worth asking around among your friends and acquaintances and getting a small campaign together.

Fax

If you will be doing a lot of business by fax you will need a separate line so that the fax can be left switched on permanently and not interfere with your ordinary telephone requirements. Otherwise, you could choose an answerphone combined with a fax, which should be able to identify whether the incoming call is from a person or a fax. Most fax/answerphones can be set to ring a certain number of times so that, if you are there, you have a chance to answer a call before the other facilities come into play.

Any modem or modem card today will include fax features. There are also stand-alone modems which will take messages and receive (but not print) faxes even when a PC is turned off.

Computers

Almost 40 per cent of households now have a computer, and it is almost impossible to work from home without one. Even if your main occupation is hand-knitting at home for a large knitwear company, the chances are that you will need to produce invoices and quotations, write letters, file away correspondence – some basic administrative work at least. A computer may help you do more sophisticated things such as find more work by accessing the Internet, or bank and shop for supplies online. If you are buying a computer for the first time, or upgrading a computer so that you can develop your business, then you need to do some analysis first.

When purchasing a computer, the key is to purchase the right **software** (the tools or programs which run on the computer) before choosing the computer itself and peripherals – the **hardware**. Think carefully about what you want your computer to do and the types of applications that will suit your requirements. If you want help with the accounts, for example, you can buy specialised software packages to help you deal with your finances. General-purpose business packages or 'office suites' include a word processor, a spreadsheet, a database, a business presentation package and extras such as a personal information manager. They provide a framework in which to work but must be tailored to your needs before you can use them – for example, you must create new templates for different types of spreadsheet. Before committing yourself, try to see software which interests you in operation. Don't be fooled into thinking that you need all kinds of elaborate applications if you will never use them. You may find a cheaper, simpler office suite such as Microsoft Works does all you need.

Take advice from friends and computer magazines and do not be swayed by salespeople pushing the latest software package (this could prove an unwise investment if the product has not been sufficiently road-tested) or the fastest computer. Depending on your level of knowledge, you might want to go on an introductory course or use a consultant – an expensive option but worthwhile provided he or she understands your requirements.

Today it is possible to transform any enterprise with hi-tech hardware and state-of-the-art software. Listed below are some of the possibilities:

Bookkeeping Programs to produce end-of-year accounts and automate VAT calculations, plus invoice- and cheque-printing systems.

Communications With the aid of a modem, your computer can dial telephone numbers for you and send and receive faxes.

Computer-aided design (CAD) Software for visualising two- and three-dimensional objects. Drawings are viewed on screen from any angle and easily altered.

Electronic banking Statements can be sent direct to your computer, bills paid and money transferred at any time of day or night.

Image manipulation Used by artists and graphic designers, this offers special effects not achievable by other means, such as 'morphing' (the smooth transformation of one image into another).

Internet For email, website management and access to the World Wide Web. You need a modem telephone connection with a socket, a computer, a modem (if your computer does not already have one), a subscription to an Internet service and suitable software. Some providers offer free web space where you can advertise your product or services.

Networking Computers in a small office can be connected so that they share information and extras such as printers and scanners

Personal organiser Electronic organisers store all your vital information, can interlink subjects – for example, people and projects – and remind you to keep appointments.

Presentation Presentation applications offer libraries of graphics and symbols, including animation features, music and sound clips. Desktop publishing makes possible professional-quality sales literature.

Specialist applications Computer assistance with specific professional applications – for example, programs interface with sewing and knitting machines to design patterns, create embroideries and adapt garments.

Spreadsheets Ideal for speculative calculations and profit management; information can be presented in tabular form and graphically.

Stock control Databases can keep track of information and pick out trends and details.

Translation software To translate documents into one or more languages.

Voice-activated software The computer can function at your voice command and also read out the words entered or received on screen. Useful for partially sighted/blind people.

Once you have purchased your computer there are several safe-guards to remember:

- Keep the computer purely for business. Do not allow other members of the family to play games on it or to introduce other software that might contain a computer virus – it could wipe out your business records.
- Invest in virus-checking software if your computer does not already have this built into the system. Every time you receive a disk from, say, a client, you need to virus-check it before accessing it.
- Regularly copy all the material stored on your computer on to back-up disks so that in the event of fire or theft you can retrieve the information. Remember, it is not your computer that is indispensable to your business but your data – you can replace your computer straight away. If possible, keep these back-ups at a separate location so that if your house or office burns down your records will be safe.
- Keep a set of paper records filed in a different part of the house, including your accounts materials. Good accounting software will print the forms required by the Inland Revenue.

M-commerce applications

Anyone who does business nowadays finds mobile phones indis-pensable. Determine what sort of user you are before you buy a mobile phone. There are three basic choices to make when it comes to choosing how you want to pay for a mobile phone: prepay (also known as pay-as-you-go), contract (which includes a line rental) and no line rental. Prepay tariffs are the simplest and tend to be cheaper for low users. You pay in advance for calls by buying vouchers, or by credit or debit card. Generally, if your call charges are over £20 per month and you're likely to use the phone for more than three minutes a day, you'll be better off with a contract. With a contract, once you've been credit-checked, you pay monthly line rental and call charges by direct debit. Most contract tariffs give you a number of free minutes each month. With no-line-rental deals, users pay by direct debit, there's no line rental charge and no commitment to any contract (though you may be credit-checked). You receive an itemised bill each month and pay only for calls made. Handsets can be expensive, however. When making up your mind, check the incentives on offer with packages (for example, free calls to voicemail). Note that all packages have high charges for calling a mobile on a different network.

The latest generation of mobile phones are at the heart of what is now called m-commerce, and this mobile technology does virtually everything that you could do at your PC at home.

Some of these 'handsets' are no longer called phones, because they do so much more. For example, GPRS handsets, 'smart phones' and Personal Digital Assistants (PDAs) offer Internet access, fast data transfer and email access, as well as full voice and mobile telephone services for anyone who is trying to conduct business on the move.

Here is what is on offer:

Data transfer services

GPRS (general packet radio service) is up to five times faster than current networks. It is cost effective, since you can stay online all day but will only be charged for the volume of data sent and received. Most services offer a flat-rate monthly payment that covers a certain number of megabytes per month, and then a fixed price per megabyte after that. Currently only Orange offers a flat-rate 'all you can eat' tariff with unlimited access for a fixed price. While access is fast, this can be an expensive way to work and is not recommended for anyone who needs to send large file attachments.

3G (Third Generation) is a new technology that went live in March 2003. It offers complete multimedia, that is, it allows the receiver to see and hear video clips, as well as audio, text, data and still visuals. However, few 3G phones are currently available and initial tariffs cost around £60 per month. The level of uptake among the public remains to be seen.

Wireless applications

Mobile web Since most mobile phones can be set up to work as wireless modems, you can use them to connect your laptop to the Internet. This is simpler than it sounds. Your laptop sees a standard modem, just like the one you use at home. Your phone then connects to the Internet using its aerial instead of a cable to a BT phone socket. You will need to specify a 'data' service when you sign a mobile phone contract in order to use this feature.

The other alternative is to use a PDA such as the Orange SPV or Nokia's 9210i Communicator, both of which have built-in email features and a web browser. Any phone using GPRS will provide the fastest mobile link. Orange offers an alternative technology called HSCSD (high-speed circuit-switched data), which is slightly slower than GPRS and priced per minute. You can also connect over standard GSM (global system for mobile communications – the basic digital mobile system) using almost any phone, although this will provide only a very slow connection.

GPRS cards These can be slotted into most laptops, offering Internet access without the need for a mobile handset. Faster uploads and downloads of Internet pages or file attachments can be done if the card is used in conjunction with a PDA or PC/laptop.

WAP (wireless application protocol) allows mobile users to access and interact with information and services (such as train and cinema timetables and newspaper listings). Although you can access special WAP pages on the Internet, it is more like teletext on your phone than surfing the Net. WAP works with hand-held digital wireless devices such as mobile phones, pagers, two-way radios and smart phones.

Wireless devices
PDA (Personal digital assistant) is a hand-held computer that is able to access email and diary functions and interact with a home-based PC.

Blackberry A hand-held wireless device that delivers email and allows the user to receive, read and reply to emails that have been sent to the home-based computer. A Blackberry 'enterprise server' is installed on the home PC and it then relays to the hand-held device.

The **Xda** or '**Smart phone**' is a combined voice and data wireless device. It offers full-colour Internet and web-based email on a PDA that also doubles as a mobile phone. It also gives access to Excel, Word and all the usual PC applications. The Nokia 9210i offers a slightly sleeker alternative with similar features. Users of the Palm series of PDAs can add a clip-on mobile modem to provide mobile Internet access.

Other portable gadgets

Phones with Java features have recently entered the marketplace in the UK. They allow customers to download applications on to their mobile phones. Java claims to bring uniformity to applications, interfaces and programming of mobile devices. It is also a multimedia messaging device, incorporating video and still images. Often used for games.

Laptop computers are getting slimmer and lighter in response to the threat from the mobile handset invasion. The biggest problem with laptops has always been the fact that the batteries don't last very long without needing a recharge and so the idea of being able to work on your laptop in the middle of a cornfield all day is a bit of a myth. Two or three hours on batteries is standard, although some laptops give you the option to install a spare battery, providing up to five hours' use. Portable solar battery chargers are on the market but these are expensive and can be fragile. In-car lighter-socket chargers are a cheaper alternative.

Adding a WiFi card to your laptop makes it possible to access the Internet at high speeds from an increasing number of locations. BT and other companies, and also some hotel chains, coffee shops and cafés now offer WiFi access. You will usually need to pay a subscription fee per day or per month, although some coffee shops now offer the service as a free incentive to their customers. WiFi cards currently cost between £50 and £100. Setting up is minimal, and as soon as your laptop enters a 'WiFi hotspot' your Internet connection will start working.

Smart Displays You may not need to do your computing away from the house but you may want to do it out in the garden on a sunny day, rather than being trapped inside. Just released in the United States is the Smart Display, a flat screen which connects wirelessly to any computer in the house, letting you use the software and files on it, in any room or outside, as long as you are within 100 feet of the main computer. At present, these are expensive.

Buying and hiring equipment

When it comes to choosing the best-value piece of equipment for your purposes do some research to enable you to shop around effectively.

Which? magazine has published surveys on most kinds of domestic and office equipment, with test results on the level of performance you can expect for your money, and with recommendations for those items offering best value for money.

Specialist equipment may have been the subject of similar surveys by trade associations. It is worth enquiring whether the association relevant to your line of work has done tests on the type of equipment you intend to buy and can make recommendations.

Similarly, you can often find informative articles in trade magazines or papers. Industrial sewing machines, for example, might be covered in clothing industry magazines or manufacturing publications – it will pay you to look in both areas.

You could also try an independent dealer who stocks most, if not all, of the makes of equipment that interest you. Go armed with a list of questions: you need to know exactly what you want from your piece of equipment so that the dealer will be able to make a positive recommendation.

What do you want to do with it? How demanding are you going to be? Will you be using it all the time? In which case, does it have a powerful enough engine? An ordinary domestic lawnmower, for example, cannot cope with being used continuously for large areas of grass – the motor would burn out.

Do you need to carry it around with you? If you are on the road a lot, do you need portable equipment? A mobile hairdresser will need equipment that can be loaded and unloaded easily, as will many others – caterers, masseurs, aromatherapists, beauticians and so on.

Do you need it to be flexible? Do you need power tools, for example, to do the small intricate jobs as well as the big hefty ones? Do you need equipment that is battery-operated, so that you can use it anywhere?

Do you need something sophisticated or can it be simple? Think carefully about what you need from your equipment. Do not be tempted to buy a state-of-the-art machine if you plan to put it to fairly basic use.

Does the price of the equipment vary from stockist to stockist? Do your cost comparisons before you buy. Look in shops and dealerships, browse through trade magazines, ask at trade associations. Are there any special deals on offer if you are a member of an association? Is the price cheaper at certain times of the year? Computers, for example, often get more expensive just before Christmas, because they have a domestic as well as a business application. Ask if there is a discount for cash. Some shops are prepared to forgo the percentage they would normally pay to a credit-card company if you pay cash (not cheque).

Do you have to have accessories? Sometimes you cannot do without them for reasons of health and safety – for example, a face-guard for use with a chain saw. Other accessories may not be important or you may be able to get them cheaper elsewhere. If a piece of equipment is being offered with the accessories as a 'free' gift, check that the price of the package really is a bargain and that you cannot in fact get it cheaper elsewhere.

Do you need to upgrade your machinery regularly? Hiring may also be a better option to avoid built-in obsolescence (see below). The older the equipment the more difficult it is to get spare parts. (You certainly do not want to buy second-hand in this case.)

Do you have to buy, or would you be better hiring? Hiring can also be a better option if you need a piece of equipment for a short time only (perhaps at a trade fair or exhibition being held at the other end of the country), or you want to experiment by offering another product or service but are not willing to commit yourself to buying machinery until you know there is a demand. If there is any element of risk in your situation, you may prefer to start off your business by hiring rather than taking out a loan and buying. You can hire almost anything. Many computer companies offer business leasing (i.e. hire) deals which may be cheaper than buying because of tax breaks. Note however that you will be expected to return the equipment at the end of the leasing period. The financial implications can be complicated, and it is worth asking your accountant to work out which approach will be most cost-effective for you.

What about back-up? If your equipment fails and will take several days to be repaired, where can you get something to tide you over? Arm yourself with that information before you buy. If you do buy, particularly if it is an expensive piece of equipment, can you get a temporary replacement clause built into the sales contract, or will you have to replace the item through your insurance policy?

Do you need an extended guarantee? Nowadays, most equipment carries with it the option of paying for an extended guarantee period. The equipment will carry a free guarantee for, say, up to one year, and you have the option of taking out an insurance which covers you for three or five years, or whatever the manufacturer feels is appropriate. However, study the small print of the contract very carefully: some extended guarantees do not cover 'wear and tear' and some exclude business use. One alternative to these guarantees would be to take out a maintenance contract with a company which, for an annual fee, will cover you for regular services and repairs. Another option is to hire your equipment, in which case it should automatically be covered for any repairs or replacements.

Care of specialist equipment

Your initial market research will determine what other equipment you would benefit from. What do your competitors use? What manufacturing techniques do they employ? Can you afford to copy them?

If you have industrial equipment that cuts, sews, planes, welds, shapes, saws or performs any function that could injure or kill, safeguards are vital. You must be able to lock it away when you are not using it, and you must make sure that no unauthorised person is able to operate it or allowed to stand near it when it is in use. If safety gear is appropriate you must have it handy and wear it whenever you use the machinery: face masks and eye protection for working with dusty materials or chemicals; eye protection when welding or using chainsaws or powerful garden strimmers; protective gloves when handling caustic or sharp materials, and so on. Never be casual about it. Just because you are very experienced does not mean that you cannot make a mistake.

Have the equipment serviced regularly, particularly if a third party is involved – as in the case of a driving school car, for instance. If you are a homeworker working for someone else, call in your employer if you have any doubts about the machinery. If you suspect a fault, switch off and do not use it again until it has been thoroughly checked by a competent person. It is better to be safe than sorry.

Do not keep machinery that uses fuel, for example a petrol-driven lawnmower or oxyacetylene equipment, in any part of the house, not even in a scullery or conservatory. And do not keep photographic film or video tapes on open shelves – they can burn very fast and give off toxic fumes. Keep them in a fireproof, damp-proof cupboard away from the house. Ask your local Fire Officer for advice and always be sure to follow Health and Safety Regulations (see page 62).

Insurance

Insure all your important equipment against damage or theft. You will need to replace it quickly to keep your business going.

Your rights as a purchaser

Cancellation

Some goods are not available instantly and have to be ordered from the manufacturer. The salesperson may tell you there is, say, a four- to six-week delivery period. If you accept this and sign an agreement, you are not entitled to cancel the order unless the goods have still not arrived after the agreed time, and you have given the seller a deadline, in writing, before cancellation, for example, 'I am informing you that if my automatic wine-corking machine is not delivered by the end of next week, I am cancelling the order.'

Delivery

Under the law it is the buyer's responsibility to collect goods unless the seller has agreed to deliver them. Mostly, companies will offer to deliver but for a charge. It makes no difference under the law whether you are disabled or elderly – the seller has no legal oblig-ation to deliver unless you are buying a piece of equipment that, for safety reasons, has to be professionally installed or built on site. The legal obligation lies with whoever installs the equipment, should a death or injury arise from faulty installation of the equipment. Bear that in mind if you decide to do it yourself. Also, there are certain pieces of equipment that have to be regularly inspected in order to comply with regulations – such as high-pressure water heaters or special electrical installations.

Return of goods

You have to have reasonable cause to return goods that you have bought, which is to say that they have to be faulty, unfit for their purpose or not comply with their description. You cannot simply return a van because you have decided you do not like the colour after all, for example.

Hiring equipment

Read the rental agreement carefully. Points to look out for are:

Insurance

Most rental companies will expect you to take out insurance to cover the cost of the goods if they are damaged or stolen.

Minimum hire period

You may want to hire something for only a week while you are at a trade fair, but the hire company may have a policy of a minimum one-month hire period.

Location of equipment

A hire company has the right to insist that the equipment is kept at one particular place, such as the home or office. The contract may stipulate that you cannot travel with it, or that you cannot keep it in a shed in your garden.

Early termination of agreement

You cannot normally be made to sign up for longer than eighteen months at a time without a chance to end the agreement by giving 'reasonable notice' as specified in your agreement. Check that the agreement you are entering into allows for an early termination. If your business folds you do not want to be bound to hiring a piece of equipment you no longer need.

Service or maintenance clause

You want to be assured that in the event of breakdown or other problems the hire company will repair or replace the equipment as fast as possible at no cost.

Your obligations

You must take good care of the equipment you are hiring: you will be liable for its cost if it is damaged through your negligence. You must also pay your rental instalments when agreed or the hire company may be entitled to repossess the goods. However, note that if you fail to pay only one instalment, the hire company can only repossess the article if your agreement says so.

The hire company's obligations

The company is obliged to supply you with goods which are suitable for the purpose for which they are wanted, and are in a safe, working condition. It is required to make some arrangements for service or maintenance, either by doing it or providing the name of a company with which it has a special arrangement. The company must replace any equipment that cannot be repaired, unless that situation has arisen through your negligence. Again, **always check the terms and conditions of any agreements before you sign them**, so that you are aware of exactly where obligations lie. Some companies require the hirer to pay for an insurance that covers the piece of equipment in the event of damage.

Hire-purchasing equipment

This is a form of hiring but the ultimate aim is to purchase the goods outright. The usual structure of the contract is that the customer pays an initial deposit and then further regular instalments (which cover the purchase price) plus an interest charge on the overall amount. The final payment is deemed in the contract to be an amount which is not part of the hire but is an 'option to buy'.

Frequently, a hire purchase agreement is between a customer and a finance company, not the trader who is selling the goods. The finance company, in effect, owns the goods that are hire purchased and therefore is the party that must be contacted and held liable for any defect in the goods.

The seller's obligations

The seller is obliged to give the goods to you in sound condition as soon as you have paid the deposit. The seller is also obliged to allow you to have full use of the goods without interference, provided all agreed payments are forthcoming.

The seller is also required by law to be a complete owner of the goods being offered for hire.

Your obligations

You must look after the goods for the period of the hire purchase agreement. (After the final payment you can do what you like with them.)

You must keep them insured for their full value against damage, loss, theft and so on, and you must not sell, pawn or hire out the goods while they are still subject to the hire purchase agreement.

If difficulties arise

The law recognises three distinct ways of backing out of a hire purchase agreement.

Cancellation This means cancelling an agreement before it starts. If you sign an agreement in your own home rather than at a place of business and if the agreement is a consumer credit agreement, there is a statutory five-day 'cooling-off' period during which you may cancel the agreement; the seller has to return any deposit or part-exchange goods (or a part-exchange allowance in cash). This is designed to protect people from succumbing to high-pressure sales techniques used on them at home.

There is no 'cooling-off' period if you sign an agreement at the seller's business premises, so you cannot cancel. You can usually cancel if you have agreed to buy something by mail order. The seller will usually specify a period during which the product must be returned if a refund and cancellation are required. The 'pressure to buy' is deemed by law to be much less in such circumstances.

Withdrawal The ability to withdraw from an agreement depends on whether or not the seller has signed the agreement. If you have signed an agreement at a seller's business premises, you cannot cancel. However, if the seller has not completed his or her side of the contract, that is to say signed the agreement undertaking to fulfil his or her obligations as a hire purchaser and given you a copy, you are able to withdraw from the agreement by notifying the seller as quickly as possible in writing. But, be warned, the seller is deemed to have completed the deal upon posting his or her copy of the agreement, so if your written withdrawal and the signed contract cross in the post, the chances are you did not get in quickly enough and you will have lost the chance to withdraw.

If your withdrawal is successful, you should be entitled to an immediate refund of any deposit paid or goods taken in part-exchange.

Termination If you have difficulty keeping up with the payments you can terminate a hire purchase agreement, usually after a certain point in the life of the contract. Most agreements stipulate that the buyer has to pay at least half the total cost of the goods plus any extras that may have been incurred such as insurance, installation charges or delivery. Once the goods have been returned there is no more to pay.

If you owe money to the seller when you decide to terminate, you will be liable to pay any outstanding amounts up to the date of official termination.

What the seller can do

If you have not kept up the payments or returned the goods, or unlawfully sold the goods to someone else, the seller is able to take certain action.

First, the seller must send you a default notice which details why you are in breach of the agreement and what the seller wants to do about it, that is, whether you must pay the money you owe and/or return the goods, or pay compensation for the value of the goods.

You have seven days in which to respond to the default notice. If you do not respond the seller has the right to ask your permission to repossess any of his or her goods that are on your property. If you do not give him or her that permission the seller can get a court order to repossess.

If there are no goods to repossess, the seller can take court action to recover whatever monies are owed in respect of hire purchase and in lieu of the goods that have gone missing.

If you agree to hand back the goods without the seller having to get a court order to repossess, you will also have to finish paying one-half of the total hire purchase price.

Financial help with equipment

Some of the organisations mentioned in Chapter 6 may be able to offer loans or grants towards the purchase of essential equipment. It is always worth checking to see what the current position is. Some of the Homeworking Units will loan certain equipment to home-workers that contributes to the health and safety of workers, such as adjustable chairs and lamps, smoke alarms, circuit breakers, first aid kits, scissors, aprons and sticky tape dispensers.

Getting support

You need the right equipment to help you work successfully from home, but you also need the right information and specialist advice to help you to function. This kind of support helps you to make the best decisions for every aspect of your new business.

All the organisations mentioned in Chapter 6 can offer lone entrepreneurs and small businesses the additional skills and support they need for growth. The Learning and Skills Councils (LSCs)★ and Business Links★ in particular help you to identify your business needs and a number of their support services are provided either free of charge or at a very modest cost. Contact Local Enterprise Councils (LECs)★ or Scottish Enterprise★ in Scotland, and Business Connect★ in Wales.

These organisations aim to provide contacts to help overcome the problem which faces many individuals who work from home – isolation. One solution to isolation is to 'network'. Networking is the process of making business contacts, building up a network of people who will become your support services, your customers, perhaps even your partners and friends.

Some of the many sources of support are outlined below, but first you need to assess the areas in which you may need support.

Help with your account books

As discussed earlier in the book, unless you are a qualified accountant yourself, it is advisable to get someone to organise your account books, and to advise on credit control, raising finance, tax and other matters. However, if you are starting small, you may need no more than some advice from your local Business Link★, bank manager or the Inland Revenue★. On the other hand, if you are starting an ambitious project it would be prudent to use the services of a professional accountant from the beginning. Whatever the size of your enterprise, it is advisable to get an accountant to audit your accounts once a year for tax purposes.

If you have no experience of accounting at all, you may need the support of a bookkeeper who will come in, say, once a week to put your books in order, enter all receipts, sales, expenses and so on.

At one time, before the high-street banks cut back on their staff, the first port of call would have been your bank manager. However, a manager now often has two or three branches to oversee and is rarely available to give that sort of advice. Some banks have trained a member of staff to be a 'small business adviser' but his or her time and experience is sometimes limited.

Your Local Enterprise Agency, LSC★ or Business Link★ can put you in touch with qualified people and also offer help with training in basic bookkeeping skills, as well as supplying you with literature produced by the government that is specifically aimed at helping small businesses to organise and maintain their accounts.

Legal support

Many people tend to retain a solicitor only when there is trouble, but a solicitor can help a lone entrepreneur in many ways. Many solicitors publish a scale of charges for uncomplicated jobs, such as writing letters to bad debtors or drawing up a contract of employment. It is worth discussing your future needs with a few local solicitors to see what charges you might incur.

For basic advice on contracts or consumer matters you can contact your local Citizens Advice Bureau or join the *Which?* Legal Service at Consumers' Association★. For a fee you get unlimited telephone access to consumer lawyers, and if your case requires written action this is available for a competitive fixed fee.

You may find yourself in a situation where you have to recover a bad debt through the Small Claims Court, in which case you will not need legal advice as the system is specifically tailored to meet the needs of people who are not familiar with legal procedures. The forms (available from your local County Court) have accompanying notes and the procedure, once you attend the court, is explained in simple language.

Your local authority will be able to offer advice on rules and regulations that may apply to your setting up in business. Local authority literature covers a wide range of occupations and explains the relevant government and EU regulations.

Most trade and professional associations have legal departments which give advice to members. They may hold seminars on legal problems which often beset their particular industry. General professional bodies, such as the Institute of Directors (IoD)★, offer free legal advice to members on any problems relating to the running of a business. The IoD publishes lots of material and runs frequent seminars on the legal liability of company directors, which apply to any company whether it comprises two people or two hundred.

Marketing

You can find support for your marketing activities from all sorts of sources, as described in Chapter 5. You can use published market research in libraries or on the Internet.

Employing marketing consultants can cost a great deal of money and readers of this book should turn to the organisations mentioned in Chapter 6 first to see if they can get such advice free or grant-aided. Local advertising agencies, however, may be within your budget. Ring them up to see if they will give a free initial consultation to look at your particular marketing problems and suggest a tentative plan of action, outlining their costs should you wish to proceed.

Selling direct to the public is governed by a code of good practice which was drawn up by the Direct Selling Association★ in collaboration with the Office of Fair Trading. The Direct Selling Association can offer advice on all aspects from door-to-door selling to party plans.

You should also contact your local Trading Standards Office, which will be able to offer you free advice on how you must sell your goods. They can also provide a wealth of literature regarding the current rules and regulations for labelling, safety requirements, trade descriptions and so on. They should be willing to advise anyone who has a business idea, but has not yet set up in business.

Mail order

The first place to go for advice is the Advertising Standards Authority★. It lays down the British Code of Advertising Practice, with which all mail-order firms have to comply. If you intend to advertise your products through a newspaper or magazine you will have to get details of the Mail Order Protection Scheme (MOPS)★, run by the relevant publication.

On the practical side of mail order – forms of packaging, times and frequency of despatch and so on – the Royal Mail★ will gladly discuss with you your proposed venture and suggest ways and means of dealing with your despatch needs. So will any of the private security/courier firms.

You may find that you need a few sessions with a specialised consultant in order to determine the best sources and types of packaging. Your Business Link★ or Local Enterprise Agency should be able to help.

Export

An enormous amount of advice and support is available for the individual who feels that his or her product may do well in an overseas market.

If you are resident in England, your first port of call should be the Business Link Office★. In Scotland contact Scottish Enterprise★; in Wales, contact Business Connect★.

The British Standards Institution★ gives technical advice to ensure that your products comply with the various overseas standards.

The Central Office of Information (COI)★ can offer advice and practical help in export publicity services to make your product better known overseas.

Most trade and business associations and Chambers of Commerce run export clubs or forums where potential or new exporters can network with experienced exporters and learn more about the procedures and pitfalls of exporting. Sometimes financial help is available in the form of subsidised overseas marketing trips or similar.

Most of the above-named organisations will be able to put you in touch with good commercial translators who will help you overcome the language barrier when starting to export to non-English-speaking countries. Also, if you intend to advertise abroad, you will need the advice of an advertising agency versed in the rules and regulations governing advertising in those countries: these regulations vary enormously and have to be strictly adhered to.

Other support

You will certainly need advice on what insurances you must have and what you can afford. An independent insurance broker is the best source of advice but do shop around – you can make quite a saving by looking at what is on offer before you actually buy.

Remember to read the small print very carefully to ensure that you are getting cover for what you need and not duplicating cover you already have on another policy.

You may need help with technology, either because you do not have the right technology to do a particular job or your existing technology needs a good service back-up. LSCs* can help here, perhaps by putting you in touch with a potential subcontractor who has the right technology to undertake a particular job on your behalf; or a local office services bureau might be able to offer the amount of support you need if a particular job has swamped you and you need help for just a short period. The place where you bought your equipment should be able to recommend a good service engineer or, if you bought it second-hand, you could ask for advice at your local Chamber of Commerce or trade association.

Last but by no means least, enlist the support of your family and friends. Apart from being extra pairs of hands when the workload piles up, they can also be excellent sources of information and fresh ideas. It is a common trap for the individual working from home to operate in a vacuum. Ideas become stale, problems get out of proportion, the ability to delegate disappears. Let others support you in whatever ways they can and you will find that you get greater enjoyment from your work.

Getting skills

You may be contemplating starting a career from home which requires you to learn a new skill from scratch, or you may feel that although you are already skilled in your field a formal qualification will inspire more confidence in your customers. Indeed, you may not be able to operate certain businesses – for example, a driving school – without formal qualifications. You may want to learn new skills to help you to diversify from the product or service range you are currently offering. Alternatively, you may be acquiring a new piece of equipment which demands a period of training to acquaint yourself fully with its finer points.

There are many places to go for the necessary training: Adult Education Institutes (evening or day classes), universities or colleges (for full- or part-time courses) or correspondence courses (for diplomas in a wide variety of skills from accountancy to interior design). Other courses can be found by contacting the manufacturers of the equipment you want to buy or by visiting your local library, JobCentre or nearest Training Access Point (TAP) – ask the JobCentre for details. Training is discussed in detail in Chapter 2.

Again, many of the organisations mentioned in Chapter 6 offer support for training in certain skills and, sometimes, grants for the same. The Department for Education and Skills (DfES)★ offers a Career Development Loan. The government helps people to pay for vocational training by arranging with some of the high-street banks to offer special loans. The government pays the interest due on the loan for the duration of the course and for up to one month afterwards. Then the borrower has to repay the loan, plus any further interest, in instalments. The borrower may train full-time or part-time, or use open learning. The loans are available for up to 80 per cent of the course fees and, in some cases, living expenses if you are on a full-time course.

To qualify you have to be over the age of 18 and not in receipt of any other support for training or education, and undertake to work in the UK or elsewhere in the European Union after the course is completed. The course has to be suitable for the work you want to do and last between one week and one year, and the loan has to be for between £300 and £5,000. Further information is available from your local JobCentre.

The New Deal programme offers help for people who want to set up their own business. Help with the business plan and a period of training is available. Work-based Learning for Adults (in England and Wales), the Training for Work Scheme (Scotland) or a Jobfinder's Grant are other avenues available for people wishing to work for themselves. Information is available through local JobCentres.

Some local LSCs★ and LECs★ may provide financial support to start-up businesses.

All companies that are members of the British Franchise Association★ undertake to offer full training in the operation of their franchises. After all, it is entirely in the interest of the franchisor to ensure that the product or service continues to carry a good name by being operated by skilled people.

Training on specific pieces of equipment should be no problem, although it may not be a free service if it requires more than half a day's instruction. Many Adult Education Institutes run computer software courses where you can learn the intricacies of desktop publishing or get to grips with word-processing packages. The advantage of such courses is that they allow you to learn at a steady pace, perhaps before you invest in the relevant software. Many manufacturers now offer training videos, often free of charge, with each new purchase of equipment. Again, these are a good idea because they provide more insight than a manual and they can be played over and over again until you feel confident you know what you are doing.

If you are a craftworker who would like to add to your skills, you can look in some of the art and crafts publications to see what courses are on offer or contact the Crafts Council*, which publishes a huge, regularly updated list of courses throughout the country.

Chapter 11

Wading through the red tape

If you asked most owners of a small business what they feared the most about working for themselves they would probably say that it was having to deal with local government, central government and EU regulations – in other words 'red tape'. A constant flow of new EU directives is translated into regulations that underpin or amend existing legislation in the UK. The burden of employment regulation has been a particular problem.

All businesses are subject to legal requirements. There are too many rules and regulations to cover in one chapter of this book; below are those that might be of most interest to someone setting up a small business or working for themselves. Tax and VAT matters, mail-order and employment legislation are dealt with elsewhere in this book, and Chapter 13 deals exclusively with legislation pertaining to converting your home or land into a business.

Legal controls

Most businesses are subject to legal controls. Below is a list of some of the Acts and regulations with which you may have to comply.

Acts of Parliament
Activity Centres (Young Persons Safety) Act 1995
Animal Boarding Establishments Act 1963
Animal Health Act 2002
Architects Act 1997
Breeding of Dogs and Sale of Dogs (Welfare) Act 1999
Business Names Act 1985
Care Standards Act 2000
Carers and Disabled Children Act 2000

Chiropractors Act 1994

Community Care (Residential Accommodation) Act 1998

Companies Act 1985

Company Directors Disqualification Act 1986

Competition Act 1998

Computer Misuse Act 1993

Consumer Credit Act 1974

Consumer Protection Act 1987

Copyright etc. and Trade Marks (Offences and Enforcement) Act 2002

Data Protection Act 1998

Education Act 2002

Employment Act 2002

Enterprise Act 2002

Estate Agents Act 1979

Fair Employment (N. Ireland) Act 1989

Fair Trading Act 1973

Food Safety Act 1990

Food Standards Act 1999

Health and Safety at Work etc. Act 1974

Human Rights Act 1998

Insolvency Act 1986

Late Payment of Commercial Debts (Interest) Act 1998

Limited Liability Partnerships Act 2000

Local Government (Miscellaneous Provisions) Act 1982

Noise Act 1996

Osteopaths Act 1993

Patents Act 1977

Protection of Animals (Amendment Act) 2000

Protection of Children Act 1999

Registered Designs Act 1949

Registered Homes (Amendment) Act 1991

Sale of Goods Act 1979

Supply of Goods and Services Act 1982

Trade Descriptions Act 1968/72

Trade Marks Act 1994

Trading Schemes Act 1996

Unfair Contract Terms Act 1977

Video Recordings Act 1993

Regulations

Companies (Particulars of Usual Residential Address)
  (Confidentiality Orders) Regulations 2002
Consumer Protection (Distance Selling) Regulations 2000
Control of Misleading Advertisements Regulations 1998
  (as amended)
Doorstep Selling Regulations 1988
Electricity at Work Regulations 1989
Electronic Commerce (EC Directive) Regulations 2002
Estate Agents (Provision of Information) Regulations 1991
Food Safety (General Food Hygiene) Regulations 1995
Furniture and Furnishings (Fire) (Safety) Regulations 1988
  (as amended)
General Product Safety Regulations 1994
Limited Liability Partnership Regulations 2000
Management of Health and Safety at Work Regulations 1999
Nightwear (Safety) Regulations 1985
Registered Designs Regulations 2001
Sale and Supply of Goods to Consumers Regulations 2002
Toys (Safety) Regulations 1995
Unfair Terms in Consumer Contracts Regulations 1999

Other

British Standards mark or European Approval mark
Local authority planning regulations
Local authority licences

Please be aware that this is, by no means, a comprehensive list. If you are contemplating starting a small business from your own home you should seek as much advice as possible about the regulations and legislation that could apply to your chosen enterprise (see below).

It can be dispiriting to someone who is simply developing a hobby into a business to find that once he or she stops selling to friends and starts selling to the general public, a tidal wave of regulation looms up. Some of the sources of information for small businesses are listed below.

The national press and other publications report that one of the biggest problems encountered by many individuals is the fact that many of the newest regulations emanating from the EU are not specific enough and are open to wide interpretation by local and central government officials.

The concerns of the business community about the standard and volume of government regulation led to the enactment of The Regulatory Reform Act in 2001. This law provides ministers with a wide order-making power to reform legislation – to 'tackle outdated, overlapping and over burdensome legislation'. Government consultation documents, including those on proposals for regulatory reform, can be found at *www.ukonline.gov.uk*

A non-statutory code called the 'Enforcement Concordat' describes for businesses and others what they can expect from enforcement officers. One of the guiding principles is that of helpfulness – staff will work on the basis that prevention is better than cure.

Take advice

One of the best places to start is your local Trading Standards Office, which will have a Department of Regulatory Services (or similar title). Even if you just have a business idea at this stage, they will be able to advise you on what legislation will be applicable to your enterprise. They will provide you with the latest literature and tell you whether any new regulations are likely to come into force in the coming months. Guidance leaflets on a number of topics are available online at *www.tradingstandards.gov.uk*. This website also lists local Trading Standards Offices.

Most of the literature originates from the Department of Trade and Industry (DTI)★, The Office of Fair Trading★, or, if the subject is food safety and standards, the Food Standards Agency★.

Useful websites include:

www.companieshouse.gov.uk
www.dti.gov.uk
www.food.gov.uk
www.hse.gov.uk/startup
www.oft.gov.uk/Business
www.ukonline.gov.uk/startingupinbusiness

You could also visit a website called *www.businesslink.org* – part of the Small Business Service, which is full of valuable information about regulatory problems. There are factsheets on the website which can be downloaded in a pdf version or ordered by telephone. The checklist for starting a business is particularly useful. Information is also available on how a business can be financed and the availability of grants, as well as on sales and marketing.

Women's Institute Country Markets* give their potential stall-holders leaflets explaining the legal requirements for different types of products. For example, preserves have to be in clear glass jars of particular sizes; labelling has to be done in particular ways and must include the maker's full name and address; and so on. See *www.wimarkets.co.uk* for more information.

Starting at the beginning

First, make sure that you are allowed to conduct your proposed business from your home. Check your lease or mortgage and your house insurance. If your proposed business is allowable, in that it is not noisy, hazardous, likely to cause offence to the neighbours or require alteration to a listed building in a conservation area, the chances are that you will be able to proceed.

If you are going to change the use of your premises (into a treatment room, tea room, shop and so on), alter the shape (build a workshop over your garage or similar) or the appearance (install a large shop window in the front or put a sign on the door) you will most likely have to seek planning permission. Most local authorities provide leaflets which explain the application procedure for planning permission.

A number of businesses cannot operate without a licence. The boxed list may be applicable to home-run businesses.

Setting up

You have to observe the legal requirements when setting up in business. The amount of paperwork that has to be done depends upon the form in which you choose to conduct business. Here are the options.

Sole trader

As a sole trader you are wholly responsible for your business and its dealings and you are also personally responsible for all debts

Licences issued by Trading Standards Departments or referred on by them to other licensing authorities

Amusements with prizes	Mini cabs
Animal boarding	Motor salvage operations
Auction rooms	Night cafés
Betting and gambling	Nurses agencies
Breeding of dogs	Open air cafés
Buskers	Outdoor boxing and wrestling
Butchers	Pet shops
Cinemas showing films	Pharmacies and poisons
Dangerous wild animals	Pools betting
Door supervisors (bouncers)	Public music and dancing
Explosives (fireworks)	Riding establishments
Game dealers	Sex establishments
Hypnotism	Special treatments[1]
Indoor sporting events	Street trading
Karaoke (for the public)	Theatres and small plays
Marriage premises	

[1]Acupuncture, aromatherapy, bleaching, body scrub, body wrap, chiropody, cosmetic piercing, ear and nose piercing, electrolysis, eyebrow/lash tinting, facials, faradism, galvanism, hair extensions, makeup, manicure/pedicure, massage, nail extensions, perming, reflexology, sauna or other baths, semi-permanent makeup, sugaring, sunbeds, tattooing, vacuum suction, vapour, waxing.

incurred. Your personal possessions, such as your home, may have to be sold to cover your debts. You do not have to submit accounts to Companies House★ (Companies Registry★ in Northern Ireland). The law affecting company directors under the Companies Act does not apply to sole traders.

Partnership

A partnership is likely to exist automatically in law if two or more people carry on a business. There are no registration formalities. The same responsibilities in law apply to partners as for sole traders. A partnership agreement should be drawn up by a solicitor to record your agreement on key matters such as sharing profits and losses, cheque-signing, partners leaving or joining, financial arrangements and so on. Under the law, all partners have unlimited liability for the debts of the business, even if they are 'sleeping' (non-working) partners or have only a small share of the profits.

Limited company

You cannot use the word 'Limited' unless your business is registered as a company. The name of the company must not be the same as another company in existence or 'too like' it. A list of prohibited names is available from Companies House★ (or Companies Registry★ in Northern Ireland) – that is, names that are not allowed by law such as Royal, Trust, Association and so on. A limited company is a separate legal 'person' that can sue and be sued in its own right.

A company must have at least one shareholder, one director and a company secretary (who could be a second director). The directors of a company are subject to various legal constraints which may make them personally responsible for any wrongdoing. Directors may also be personally responsible for their own negligence. If a company director gives a personal guarantee for a company's bank loan, he or she will be personally liable for the full amount in the event that the company goes bust. Unlike the company, he or she will not be covered for limited liability.

Not taking every step to protect creditors should your company be in financial difficulties could lead to personal responsibility if the company is wound up. The court may be obliged to disqualify unfit directors of insolvent companies.

The law states that the accounts of a limited company showing a true and fair view have to be submitted each year to Companies House★ (Companies Registry★ in Northern Ireland) to be available for public scrutiny. Depending on the size of the company, the annual accounts may have to be audited. Directors' meetings must be properly minuted and shareholders must have an annual meeting. However, resolutions can now be passed which enable companies to dispense with the holding of annual meetings.

The requirement for company directors to disclose their home addresses at Companies House has provided an easy route for activists to obtain personal details. Measures have been introduced that allow company officers to keep home details private, but only where they can demonstrate actual or serious risk of violence or intimidation. The Secretary of State is able to grant a Confidentiality Order, under which a service address replaces the usual residential address.

Limited liability partnership

Confidentiality protection is also available to members of limited liability partnerships (LLPs). Despite their name, LLPs are not partnerships at all, but types of corporate body that offer the protection of limited liability but whose members are taxed as a partnership. LLPs are available for all commercial ventures, including business start-ups, so long as there are at least two members. Like companies, details of the members are registered at Companies House*, but unlike companies the agreement between the members is private. LLPs offer the opportunity for internal flexibility for the members, with no formal share capital structure. However, the 'price' for limited liability (in the same way as for a company) is the requirement to file annual accounts at Companies House.

Further information about companies and limited liability partnerships can be found at the Companies House website *www.companieshouse.gov.uk*.

Trade name disclosures

Whether you are a sole trader, partnership or company, you may wish to use a trade name, for example 'Quick and Sure Builders'. If a business or company uses a trade name in Great Britain that differs from the surname or surnames of the proprietor or partners, or the registered corporate name, certain particulars must be disclosed in business communications and at the business premises. Details must be given of the name(s) of the proprietor(s) or of the corporate name, and an address for service of documents. The registered number, place of registration and registered address of a company must always appear on its business letters and order forms.

You must also take care not to use a business name that somebody else is using, where there might be confusion and loss of business to the other trader.

Registering domain names

Domain names for websites have to be registered with an international organisation called the Internet Corporation for Assigned Names and Numbers (ICANN), otherwise there would be a great deal of confusion if many websites had the same names – particularly as the Internet is a global marketplace. Registering domain names is usually done through companies that specialise in this business and they can be found, of course, on the Internet. The cost is usually around £10–£15 for a UK-only name and £20–£40 for a global name. Because of the often short life span of dotcom companies, it is usual to register a domain name for just two years and then renew at regular intervals, should your business be fortunate enough to keep going.

A good book to get is *Tolley's Domain Names – a Practical Guide*, which explains the legal and commercial considerations, regulations and best practice and procedural issues relating to domain names.

Understanding domain name suffixes

.co.uk	for UK commercial enterprises
.org.uk	for UK non-commercial enterprises
.me.uk	for UK personal domains
.plc.uk and .ltd.uk	for UK registered companies
.name	for global personal domain
.info	for global domain for any purpose
.net	also for global domain for any purpose
.us	for USA general purpose
.org	for global non-commerce organisation
.biz	for global business domain
.com	for global general domain

Buying an existing business

The main thing to note if you are buying a business is that, if it has employees, the new owner must maintain their existing conditions of employment and their employee rights (see Chapter 14).

Co-operatives

There are two types of co-operative. Under the Industrial and Provident Societies Acts 1965–78, an Industrial and Provident Co-operative must have at least three members. Under the Companies Act 1985, a limited company co-operative need only have one member. The principles, however, are the same. Every employee who is a member owns one share of the business, everybody has equal voting rights and the profits are shared.

Health and safety

This is probably the major area where you can fall foul of the law. Since 1974 various Acts of Parliament have introduced regulations which address the health and safety of employees at work, the health and safety of children and the elderly in specific places such as nurseries and nursing homes (see Chapter 13). In addition, there are many regulations which are designed to protect the consumer from bad hygiene, faulty goods and lack of fire safety.

The Management of Health and Safety at Work Regulations cover (with some exceptions) all workers, including mobile workers and homeworkers. Employers and self-employed people must assess the risks involved in their work activities. Employers must make arrangements to implement necessary measures, appoint competent people and arrange for appropriate information and training.

For further information on health and safety matters contact the Environmental Health Services of your local council or see the website of the Health and Safety Executive at *www.hse.gov.uk*.

Food safety

The whole area of food safety is a minefield. You must be prepared to invest time, patience and money getting it right and complying with all the regulations. The Food Standards Agency★ is responsible for ensuring that food is safe for human consumption right from the farm or garden through to the processing and packaging. For instance, the Agency controls the quantity and type of pesticides used, and makes regular checks on harmful chemicals, radioactivity or poisonous metals that could contaminate or come into contact with anything produced on a farm, market garden or fish farm. It also enforces regulations on what food additives may be used, and monitors whether the packaging is safe or whether it may leave residues on the food or drink.

The local authorities, in the form of Environmental Health Officers, then take over to ensure that food prepared further along the chain, in commercial or domestic kitchens, is safe and that food sold in shops complies with all necessary legislation. Legislation covers, among other things, such areas as the temperature at which food must be stored, the type of utensils to be used, the system for disposing of waste, the cleaning of walls, worktops and equipment, the banning of animals from food preparation areas, and the personal hygiene of those preparing food.

Food Safety (General Food Hygiene) Regulations 1995

These regulations affect anyone who owns, manages or works in a food business. They apply to anything from a sandwich van to a restaurant, from a village hall where food is prepared to a supermarket. These regulations cover every process that deals with the preparation and sale of food including: processing, manufacturing, transportation, distribution, handling, packaging, storage, selling and supplying. They do not apply to food cooked at home for private consumption. Wherever food is sold two basic rules always apply:

- there should always be adequate facilities to prepare and serve food safely
- food handling procedures should avoid exposing food to risk of any contamination.

For further advice about the regulations, contact the Environmental Health services of your local council.

Food Safety Act 1990

The Food Safety Act empowers Environmental Health Officers to enter food premises uninvited and to inspect the food and the premises, to take samples away for investigation and, if necessary, to ask a Justice of the Peace to condemn food as unfit for human consumption. They may demand that improvements be made to premises that they consider unhygienic and, if those improvements are not made, or if the state of the premises is bad, they may close a business down very quickly. It can only be reopened when the local

---

CASE HISTORY: Ranjit

Ranjit and his wife make bhajis and samosas and deliver them to shops and garages as snack food. Ranjit had to have his kitchen inspected by the Environmental Health Officer and it had to be refurbished to comply with the regulations. New tiling, a new sink, a new refrigerator and extra ventilation cost Ranjit almost £2,000. He was told that his products would have to be packaged according to the regulations, with detailed labelling listing ingredients, storage instructions and so on. Ranjit bought a machine that heat-sealed polythene packets and he prints out the labels on his computer. Fortunately, after all that investment, the business is doing well and showing a profit. The kitchen facilities have to be regularly inspected and Ranjit has set aside a sum to allow for yearly refurbishment.

---

authority certifies that it is no longer a threat to public health. (There is a right of appeal and the right to compensation if a business has been wrongfully penalised.)

The Food Safety Act covers the safety of food from its point of origin (farm or garden, say) right through to its point of sale. You break the law if you sell or manufacture food that:

- is unfit for human consumption, for example, produce that is rotten, mildewed or contains chemicals or additives that have been ruled unfit for human consumption
- is rendered injurious to health, for example, by poor sterilisation of equipment
- is so contaminated that it would be unreasonable to expect it to be eaten, for example, food that has become tainted by the flavour or smell of another substance stored close by
- is not of the nature, substance or quality demanded by the purchaser, for example, jam which has not set properly or is not covered by a proper lid
- is falsely or misleadingly represented, for example, something labelled 'chocolate cake' which contains no chocolate
- is sold after its 'use by' date, in the case of any highly perishable food which has, by law, to be marked with a 'use by' date. (It is

---

CASE HISTORY: Patricia

Patricia runs a wedding and celebrations catering business. She plans the menus with the clients, buys in the food and her workers (casual staff) prepare the food on the day at the venue (village hall or social club). Patricia only caters for functions that are taking place at halls where she knows the kitchens have been approved by the Environmental Health Department. However, one afternoon an inspector made a spot check on her operations and was not pleased with what he saw. His report stated that raw and cooked food were being prepared in the same area; one helper had a cut on her finger which was not covered with a waterproof dressing; food that had been prepared for the buffet had not been covered up – it was just in open bowls or on plates on the worktop; one helper was smoking in a room adjacent to the food preparation and the door was open; the refrigerator where the cold meats were stored was not functioning to the required temperature. The Environmental Health Officer advised Patricia that unless she employed people with food hygiene training or sent her existing staff to be trained, he would close her business down. She had no choice but to send her five regular staff for two days' training each and to change her working habits.

---

not illegal to sell food once its 'best before' datemark has expired – the mark merely alerts you to the possibility that the food may be past its best.)

- is sold in contravention of any other type of datemarking, including the falsification of a datemark.

Organic produce

The production and sale of organic foods are controlled by European and UK legislation which applies to every stage, from farming practices to packing and labelling. Organic growers, processors and importers must be registered and regularly inspected. In the UK, the United Kingdom Register of Organic Food Standards (UKROFS)★ administers the regulation and carries out inspections with six other certification bodies, including the Scottish Organic Producers Association (SOPA)★.

CASE HISTORY: Doreen

Doreen keeps ducks and sells the eggs 'at the garden gate' of her home. She knows that as long as she sells her eggs on a casual basis in this manner she does not have to label or weigh them. She may not put them in other people's boxes, nor may she sell cracked or deformed eggs. Doreen decided to invest in a stock of 100 plain six-egg boxes and had some basic stationery labels printed with her name and address and telephone number, which she sticks on the corner of the box. This has two purposes: she complies with the regulations for commercial egg sales in that she provides her name and address to the customer and, also, customers can ring her to see if she has any eggs available before they make the trip out to her house. She is also required to stamp every box with the date when the eggs were laid.

Organic farmers follow a set of principles which aim to minimise damage to the environment and wildlife. They use crop rotation and natural fertilisers to help soil fertility and often grow a mixture of plant varieties in fields to help control the spread of pests and disease. The result is that organic food is produced without the use of artificial fertilisers or chemical pesticides and it does not contain genetically modified ingredients.

Organic meat has to come from animals that are treated with concern for their welfare. They are given antibiotics and conventional medicines only when there is no alternative.

If you want to grow and market organic produce you should contact the Soil Association★, which will give you information about what is required to bring your production up to the necessary levels to earn Soil Association approval. After rigorous inspection you may be allowed to display the Soil Association symbol on your products.

Toys

The regulations covering the safety of children's toys are quite extensive. First, certain products are not regarded as toys for the purpose of the regulations, although they may be subject to their own safety regulations. Such items include Christmas decorations, fashion jewellery for children, detailed scale models and jigsaw puzzles with more than 500 pieces (or without a picture) that are intended for adult specialists, folk dolls and other decorative dolls intended for collectors, sports equipment, air guns and air pistols, slings and catapults, certain video toys, toy steam engines and babies' dummies. If there is any chance that they might be mistaken for a toy, they must be clearly marked with the words 'This is not a toy'.

The Toys (Safety) Regulations state that there are several areas of risk that have to be guarded against with toys, including the construction of the toy. You can cover these areas by asking yourself the following questions: Where are the toy's weak points? If it gets broken, will a dangerous component such as a nail or screw be exposed? Are there any sharp edges, protrusions, cords, cables or fastenings that might pose a risk? Could a small toy be swallowed by a very young child? If a toy heats up could it become overheated? Could the child or part of the body become trapped inside the toy? Does the packaging present a risk of suffocation?

The regulations also cover the flammability of toys, the chemical and electrical properties of their components and their labelling. For example, toys which might easily be swallowed must be marked 'Not suitable for children under three years'; and functional toys – scaled-down versions of adult appliances – must bear a warning that the toy should be used only under the direct supervision of an adult. Activity toys must be accompanied by instructions with diagrams for correct assembly, and potentially dangerous toys should carry instructions of action to be taken in case of an accident.

The making of stuffed toys is popular among homeworkers. Any toys made for small children (who are likely to put them in their mouths) must be made from colourfast, non-toxic materials, and all stuffings must be of low flammability. The biggest problem relating to stuffed toys is that eyes and noses can be removed. Guidelines issued by WI Country Markets recommend that features on toys for very small children are embroidered, while safety eyes should be used for toys for older children. There are also guidelines on packaging for such toys.

Since January 1990 all toys manufactured in Europe, or imported from outside the EU, must carry the 'CE' mark which shows that the toy has been manufactured to the required safety standard. The name, trademark and address of the manufacturer must appear on the packaging.

If you think that all this is over-cautious, note that lack of compliance with the Toys (Safety) Regulations can mean three months' imprisonment or a fine of up to £2,000. For full details of how to go about making toys that comply with the law, seek advice from your local Trading Standards Office (the address will be in the *Yellow Pages*).

Character copyright

Remember also the laws of copyright: if you are selling toys for personal gain, even if it is only at a local craft fair, you may not reproduce character toys (Paddington Bear, Winnie-the-Pooh, Noddy and so on) as the rights to the sale of these characters belong to their creators and their merchandisers. Any knitting or sewing patterns sold to you for these character toys are for private creation only, not for resale. (See also 'Protection of intellectual property', page 223.)

Clothing

According to EU guidelines, all garments *should* carry labels which show the following:

- the name of the manufacturer or the trade name
- the size of the garment
- the country of origin
- the fabric and percentages, for example, 25% cotton, 75% polyester
- washing/cleaning instructions
- any special warnings, for example, 'wash dark colours separately'.

However, nightwear and babywear *must* comply with the above guidelines. Children's nightdresses, nightshirts, dressing gowns and bathrobes (except bathrobes made from 100 per cent terry towelling) must be made of slow-burning fabrics (to British Standard 5722). If you are making such garments, you must purchase a fabric that has passed the low flammability test and ask your supplier for a copy of the certificate.

Children's pyjamas, bathrobes made from 100 per cent terry towelling, all adults' nightwear and all clothes for babies up to three months old must carry a permanent label stating whether or not the garment has passed the low flammability test. If it has, the label should read 'Low Flammability to BS 5722'. Because low flammability does not mean fireproof, the label may also read 'KEEP AWAY FROM FIRE'. If it has not passed the low flammability test, a garment should have a label saying 'KEEP AWAY FROM FIRE'.

Any nightwear that is treated with flame-retardant chemicals must carry a label with the words 'Do not wash at more than 50°C. Check suitability of washing agent'. Any advertisements of such clothing including purchase by mail order must give information about the flammability performance of each garment featured. The Department of Trade and Industry (DTI)★ is also very particular about the size and style of the print used on the labels, so if you are planning to develop a nightwear or baby clothes business, get as much advice as possible from your local Trading Standards Office.

Furniture

The Furniture and Furnishings (Fire) (Safety) Regulations 1988 (as amended) apply to:

- domestic upholstered furniture, including sofabeds and children's furniture
- nursery furniture containing upholstery
- garden furniture containing upholstery
- scatter cushions and seat pads
- pillows
- secondary covers for upholstered furniture (loose and stretch covers)
- cover fabric and filling material supplied for use with furniture and furnishings (including DIY use).

Please note that this is not a definitive list.

If you supply any of the above, as a manufacturer, upholsterer, importer, wholesaler, retailer or auctioneer, you need to understand the full implications of the regulations. The regulations also apply to the hire of furniture and furniture in accommodation – which affects anyone in the renting business.

Pillows, scatter cushions, seat pads, baby nests, secondary covers for upholstered furniture, beds and mattresses should have labels permanently attached which explain about flammability.

Other new furniture must carry two labels – one permanent, the other a swing ticket. The ticket gives basic notice of compliance with fire tests and carries the warning 'Carelessness causes fire'.

As with toys, the furniture and upholstery labels have to comply with certain standards and it is best to seek advice from your Trading Standards Office.

Consumer Protection Act 1987 and the General Product Safety Regulation 1994

A consumer can sue a manufacturer, importer or any person who puts his or her name to a product if a defective product causes death, injury or damage to property.

The producer of the goods (any of the three categories mentioned above) is liable unless he or she can prove the following:

- he or she did not supply the goods (for example, they were stolen or forged)
- when the product was manufactured the scientific or technological state of knowledge was such that the defect was not discoverable; the defect took some time to surface; and it was only obvious that it would occur at some point with the benefit of hindsight and advanced knowledge (this is known as the development risks defence)
- the defect was attributable to the law. For example, a manufacturer of toys used a special non-toxic paint on his product in order to comply with the EU regulations on such matters, but subsequently that paint reacted with the base material and caused cracks to appear in the product, creating sharp edges in the toy which cut a child's face
- the defect was caused after it left the producer's hands – for example, a retailer mishandled or badly stored the product and caused the defect
- the supplier is not in business but is a private individual. Trading Standards Departments will make an exception in the case of

individuals who supply home-made toys to bazaars and fêtes and individuals who sell second-hand goods
- the defect was caused at a later stage in the manufacturing process of the whole product.

CASE HISTORY: Kelly

Kelly made cosmetics to a very high standard in her own kitchen. She sold rosewaters, orange flower waters, bath essences, bath oils and so on with great success. However, one day she was contacted by the Environmental Health Department and was subsequently fined quite heavily because a customer who was allergic to lanolin had suffered a painful rash on her skin as a result of using Kelly's face cream. The product contained lanolin but Kelly had omitted to put that fact on the label because she did not realise that the regulations demanded it.

Sale of Goods Act 1979 and Supply of Goods and Services Act 1982

Goods sold must:

- be of satisfactory quality, that is, they should meet the standard a reasonable person would regard as satisfactory, taking account of any description, the price and other relevant circumstances (they must be fit to sell)
- be reasonably fit for any particular purpose made known to the seller (if the buyer is told computer software is compatible with a particular type of computer, it must run on that computer)
- correspond with the description (if the advertisement says that this product will do certain things and it does not, it is not what was described).

If the goods are not any of the above, the customer has a right to claim a refund or compensation. In a consumer sale, the buyer may be able to choose instead a repair or replacement; and, in the first six months, it will be assumed that the goods were faulty at the time of sale. Consumers also have similar remedies where installation by a retailer is not satisfactory. Consumers may also be able to claim against the retailer that goods are unsatisfactory where they do not match public statements on specific characteristics (particularly in advertising or on labelling) made about them by the retailer, manufacturer, importer or producer. However, if any defect was brought to the customer's attention before he or she purchased the item (for example, fire-damaged material in a sale), he or she has no right to expect compensation in relation to that particular defect. Also, if a customer asked whether, say, a certain tool would be right for a certain job and was told that it probably would not, he or she has no right to a refund if he or she chose to ignore the sales person.

If a manufacturer or retailer gives a consumer a free guarantee with the product sold, that guarantee is legally binding on the person offering it. The guarantee must also be available for viewing by consumers before purchase.

Services must be provided:

- with reasonable care
- with reasonable skill
- within a reasonable time
- at a reasonable charge.

A trader can be sued for breach of contract if it is proved that he or she failed to exercise reasonable care or reasonable skill.

Terms of business

The likelihood is that you use standard trading terms if you supply goods or services. Is there a risk that the small print might be challenged? Do you have any protection when dealing with other businesses?

By law, a trader cannot exclude or limit his or her liability for death or personal injury arising from negligence. He or she can exclude or restrict his or her liability for other loss or damage resulting from negligence only if the exclusion clause meets a 'test of reasonableness'.

A trader dealing with a consumer or dealing on his own written standard terms of business cannot in the contract exclude or restrict liability unless he or she can show that the clause satisfies the reasonableness requirement. Relevant issues include the clarity of the language used and whether the layout of the contract document is easy to follow.

Consumer contracts with members of the public acting for non-business purposes have additional protection under the Unfair Terms in Consumer Contracts Regulations 1999. The Regulations say that a consumer is not bound by a standard term in a contract with a seller or supplier if that term is unfair. The Office of Fair Trading (OFT)* has the power and duty to 'name and shame' businesses when it considers that standard terms in consumer contracts are unfair. Reports are regularly published by the OFT of cases where standard contract terms have been changed or dropped as a result of enforcement action. Statutory regulators, Trading Standards departments and the Consumers' Association can also intervene.

The regulations governing unfair terms in consumer contracts include a 'grey list' of common types of unfairness. These include, for example, terms that seek to exclude or restrict liability for the supply of defective goods, or which impose price increases. Even the size of the small print itself can be challenged if the majority of consumers would find difficulty in reading the contract.

Fairness when dealing with consumers is not the only issue. Businesses are also required to set out their terms of business in plain, intelligible language. Any doubts over unclear terms are resolved in favour of the consumer.

However, if a contract is individually negotiated, it is expected that the agreed terms will be acceptable even if, in a standard format, they might have been regarded as unfair. If the language is clear, alleged unfairness cannot be used to strike at the contract itself.

The laws that protect consumers from unfair treatment reflect a consistent approach to consumers' rights throughout the EU. However, business-to-business contracts (B2B) are still regulated by traditional English legal concepts that take no account of general principles of unfairness. Customers (large or small) under B2B contracts incorporating standard terms of business are generally protected only if those terms seek to exclude or restrict liability unreasonably.

Distance selling and e-commerce regulations

As described in detail in Chapter 12, there are stringent regulations that apply to distance selling – selling over the telephone, by mail or fax, or on the Internet. Contracts have to be very specific in order not to infringe the consumer's rights. The Electronic Commerce (EC Directive) Regulations 2002 apply to online trade and advertising (for example, on the Internet, by email or by mobile phone). The regulations concern matters such as the information that must be given to consumers when you advertise or sell online, and how to conclude contracts online. Email advertising is also regulated.

Enforcement of consumer law

Regulators such as the Office of Fair Trading are able to apply to the courts for a 'Stop Now order' (to be renamed a Consumer Enforcement Order) requiring traders to stop breaching consumer laws (for example, on unfair contract terms, distant selling, and sale of goods rights). Written assurances instead of court action can be sought.

Data Protection Act 1998

This Act requires anyone who keeps personal information on other people to register (notify) with the Office of the Information Commissioner★ and explain the use to which this information will be put. Eight data protection principles must be observed. The Act also gives private individuals the right of access to the information held on them in order to check its accuracy.

You may find yourself in the position of being a self-employed teleworker who amends mailing lists or credit information. This would constitute personal data that would need to be protected by appropriate security and confidentiality standards. The Act also, in some measure, safeguards against this data being misused.

Protection of intellectual property

Where possible, ideas, inventions and designs should be protected by registration.

Patents

The Patents Act 1977 allows any object that has been invented and is capable of commercial application to be patented. It is advisable to do this through a patent agent because the papers necessary for an application for a patent are, in fact, legal documents. Patents have to be taken out around the world in order to protect an invention from being copied. The protection lasts for 20 years and is renewable. It is possible, of course, to market an invention that has not yet been patented while the application is pending. 'Patent pending' is seen on many gadgets and devices.

Designs

Designs are capable of protection under the Registered Designs Act 1949, as now in force following the implementation of the European 'Designs Directive'. Previously, design registration had applied to a specific article. Protection now applies to all products covered by the Act in which a registered design is incorporated.

Design means 'the appearance of the whole or a part of a product resulting from the features of, in particular, the lines, contours, colours, shape, texture or materials of the product or its ornamentation'. Computer desktop icons, parts of products, and component parts visible in normal use are registrable. Handicraft items – not just products made by industrial processes – are also now covered. Special rules apply to determine whether a design meets the required tests of being new and having 'individual character'. Design registration gives the owner a monopoly on the product design for a limited period. Purely functional designs that are not capable of registration may have some protection as unregistered designs.

Trademarks

Trademarks – logos, designs or names adopted by companies to make their products or service memorable – can be registered at the Patent Office★. No one else can use them once they are registered.

Copyright

Copyright of works such as original literary material, films, music, works of art and software does not require registration. Copyright is automatic if you create something original, and generally lasts for 70 years following the author of the work's death. It is recommended that you put the copyright sign, the date and your name on each piece of work that you create. Copyright holders can exploit the right by selling copies of the work or by licensing someone else to do so in return for a fee, usually called a royalty. You can sue another individual or an organisation if you feel that they have 'copied' your original piece of work or reproduced it without your permission.

Database right

Databases may have copyright protection where there is 'intellectual creation', but a separate database right also exists if there has been a substantial investment in the contents of the database.

Ownership of intellectual property

The owner of a new copyright work is usually the person who wrote it. Self-employed people usually own the copyright but if an employee creates the work, ownership will turn on whether the work was created in the course of employment.

Cyberpiracy and cybersquatting

There have been increasing problems on the Internet with cyberpiracy (someone using someone else's domain name or creating a very similar one to fool customers into thinking that it is the real thing) and cybersquatting (someone hacking into someone else's site to broadcast to the existing customer base). Cybersquatting, in particular, has caused a great deal of unpleasantness. For example, reputable sites (the HTML validation service WebCheck and the cancer charity Marie Curie, to name but two) have had their websites hijacked by peddlers of pornography.

The Americans approved new legislation in 1999 – the Anti-cybersquatting Consumer Protection Act (ACPA) and the US Administration and the United Nations' World Intellectual Property Organisation (WPO) believe that this legislation will allow for action to be taken outside of the USA, although there has yet to be a test case.

The ACPA means that the owner of a trademark (including a personal name) can bring a civil action if a person has a bad-faith intent to profit from that mark, registers, traffics in or uses a distinctive and recognisable domain name, or uses one that is identical or confusingly similar.

Chapter 12

Your business relationships

Customers, clients, agents, suppliers, employees – all must be kept happy, and it is sometimes the 'people' side of business that is the most difficult to handle. However, if you can cultivate good business relationships they can be worth their weight in gold – to be able to have confidence in a colleague, to have a rapport based on mutual respect and trust, can be like a good marriage. In view of how much of your daily time you have to devote to work, the relationships arising from it are very important.

Relationships with your customers

This can be the most unpredictable area of your business relationships. After all, your dealings with agents, employees, suppliers and so on are controlled to a certain extent by contracts which state how you will all perform. You cannot do that with customers – or can you?

You can, in fact, draw up some sort of contract which customers and clients have to respect. It is your terms of trading – in other words, what you contract to supply and how they must pay for it. It can be a note of agreement between yourself and a client, a notice pinned up in your workshop or a statement of terms printed on your invoice. You can clarify the relationship between you and your customer in several ways.

Confirmation of an oral contract

Suppose you go to meet a potential client and he offers you a project. You discuss the requirements of the job, the payment and the timescale over a drink in a pub. There are no witnesses. He may be a very nice man and you may feel instinctively that you can trust him, but there could have been a misunderstanding over some of the finer points of the project you are about to embark upon. So when you get home you should immediately commit to paper your understanding of the terms and conditions of the job on offer and send it to him for his confirmation. That way, everyone is happy with what was discussed. You have a written contract.

However, if you are selling a product or service to a consumer, take advice about the terms that you wish to place in your standard contract, as the current law states that certain types of terms, which act against the consumer's interest, may be unfair and unenforceable. Your local Trading Standards Office can advise you on the matter.

CASE HISTORY: Tanya

Tanya is a registered childminder who looks after several children at different times during the week. She presents all her parents with a form which they sign before she takes charge of their children. It gives permission for the children in her care to be taken out shopping, to be taken in the car (suitably fastened in), to be allowed to watch children's television for an hour or so, to be reprimanded if naughty and so on. She also asks the parents to give her a complete list of dietary requirements for the children and insists that parents telephone if they will be delayed in picking up their child. Also, for safety reasons, she requires a named person to be available to pick up the child if the child becomes ill when parents are out at work. These 'regulations' may seem rather pedantic but Tanya enjoys a very good relationship with all her customers because everyone knows exactly what the rules are and they are happy with them.

Explanation of payment terms

If you are selling products directly to the public, whether door-to-door, by mail order, from a stall or in your own shop, you must make it very clear to the customers what forms of payment are acceptable. Notices like 'Cash sales only' or 'Sorry, we cannot accept credit cards' or 'Cheques only accepted for amounts over £10' must be prominently displayed or printed on your literature.

If you are working from home and just starting out, you cannot afford to lose control of your cash-flow. That means that you must have money coming in – real money, not promised money – before you can afford to invest more money in building up your stock.

Right at the beginning you have to decide what your payment terms are going to be. If you are selling from a stall in a market then your payment is instantaneous – or at least it should be. If a cheque is incorrectly filled in or it bounces, you are in trouble. Therefore, insist on the cheque being backed by a guarantee card (some still cover £50 but most now cover £100 and some cover more), or at the very least ask for the customer's name, address and telephone number to be written on the back of the cheque, and write these down in a book before you present the cheque to your own bank in case it bounces. That way you will know where to get hold of the customer to demand another payment or your goods back.

CASE HISTORY: Harry

Harry makes beautiful nursery furniture which is custom-made for each child, with the appropriate name carved into it. He therefore insists on a deposit on an article before he starts work, then an approval visit by the customer before the child's name is put on the item of furniture, with a further payment at that point. For his part, Harry promises to complete the work within a specified time and guarantees the item of furniture for two years.

If you are starting a new venture you might find it wise to trade on a 'cash only' basis. Banks charge business accounts a fee for each cheque processed and many small shopkeepers, for example, now refuse to take payment by cheque for sums less than £10.

Selling door-to-door

Selling door-to-door is the same, unless you are selling such a large range of stock that you cannot carry it all with you and products have to be ordered. In this case you want an order form signed by the purchaser, which is, in effect, a binding contract with the customer before you order the goods. Note that the law is quite specific regarding consumer's rights for doorstep sales.

CASE HISTORY: Alison

Alison makes designer wedding dresses, none of which is exactly alike. She therefore charges her clients a separate fee for the drawing up of the design. When they have approved the design and selected the material, she asks for a one-third deposit of the total cost of the dress. This pays for all the materials and trimmings. She then insists on several fittings and the final two-thirds payment before the trimmings are put on. Sadly, some of her clients have called off their weddings because their relationships have broken up, but Alison takes the view that they will undoubtedly find another partner and can therefore keep the wedding dress in the wardrobe for the next occasion!

- If the goods or services you sell cost more than £25 and you were not invited to call, then the consumer has seven days to change their mind and cancel the sale. If they responded to an advertisement or a leaflet dropped through the door, then this counts as an invitation to call.
- However, if the consumer agrees to a visit after you have telephoned them or your representative called and arranged a sales appointment, then the seven days' 'cooling-off' period applies.
- By law, the seller must give the consumer written details of the right to cancel. Failure to do this is a criminal offence.
- If the consumer cancels the contract, he or she may get back any money that was paid out. But, if certain goods have already been received (such as perishable food items) or some services have been carried out, then these will have to be paid for, even though the full contract has been cancelled.
- Any non-perishable goods that have been delivered must be looked-after and available for delivery if the contract is cancelled.
- If the goods or services are bought on credit then the cancellation period is limited to five days.
- If the goods or services are faulty then the consumer has full rights to complain and seek redress under the law.

Distance selling

When starting a mail-order business, it is sensible to ask for payment upfront if possible. You cannot afford to 'sell from a distance' without some guarantee of payment. In return, you have to offer a trial period with full cash-back rights if the product is not suitable. Most small mail-order concerns operate in this way – you have to be a very large going concern before you can afford to part with goods and wait for payments to come in in stages.

CASE HISTORY: Paula

Paula set up an Internet business marketing Afro-Caribbean cosmetics and was able to get a grant and full support from an organisation which gives grants to young people trying to start businesses. She also received expert help to set up her website so that it would address the needs of her target market. The website is in three languages – English, Spanish and French, as she targets Afro-Caribbean women in the UK, North and South America and parts of Africa and North Africa where French is spoken. She actively encourages her customers to email her with suggestions or queries about the products available, so that she can refine and add to her product list.

The Consumer Protection (Distance Selling) Regulations 2000

Because of the increased use of the Internet as a sales medium, these regulations were created to protect consumers from problems that can arise from distance selling. These regulations apply to businesses/individuals who sell goods or services:

- on the Internet or digital television
- by mail order, including catalogue shopping
- by phone
- by fax.

The key features of the regulations are:

- the consumer must be given clear information about the goods or services offered

- after making a purchase, the consumer must be sent confirmation
- the consumer has a cooling-off period of seven days (see exception above)
- the regulations do not apply to business-to-business selling.

Regulations governing Internet sales

The EU has published certain guidelines (available through Trading Standards Offices in the UK) to protect consumers who shop online through computers, digital TVs or mobile phones.

Safe payment

The usual consumer rights apply online. In the EU, credit-card companies must refund consumers if their credit or debit cards are used fraudulently. If goods fail to arrive or are faulty, the credit-card company should refund consumers for any single item costing over £100.

What the seller should offer

- Full security features on a website. This should be denoted by the closed padlock symbol at the bottom of the screen, which shows that the consumer's details are protected when sent. Most reputable sites also display the TrustUK e-hallmark. For further information read *Which? Way to Drive Your Small Business*, or contact your local Trading Standards office for advice on safe Internet marketing.
- The consumer must be given full details before buying. These are:
  - Your name or company name and full postal address
  - A full description of the goods or services
  - The price, including all taxes
  - Delivery costs where they apply
  - Arrangements for payment
  - Arrangements for delivery (normally within 30 days unless the contract says otherwise)
  - The right to cancel the order and whether the seller or buyer will be responsible for returning the goods
  - For services, the minimum duration of the contract, if the service is to be provided over a period of time
  - How long the offer or price remain valid

- A facility whereby any order is confirmed immediately by email
- You must give the buyer assurance that personal details will not be used for direct marketing, or at least give them the option to decline
- Other high street rights apply to consumers buying on the Internet. In other words, goods and services must be of a satisfactory quality and adverts and descriptions must not be misleading.

There are certain situations where the right to cancel does not apply, for example: the immediate downloading of software or data because it is deemed to have been used the moment it takes up residence in the purchaser's computer; services which it has been agreed will start before the seven-day cooling-off period has finished; goods made to personal specifications (for example, engraved with initials); goods liable to rapid deterioration (fresh food or flowers); sealed audio or video recordings or mailed software which have been opened; betting, gaming or lottery services.

The regulations do not apply, at the moment, to financial services sold on the Internet, auctions or sales of land.

Credit cards

These are an increasing problem nowadays for small traders. Credit cards are being used more and more to pay for purchases, to the extent that some people rarely carry cheque books or cash. Being able to accept the major credit cards can boost your sales enormously and it is, of course, guaranteed and 'instant' payment. If you decide, at the outset, that you are going to do business on the Internet then you cannot manage without a credit-card facility.

So at what point in your business activities do you start accepting credit cards? Unfortunately, it may not be up to you. Because of the prevalence of fraud in recent years the credit-card companies have become more particular about accreditation – particularly if you want telephone, postal or Internet facilities, because these are, apparently, the most vulnerable areas of fraud. This is a pity, because most small mail-order businesses would dearly love to have a credit-card facility. Another problem is that there is a certain amount of prejudice by the credit-card operators against home-run businesses (they feel that they lack credibility and stability) and they also prefer to do business with traders who have been operating for at least a year and can provide a copy of one year's accounts as proof of creditworthiness.

Whether you are trading on the Internet or not, the first place to discuss Card Merchant status, as it is called, is with your bank. If you are a start-up or Internet business and have no track record of trading, then you may have to speak to a specialist in e-commerce within the bank, who will probably want to look at your business plan and see if he or she can sort out a deal for you on that basis. You will have to give guarantees, of course, in the same way as you would if you were receiving a loan. If all goes well, then the credit-card company will be able to advise you on the mechanics of receiving and banking payments. Your Web-hosting service will be able to advise you on how to set up a secure system, which is encrypted to protect you and your customers from hackers.

A credit-card facility, of course, costs you money, which you have to build into your prices. As well as an initial registration fee, which can vary between credit-card companies but is around £300 on average, a small trader can pay up to five per cent on every transaction. Some credit-card companies offer the first six months of trading free, as an incentive. You can charge extra for credit-card transactions over cash or cheques, so there may be scope for passing on those costs to customers who value the facility. However, if you cannot build this into your price because the competition is too fierce, this five per cent is quite a large chunk out of your profits.

Debit cards

Debit cards, such as Visa, Delta or Switch, were introduced to replace cheques, rather than credit cards. These plastic cards are presented by the purchaser to the trader who debits the purchaser's bank account for the necessary amount via a computer terminal. It can take up to two days for the amount to be debited from the purchaser's account, whereas a cheque can take up to five working days. The advantages to the trader are no more bouncing cheques or bad debts. It is as good as cash to the trader.

Until recently, a debit-card facility was not really an option for small businesses because of the cost of purchasing or renting the computer equipment to effect the transaction. But small hand-held terminals are now available and it is no longer uncommon to see even street market vendors offering debit facilities.

Offering such a facility is, up to a certain point, cheaper than operating a credit-card facility. Credit-card companies charge a percentage on every purchase; debit-card transactions are done on a flat fee basis. Therefore, if you provide high-cost goods or services or operate a business where customers buy in bulk from you on one purchase, a debit-card transaction will cost you less than a credit-card transaction. It is impossible to quote even an average fee for the service as debit-card facilities are all operated through 'providers', in other words, most of the high-street banks, which all charge different rates and offer different deals. It is worth discussing it with your bank manager to see whether it is a viable option for your business.

Credit terms

If you are prepared to offer credit terms (rather risky for a fledgling business, but you may have no option), you must take several steps first.

If the customer is another business, you must check his or her creditworthiness. Ask for references from other suppliers, wholesalers or even the customer's bank, and check them thoroughly. Ask the other suppliers if they give the customer in question credit terms and, if so, for how long, and whether they have ever had any trouble with payments.

It is very easy, nowadays, to check on the financial health of a company, particularly through the Internet. An organisation such as CheckSURE* offers free UK business credit information on nearly four million UK limited liability companies, partnerships and sole traders. A more detailed report can cost from £6 to £10. Alternatively, for the sum of £5 you can purchase online a company's latest accounts and annual return from Companies House*. Lots of other information is free on the Companies House' website too, such as a history of company transactions, basic company details and insolvency details. However, to a certain extent, these details are historic and in order to check the current situation, you need to try to speak to some of the company's suppliers and customers to find out if the bills are being paid. You probably cannot afford to let smaller business customers have more than the standard 28 or 30 days' credit before payment is due.

Incentives

The most significant incentive you can offer any customer is a discount for a cash payment or prompt payment. It may be worth it to you to offer, say, five per cent off the normal price of a product just to get an instant payment of real cash, or for a business customer to settle ahead of the usual 30 days' credit period.

Customers' rights

Apart from the statutory obligations that you will provide customers, in good faith, with goods that have no defects and are fit for the purpose for which they are described and, in the case of service, that you will exercise reasonable care and skill and will do the job in a reasonable time, the customer has a right to expect several other things.

Courtesy

Everyone has the right to expect that they will be treated with courtesy when they are doing business with you. There may be a few eccentric artists or crafts people who can get away with being surly and taciturn and still sell their work, but it would be rash to count on being able to do that yourself. 'The customer is king' goes the saying, and it is right; without customers, you don't do any business. Saying, 'Can I help you?' when they are browsing round your workshop goes a long way. Similarly, a 'thank you' when they have completed their purchase costs you nothing and means a lot.

Attention

Customers have the right, first of all, to be able to get your attention. How many times have you stood at a shop counter or sat in a café and fumed while two assistants carry on a personal conversation and ignore you? Secondly, customers have the right to expect your attention to detail. If they want to give you instructions as to how a service should be carried out, they will expect you to pay attention –

even write it down – so that you can get the job right. If you are making a product, customers have the right to expect that you have given it your full attention and not skimped or made mistakes. If they ask for your professional opinion on whether a certain product will do the job they have in mind, they have a right to expect that you have given some attention to learning about the products you are selling and can advise with expertise.

Friendliness

Customers are encouraged by smiles. If customers at a craft fair have a choice between two stalls selling cushions, the one with the stallholder who smiles and chats will always win out over the gloomy one. However, friendly chitchat can be overdone – if there are customers queuing up some may become impatient and go elsewhere.

Efficiency

Customers have the right to expect, particularly when ordering through the post or over the telephone, that the order will be despatched quickly and efficiently. Similarly, all queries and accounts should be dealt with efficiently. You may be the most charming salesman or woman in the world but if your paperwork is a mess and you have no filing system, you will lose customers because they have been frustrated by your lack of organisation.

Action

If a customer has a justifiable complaint he or she has a right to expect some action. If you are working from home on your own, you are the boss and the buck stops with you. Junior personnel might be able to get away with saying 'I'll have to ask the manager', but you can't. You have to learn to make quick decisions and act upon them.

Dealing with complaints

You will get complaints – some reasonable, some unreasonable. Some you can deal with and resolve amicably, others you cannot. The main thing is that you must, if you are going to work for yourself, develop a thick skin. You cannot afford to treat each complaint as a personal insult and lose your temper. You must be able to admit that you, or one of your staff, has made a mistake and be able to apologise and take action.

Some customers are troublemakers – they are never happier than when they are complaining. Keep a cool head and refuse to get angry, even if the person gets abusive. This frequently happens on the telephone. If you have an angry customer in person in your workshop, try to take him or her aside, somewhere quiet, away from other customers, to resolve the matter.

If the customer has returned a product which has broken or is defective, you must establish whether he or she wants a replacement or a refund. Bear in mind that, in most cases, the customer is entitled to a full refund and does not have to accept a replacement product unless he or she specifically wishes to do so. If the customer has bought the wrong product because one of your staff advised him or her badly, you have no choice but to exchange or refund.

If the customer wishes to return a product for a less valid reason, for example she thought the jumper would match a skirt but it did not, you must explain, in a friendly manner, that she should have brought the skirt with her when buying the jumper and that as the jumper is of perfectly good quality you are under no obligation to change it or refund money. If she is a very good and regular customer, it is up to you whether you allow her, just this once, to change the item. In practice, most retailers do allow exchanges and refunds but, if you are a very small retailer, you can reserve the right to adopt a firm policy.

If you provide a service and you have plainly fallen down in the quality of that service, the customer has the right to an amended bill or to have the work done again free. If you have caused irreparable damage by your poor service, the customer has the right to sue you for full compensation. You could settle out of court, but the legal procedures for this are still expensive and time-consuming.

From the very beginning of your new enterprise it is prudent to print, perhaps on your receipts or invoices, the terms and conditions under which you will accept responsibility for the return of goods or non-payment of services. Remember that these terms and conditions must comply with the law. The customer must produce proof of purchase but you cannot specify the production of a till receipt before you will refund the money, nor can you insist on replacement goods rather than a refund. Draw your customer's attention to the terms and conditions when making the sale or agreeing to provide a service. Don't make a rod for your own back with such promises as: 'If you can get this product cheaper anywhere else we will refund the difference' – only the major department stores can afford to do that. Similarly, never make claims for your service that you may not be able to keep because of changing circumstances, such as 'guaranteed 24-hour turnaround on all jobs'. This will give the customer the right to refuse payment if you take a bit longer.

Internet customers

Although you are not conducting business face-to-face, customers on the Internet have a right to expect a website to be user-friendly, with all the relevant information properly signposted, not too many pages to your site and a facility to purchase with ease and not panic. It helps if the language of your site is friendly and informal and you do not use jargon.

Listen to customers

When a customer does complain, try to learn from it. Complaints can be a positive aid to your business. Try to view it as a method of quality control for your business. If, for example, you are running a mail-order business selling products that you buy in rather than make yourself, you should review your product range if one particular item causes a certain number of complaints.

If your attitude or the attitude of your staff causes complaints, you must do something about it. If your service is sloppy and meets with dissatisfaction, you need to rethink what you are doing. Perhaps you should concentrate on providing those services you can do really well? Perhaps you are trying to do too much yourself and need some assistance? Would you benefit from some refresher training? Do your staff need some customer relation training?

What customers say is a continuing source of market research. Their ideas, preferences, tastes and irritations will point the way for you to improve your product range or service. But you must listen to them. It is too easy to get caught up in the day-to-day business of earning money and to dismiss comments made by customers during the course of work.

Occasionally it is worth conducting a small survey among your customers to find out if they are satisfied with your efforts. Use the mailing list you have compiled of all your customers. (Compiling mailing lists is covered in more detail in Chapter 9.) Even if you sell from a stall you can invite cash customers to write down their name and address in a book if they would like further information about your products. By building up a mailing list you can then, at some point, include a short questionnaire (with a stamped addressed envelope) and invite comments about what products customers are particularly interested in, what times of year they purchase, how much they are prepared to spend and so on.

Bad debts

This is the unpleasant side of customer relations – when the agreement has broken down and the customer has failed to pay. This is not a problem, of course, for strictly cash-on-the-nail businesses, but many sole traders have to rely on the invoice system and it can be heartbreaking, not to mention hazardous, for a very small business when a customer does not co-operate.

If you have tried without success to get the customer to pay by making phone calls and writing letters, the next step is to appoint a solicitor to write a letter threatening legal action. If this fails, you have to decide whether to write off the bad debt or whether it is worth pursuing it through the courts.

Since April 1999 the civil justice system has consisted of three levels of court action based, principally, on the value of the case, but they are supposed to be flexible.

The first level is a small claims procedure for cases worth up to £5,000, with a £1,000 limit for personal injury and housing disrepair cases. Eviction and harassment cases are excluded. The court proceeding is informal, lawyers are not necessary and legal representation costs are not recoverable.

The second level is for cases worth up to £15,000 and this level operates a 'fast track' system to cut down on waiting time. The procedure in the court is slightly more complex, with some reference to the rules of giving evidence, and legal representation is probably advisable.

The third level is for cases which, by their complex nature or the sums of money involved, require 'hands-on judicial case management' (in other words, some personal attention).

How can customers be made to pay up?

If a court decides in your favour, you can choose from the following methods of recovering your money, but you will have to pay fees for these services.

Garnishee order The court orders a debtor of your debtor to pay his or her money directly to you rather than to your debtor.

A warrant of execution Sending the bailiffs in to take away any of your client's goods which he or she fully owns, and the sale of which will cover the debt to you.

Attachment of earnings This can be of use only where the debtor is a salaried employee because the order instructs the debtor's employer to deduct regular sums from his or her wages and pay them directly to you.

Charging order The court makes an order which, in effect, means that if your debtor sells his or her house or land, what is owed to you has to be deducted from the proceeds of the sale.

If you are in doubt about any of the above procedures contact your local Citizens Advice Bureau for advice. Obviously, if your bad debt is less than £100 there is very little point in spending as much again in pursuing it through the county court. You just have to chalk it up to experience and never do business again with doubtful payers.

Weed out the bad customers

Some customers are just not worth tolerating. For example, one artist regularly sold small paintings to a local woman but her cheques periodically bounced. The customer always rectified the matter but every time one of the cheques bounced, the artist's bank charged her £5. She has since changed her bank to one that does not charge her for other people's bouncing cheques and she has also got tough with the regular customer by saying that she can sell to her only on a cash basis.

If you have a customer who always disputes your invoice, beware – this may be a delaying tactic. Take it as a warning sign that the customer's cash-flow is unsteady. It may be prudent to drop him or her.

You should invoice immediately after the service is provided or delivery has been made and you should send a statement as soon as the credit time has elapsed, for example, after 30 days. Find out what the payment timings are. For example, some companies pay by computer and the computer prints all the cheques on the 15th of every month. Therefore, if your invoice has not arrived and/or the data has not been fed into the computer by a certain date, you will not get paid that month, but will have to wait for the next data input.

Always check with your potential customers what their expectation of credit is. You would be amazed at the number of companies that say, 'We never pay on receipt of invoice, only on receipt of statement, it's a company policy.' In other words, they expect 60 days' credit. Other, usually large, companies state flatly that all their suppliers give them 90 days' credit. This is fine if your cash-flow can stand it, but you must decide whether doing business with such customers will put too much of a strain on your resources.

Factoring

If your business has expanded successfully and you do not have time to chase up bad payers or even to keep an eye on your credit control situation every month, factoring could be the solution. It is cheaper than paying off an overdraft or hiring someone full-time to chase up invoices.

Factoring means that a specialist company buys all your invoices from you the day that they are sent out, and initially pays you 80 per cent of their total value. You get the bulk of the cash while the factoring company has the headache of chasing up the invoices. When payment is made you get the other 20 per cent, less the interest charged on the 80 per cent paid in advance to you (usually between 3 to 4 per cent above base rate) and an administration charge of around 2 per cent of the total value of the invoices.

Factoring is not an option for everyone because factoring companies are usually only interested in businesses with a turnover of more than £50,000. But that is not so far out of reach for some of the readers of this book – it is not unknown for consultants or specialist teleworkers to make that kind of turnover in a year. Banks can usually provide a list of factoring companies.

When you take on a factoring company you decide just what level of service you want from them. They can chase up all your invoices and they can also manage your sales accounts and run credit checks on potential customers. Bad debts seem to disappear when factoring companies handle accounts. Bad customers tend to respond better to a letter from a factoring company than from a small business.

Relationships with your suppliers

In this instance you are the customer and therefore you need to be reassured about several things.

The supplier's financial health and reputation

If you do not already have a supplier lined up, you can find one from directories of suppliers in a reference library, for example *Kompass Directories*, and *www.UKTradeWorld.com* stocks directories for all over the world; you can order them online. It is then a question of asking around among other business people or trade associations to see whether that supplier is reputable. A good supplier should be willing to give you the names of regular customers so that you can have a reassuring chat with them. You can, of course, pay for a credit check to be run on a supplier (the same procedure is discussed earlier in this chapter), but this would really only be necessary if supplies from that quarter were so crucial that you could not operate without them.

If it is possible, or relevant to your business, you could check up on the premises of all the major suppliers you are likely to use – you can tell a lot by the way business is conducted there. Are they neat and tidy? Is the order-processing system efficient? Are the staff helpful and well trained? Do they give you unbiased advice? Obviously, if you are buying small quantities of materials from suppliers scattered all over the country, this will not be a viable option.

The supplier's reliability

It can be worth writing to suppliers to explain what your requirements might be, then see what sort of written response you get. If a supplier sends back an impressive reply – that is to say one that is helpful, enclosing price lists and details of services – you should feel confident enough to proceed. If, however, the response is indifferent, the chances are the service will be too. Check with other customers as to whether they have ever had any problems with the supplier's reliability.

The quality of the goods

If you are buying raw materials such as textiles, stuffing or wadding you need to know exactly the composition of the material, its colour fastness, flammability and so on in order that you can buy what is best for your product. You must be assured that similar-quality goods will always be available – you do not want to find yourself suddenly without a source at a crucial moment.

The promptness and flexibility of delivery times

If you will need your materials to be delivered, it is important that you know how flexible or inflexible the supplier's schedules are. For example, perhaps he or she delivers to your area only on Thursdays and this is not ideal as you require delivery early in the week and possibly more than once a week. Does he or she always deliver on time? Only experience of the delivery service will tell you that. There is nothing more frustrating than having to stay in all day because a delivery time cannot be given and it means that you cannot make any sales appointments for that day. Delivery charges have to be taken into account, too. Perhaps a supplier offers free delivery for orders over a certain size? Can you buy and store such a quantity of goods to make this saving?

Credit terms and discounts

What credit terms will the supplier give you if you supply references? Is there any discount offered for cash and carry, cash on delivery or early payment of invoices? Do the prices include delivery or is that an extra charge? If you are buying large items what warranty is on offer? Does the supplier ever run special offers that might be of value, say two for the price of one on certain lines or discounts for bulk buying?

Location and communication

If you are considering using a supplier who you will need to visit at least twice a week, location is important, and that in itself may eliminate the competition unless suppliers further afield have reliable and efficient communications and are willing to deliver small quantities frequently. Wherever the supplier is (and you may need a specialist supplier who is at the other end of the country and only contactable by phone/post/fax/email), he or she must have good communications and respond promptly. You want to be able to leave messages, send a fax, speak to an efficient member of staff on the telephone and feel confident that your supplier is dealing with your request. You do not want to do business with someone you can never get hold of, or who keeps goods in an anonymous lock-up warehouse which you can view only by appointment, or who does not appear to have any staff, paperwork or detailed information on his or her goods.

Competition

If you are lucky enough to have several suppliers nearby you can afford to shop around and compare prices. It may be that you end up going to one warehouse for cut flowers, say, another for dried flowers and another for florists' accessories.

Any special terms

These can be important when you are starting up. You may not be able to get any credit terms until you are more established and can order in larger quantities. The supplier may have a minimum order rule; below that amount you have to pay cash upfront. It is not worth compromising your cash-flow by overstocking just to get credit, unless you are absolutely sure that you can shift all your products. With certain 'short-life' goods that have to be bought little and often – such as fresh flowers or fruit and vegetables – you may be able to open an account with the wholesaler which is settled at the end of every month.

Your relationship with your suppliers is more or less the same as your customers' relationship with you. It has to be based on trust, unless proven otherwise, and each of you has an obligation to the other which basically hinges upon open communication, courtesy and an understanding of the terms and conditions under which you are trading with each other.

Your relationship with your bank

'What relationship?' is often the response. Exactly. Do you want to go through your working life having a relationship with your bank that is merely one of debtor and creditor? There is so much more you could develop in the way of a relationship but it needs the combined effort of you and your bank.

First, it is a question of communication again. Banks have been guilty in the past, and some of them still are, of not communicating with their customers. Charges were made or raised without the customers being informed; conditions of loans and overdrafts were changed without prior notice or consultation. A code of practice was introduced in 1992, and updated in July 1997, to improve the service offered by banks and building societies. And the industry is still the subject of complaint and scrutiny.

However, it is a two-way process. Small businesses and business borrowers must keep the banks informed of their financial progress. There is no point in hiding a financial problem from your bank manager – he or she may be able to help if you discuss it. Some banks have made the provision of information a condition of business. However, this has not been made easy for the average bank customer by the decision of most of the high-street operators to hand over their communications to centralised call-centres. Trying to get someone to answer complicated questions can often be time-consuming and frustrating. It is much better if you can bank right on your doorstep and make a personal call to speak to someone face-to-face, if you need to.

You can start off a good relationship with a bank or building society by choosing the right place to put your account and get your loan. If your business has relatively few monthly transactions – for example, you are a writer and receive cheques at infrequent intervals – some banks and building societies may offer free banking for longer than one year.

Finding the right account, which does not impose astronomical charges upon you, will get your relationship with your bank off to a good start. Business accounts have much higher charges than personal accounts – if you do not have lots of cash and cheque transactions you may be able to get away with having a personal account for your business.

As mentioned above, try to choose a local bank or building society where someone is available to offer advice. A branch in a large town may have a Small Business Adviser who can help. If you are involved in one of the government schemes or receiving grant aid from another body, you may find that your bank has a member of staff who deals specifically with that sort of account customer. Invite your bank or building society contact to come and view your home and your work, and perhaps to have lunch. But beware! It has been known for a customer to pay for the lunch and then receive a bill for the bank manager's time and a consultancy fee too!

There is a lot of bad feeling about the high-street banks, which has not been eased by the continuing policy of closing small branches and depersonalising large branches by replacing people with cash machines. Business customers seem to get a rough deal with many banks. Few banks offer business accounts and there is far less competition for them than for personal accounts where customers can shop around for the best deal. One small shopkeeper has complained that he has three accounts at his local bank and the manager still does not know his name. It is worth trying to build up a face-to-face relationship with your lending institution.

Make sure that when you take out an overdraft facility or a loan you keep copies of all correspondence from your bank that indicates changes in interest rates and charges. Check your bank statements carefully; if you think you have been overcharged challenge the bank. If you have a complaint, write to the branch or area manager of the bank or building society. If this proves unsatisfactory, take your complaint further by writing to the head office, then to the Financial Ombudsman Service★.

Chapter 13

Using your home and land as a money earner

In Chapter 2 we discussed whether it would be your skill, time, effort, ingenuity, specialist knowledge, qualifications or personality that would be your main asset in making money from home – or a combination of those factors. Having read this far in the book, it should come as no surprise to you to learn that you cannot substitute a piece of property or land for any of the above. In fact, if you are going to turn your home or land into a money-earning enterprise you will need all of these assets in spadefuls.

Your house

What could you do to create a feasible business? Let's start with your house; there are various scenarios you could think about. For example, your house may be very large – too large for you and your spouse now that the children have left home – but you do not want to move. What are your options?

- Run a business yourself from part of the house.
- Turn the whole of the house into a full-time business.
- Run a full-time tourist venture which opens up the house to the public.
- Run an occasional tourist venture which opens up the house to the public.
- Rent part of the house to someone else for their business purposes.
- Capitalise on some special occasion or certain times of the year and turn the house over to other people.

Let's examine each of these options in more depth.

Run a business yourself from part of the house

A trend among cost-conscious businesspeople in America has been to relocate their small businesses from their expensive city-based offices into their own homes – provided their homes are large enough and they have a small number of staff who are amenable to the suggestion. This has been particularly noticeable among male business owners in their mid-fifties. After a lifetime of commuting and working long hours, many of these businessmen choose to relocate their businesses into part of their home in order to enjoy their remaining working life and maximise their leisure and family time. It will not be long before this preference develops in the UK, particularly among small service companies that have no particular need to be located in an expensive city centre.

Of course, finding yourself rattling around in a big house after the children have left can neatly coincide with your decision to develop a new career, start a small business, or retrain after redundancy or early retirement. If you are in the fortunate position of having paid off the mortgage it makes sense to devote part of the house to your new business – be it office space or a treatment room where your clients visit.

Turn the whole of the house into a full-time business

You may, for example, choose to turn your large house into a residential home for the elderly or handicapped adults or into a small private school. These options would be attempted only by people with the necessary qualifications – although, in theory, it could be possible to appoint a qualified manager to run the enterprise. However, it is more likely that someone would buy a property that was already converted for such a use or buy a large property with a view to converting it.

Taking in lodgers is a full-time venture, even though you may not be cooking for them, as with a bed-and-breakfast business.

In certain areas of the country bedsitting rooms are in huge demand – university towns for example, near major teaching hospitals and in towns with English language colleges for foreign students.

Your local council will advise you on the current standards required for rented accommodation, if you are interested in taking in lodgers.

You will need to approach your insurer before you embark on installing kitchenettes or extra bathrooms for the bedsits. Such conversions will affect the premiums on your buildings insurance.

If you decide to take in only one or two lodgers you could take advantage of the Rent-a-Room Scheme. Under this, you can earn up to £4,250 a year tax-free in rent on furnished accommodation, provided it is in your main residence. This exemption does not apply to rooms used as offices – only to living accommodation. Further details can be obtained from the Department for Transport, Local Government and Regions (DTLR)*, in particular the booklet entitled *Letting Rooms in Your home – A guide for resident landlords*, which has information about the legal requirements and tax situation. Other sources of information are your local authority, the Citizens Advice Bureaux and the Inland Revenue.

CASE HISTORY: Sanji and Meera

Sanji and Meera have a very large house in a university town in the north-east of England. When their children left home they decided to convert all the rooms above the ground floor into student bedsits. They obtained advice from the local authority building inspector, the Environmental Health Officer and the Fire Safety Officer before they did the conversions. Each room (there were six former bedrooms) was equipped with a sofa-bed, dining table and chairs, wardrobe, and a mini-kitchen in an alcove. The bathroom and lavatory on each floor were renovated. They also converted two large landing cupboards into shower rooms. Each bedsit is supplied with a fire extinguisher and a fire blanket. Further adjustments had to be made to conform with fire safety regulations. However, despite investing over £80,000 in the conversion, Sanji and Meera recouped that money in three years and now make a considerable profit each year.

Run a full-time tourist venture which opens up the house to the public

The most common approach is running a bed and breakfast (B & B) or a small hotel from your home. As this involves having people in your home all the time it is probably the hardest transition to make. One minute the house is yours, your pride and joy, so is the lovely garden that you have worked so hard on – the next minute there are strangers disrupting your peace, criticising your wallpaper and sunbathing in your garden when you fancied a few quiet minutes there yourself. Many people prefer to purchase somewhere new to start up their business. But few people realise just how demanding this sort of business can be. The English Tourism Council* provides tourism business advice publications such as *The Business Development Toolkit* and *The Pink Booklet: A practical guide to legislation for accommodation providers*. Their website (*www.englishtourism.org.uk*) also gives intelligence reports on various sectors of the tourism market and advice on funding sources for tourism.

To find out if you have the necessary personality and stamina, ask yourself the following questions:

- Are you in good health?
- Can you work long hours – often from 7 a.m. till midnight?
- Do you mind sharing your home with strangers?
- Do you have the full backing of your family?
- Are you adaptable – and can you make decisions on the hop?
- Is your lifestyle dependent on a regular income?
- Have you any relevant experience in dealing with customers?
- Have you good social skills – happy to chat anytime?
- Are you adept at bookkeeping and accounts?
- Can you seek and accept advice?
- Are you willing to take a risk?
- Can you plan ahead?

Be honest with yourself. If you can't say 'yes' to the majority of these questions, then perhaps you should think again about starting up a small tourist concern.

According to the English Tourism Council, many people in the past have viewed a small-scale tourist business such as a guest-house, B & B or small hotel as an early retirement option, but now more and more people in their thirties and forties consider it a positive mid-life career change. However, the reality is different: the failure rate is very high, with one in four people selling up within three years.

If you have particularly stunning gardens or your property is extensive enough to open a small museum or some other tourist attraction on it, then you might find that you could cope with the public intrusion. Many people with extensive gardens open them to the public for some part of the year. For some of these people, the charge to the public to enjoy the gardens helps to pay for extra help in the garden during autumn and winter. Charging admission to your garden is unlikely to generate a great deal of profit but it may provide a forum for your other activities such as selling plants, crafts or rearing animals. You usually find that gardens and houses open to the public are linked with several other ventures as well.

CASE HISTORY: David and Richard

David and Richard own a beautiful fifteenth-century house which was once a convent and has extensive gardens and orchards. They realised that in order to pay for the upkeep of the house and gardens they would have to make the property and land pay for itself. David's interest has always been herbs and therefore they decided to create a large medieval-style herb garden and capitalise on the fact that the nuns in the convent used to tend the sick. They invested some money in buying in some herbal products and set up a shop selling those along with plants from the herb garden. They then turned the old refectory into a modest tea room, after consultation with the Environmental Health Department. Further work in the gardens involved re-planting the apple orchard and getting a local manufacturer to press apple juice and cider from the resultant apples. After five years, the business began to show a small profit but the main thing was that it paid for the continued upkeep and occupation of a historic house and gardens.

Another form of full-time tourist venture, which does not involve having people in your home all the time but does require that you comply with regulations, is to turn the front of your house into something like a tea or coffee shop. If you can reconcile yourself to losing the ground floor of your accommodation to this enterprise and you can get planning permission and cope with having to refit your kitchen to accord with health and food safety regulations, then a tea shop may be a possible option. The hours are much shorter than, say, running a full-scale restaurant, which means that you have to open in the evening. The average opening hours for a tea shop are from 10 a.m. until 5 p.m., which is much more civilised than running a B & B, where you are on call all the time.

Running an occasional tourist venture which opens up the house and/or land to the public

Examples of this would be properties which, say, have a large amount of land and can host occasional events (for which they charge rent) such as rock concerts, horticultural shows, horse shows, garden festivals, product launches and so on. Maybe you have a ballroom or magnificent library or entrance hall in your house, which you could rent out for dances and wedding receptions. Or you may have a warm, dry barn, with power supply, etc., which can be rented out for theatre performances, barn dances or flower shows.

If you have a heated indoor swimming pool you could investigate with the local education authority, social services or health authority whether they would be interested in renting time in your pool for school swimming, handicapped children and hydrotherapy sessions. You would need to seek advice from the Environmental Health Department to ensure that your pool and its surrounds comply with regulations regarding safety and equipment.

Rent part of the house to someone else for their business purposes

This effectively means that you would have to cease to use that part of the house, but, depending on the business that moves in, it may not intrude too much on the rest of the house and your garden. This is obviously made easier if you have a self-contained area of the house, such as a granny annexe. Remember, however, that you may also have to be able to accommodate extra parking of cars; always try to ensure that you are able to get in and out of your own property at all times. You do not want the inconvenience of having to ask someone else's client to move his or her car every time you want to go out. For example, if you decide to set up or rent out space to a children's day nursery, crèche or playgroup in your house, be aware that the amount of parking required by parents and carers depositing and collecting children at certain times during the day can be extensive.

Other enterprises that often rent rooms in private houses include medical practitioners, alternative therapists, hairdressers and dog-grooming parlours, but less parking space is required for these businesses.

Any of the businesses mentioned above may require your premises to be modified. If you rent space to a hairdresser, a couple of washbasins and an extra power supply would be needed. A children's care facility would need all kinds of equipment. Obviously any incoming business would provide and pay for any modifications, but as the owner of the property you should be very careful that the modifications would not permanently affect your property. For example, if you decided to terminate the arrangement and sell the house as a private residence, you would want the outgoing business tenant to remove all fixtures and fittings and leave the property in a good state of repair. Therefore you should make sure that it is written into the commercial letting agreement that the tenant must install and remove fixtures to your satisfaction at the commencement and termination of the letting period, if required.

All of the enterprises mentioned above would be regularly inspected by the relevant local authority department which also, in some cases, licenses them to operate. This may involve the rest of the house if, say, the Fire Safety Officer wanted to satisfy himself that the power supply in the business premises did not compromise the rest of the property and vice versa.

It would be prudent to ask advice before renting out your premises to anyone. Don't forget that you would have to consult with your insurer, which might take a dim view if it discovered, for example, that you were living over a cabinet-making business which stored lots of flammable materials and you did not inform them of this new hazard.

Capitalise on some special occasion or certain times of the year and turn the house over to other people

In 1999, for example, thousands of home owners in Cornwall and the Island of Alderney rented out their homes to all the eclipse-watchers who converged on the south-west of England. Unfortunately, solar eclipses from which you can profit are few and far between, but other opportunities exist, particularly if you live in an area which hosts special events. Many people who live in and around Henley on Thames, for example, rent out their houses and go away on holiday while the Regatta is on in early July. Similarly, inhabitants of Goodwood, Newmarket and Ascot are able to rent out rooms and houses when the horse racing is on. Arts Festivals are another example: people around Edinburgh make quite a bit of money renting out their properties while the Edinburgh Festival is on, as do people who live near Glyndebourne, Hay on Wye and Greenwich. Christmas and New Year are periods when large families want to get together in a large house in the country to celebrate, because none of them has a house which is big enough to accommodate the whole tribe – and they are prepared to pay premium rates for a location which is beautiful and affords good country walks and wonderful views.

If you live in a location popular with tourists you may be able to rent out a room or even the house during the tourist season, or even all year round in some cities. Many tourists prefer to stay in a private house than a hotel. However, where do you live while you rent your house? If you are lucky enough to have a self-contained annexe, you could move in there for the duration of the special event. If the event is on for quite a short period (two weeks or less) and you cannot stand the disruption it causes in your normally tranquil town, then you could rent out your home and go on holiday (and still make a profit from the deal).

CASE HISTORY: Lynn and Nigel

Lynn and Nigel were left a house with fairly extensive grounds on the Isle of Wight by an elderly relative. The property also benefited from a bungalow at the bottom of the garden. When they discovered that they could rent out the main house for at least £500 a week during the summer season (and for more just before and during Cowes Week), they decided to sell their house in Portsmouth and move to the island permanently. They live in the main house during the winter and move into the bungalow in the spring and summer and part of autumn. They find it a very suitable arrangement and the rentals generate a healthy income.

Looking for the right property

Alternatively, you may be thinking about selling up and buying a larger property, either in a rural or seaside area, or anywhere generally cheaper, with a view to setting up a business. Don't forget the value of outbuildings, if you think you can make use of them (see page 260). What should you be looking for?

First you have to know what kind of business you want to run. Regulations governing the use of buildings, the quality and the standard of the business and many other pertinent regulations are far-reaching and stringent. The following requirements are typical of a local authority's checklist for two of the most popular business uses of large houses – a residential care home for adults and a day nursery – and demonstrate the myriad regulations with which you must comply. They also show that such an undertaking is not to be taken lightly; failure to comply with regulations results in prosecution.

A residential care home for adults

The proposed premises must be suitable in construction and situation. Registration will not be approved unless applicants show that:

- the use intended is covered by a grant of planning permission
- the building does not contravene building regulations
- the Food Act 1984, Food Safety Act 1990, Food Hygiene (General) Regulations and other relevant regulations are complied with
- the building complies with all current fire regulations
- the electrical installation is safe and inspected by a competent contractor. A certificate issued by the inspecting contractor must be available for inspection at the home
- gas or oil appliances, lifts, fire alarms, emergency lighting and other major items are regularly maintained. Certificates must be available for inspection at the home
- there is adequate external amenity space within the site so that residents can take exercise and enjoy fresh air
- there is reasonable access to public transport, shops and other facilities
- there is adequate car parking

- there is full access for emergency vehicles
- there is adequate insurance cover: employer's liability, public liability, premises and contents. Certificates must be available for inspection at the home and premiums must be paid up to date.

There are additional standards on facilities and amenities such as handrails, lifts, lavatories, baths, showers, bedrooms, day rooms, hand basins, telephones, call systems, laundry facilities, storage, types of furniture, temperature of rooms, lighting, windows, adequacy of staffing levels and other matters.

Day nursery/crèche/playgroup/nursery school

The Social Services department inspectors will have to approve the following requirements and ensure that they comply with the relevant Acts:

- entry and exit from the facility must be secure – to prevent children leaving unattended and unauthorised persons from entering
- children must have sufficient space for playing and quiet time required under the Acts
- hygienic nappy disposal and potty sterilisation
- suitable and safe floor coverings
- the availability of a sink in the playroom
- sleeping arrangements (for daytime naps)
- buggy storage
- toy storage
- outdoor facilities (either attached or use of public facilities nearby)
- first aid equipment and training
- adequate refreshment provision for the children and a separate place for taking refreshment
- food is prepared and stored to safeguard children with allergies and medical conditions
- compliance with fire regulations
- compliance with building regulations
- compliance with health and safety regulations
- compliance with food hygiene regulations
- compliance with the Children Act 1989.

As you can see from all these regulations, undertaking this sort of business in your home is not for the faint-hearted. It would be worth your while to look for a building which has already been converted for the specific intended use.

Less ambitious requirements

Even a hairdresser operating from a small salon in his or her front room is subject to various local by-laws relating to the conditions in which business is conducted. All local authorities will have by-laws under Section 77 of the Public Health Act 1961 which stipulate that all surfaces in the salon – walls, floors, seating, etc. – should be in good repair at all times and capable of being washed. Rules govern the disposal of rubbish and the availability of washing facilities, toilet facilities, water supply and cleanliness of utensils.

The regulations are particularly stringent when it comes to services which involve the use of needles such as acupuncture, ear piercing, body piercing and tattooing. Because of the potential public health risks, any such operation being conducted from someone's house would be subjected to a mountain of hygiene regulations and frequent inspections.

Any home-based operation which involves the preparation of food is also subject to a battery of regulations. If this is your chosen business, you will obviously be looking for a house with a kitchen of a very high standard.

Even if you were merely intending to run an office-based business from home you need to think about suitability when viewing premises. If you are likely to have clients visiting you, it rather detracts from your company image if they have to go through your kitchen and utility room into a lean-to construction in order to conduct business. On the other hand, if they come into a large double-fronted house and your office is to the right of the front door in the spacious room that once would have been the front parlour, this creates altogether a different image. If you are likely to have business visitors you must consider accessibility and parking. Much as you would love to buy an old chapel in the Welsh hills, if your customers need to visit, they may be put off by the long journey and the inaccessibility of your premises and may even start to look for someone else closer to them with whom to do business.

Similarly, if you invest in a town house in a city centre and there is no parking to be had anywhere, customers may be discouraged.

Registering as a marriage premises

If you live in a minor stately home or just have a beautiful location that lends itself to wonderful wedding photography, you could consider applying for registration as a place where marriages can be held. Conditions for premises are contained in the Marriage Act 1994 and the Marriage (Approved Premises) Regulations 1995.

If you decide to apply to your local authority for a licence, then you have to publish notice of your intent to apply in a public place for 28 days. Within seven days of applying for a licence then you have to put an advertisement about your application in a local newspaper. A copy of the advert must be sent to the local authority.

You have to have planning consent from your local authority planning department for the change of use before applying for a licence. After you have applied, your premises will be inspected by the local authority, the Fire Safety Officer and possibly a Building Control Inspector. Members of the public, obviously, have the right to object to your application. One consideration will be whether you can accommodate a lot of cars on your land and whether this increase of traffic would cause a problem to the public or your neighbours.

CASE HISTORY : Michael and Sharon

Michael and Sharon bought a large public house, which the brewery had sold off as a potential private dwelling. The kitchens and bars were still intact in the property and it had sizeable gardens. They decided to keep the smaller bar and the kitchens, make the rest of the property into their living accommodation and apply for a licence to hold marriages. After several inspections by various council officers and some further work to upgrade the kitchens, the licence was granted. The venue is so popular that every Friday, Saturday and Sunday is booked for marriages throughout the spring and summer. The gardens are large enough to erect a marquee, if needed, and catering is supplied by outside companies who come in for each event. Michael and Sharon are able to have their home to themselves for most of the week.

Everything is then considered by the local authority's Licensing Committee. This takes time, so you have to be patient.

If you intend to host wedding receptions as well, then you will need a liquor licence and/or special events or entertainment licence.

What about your outbuildings?

If you would rather have your house to yourself and not host your own or anyone else's businesses from there, then you could consider renting out your outbuildings.

A dry, warm barn with a power supply can be a great asset – not just for renting out for those occasional barn dances but, perhaps, for something more permanent, as the premises for a small business, for example. Barns in remote places are often just what craftsmen and women and artists may be looking for.

The eight Regional Development Agencies (RDAs) administer Redundant Farm Building Grants which have enabled thousands of rural buildings to be converted into productive sources of income for their owners.

Applications to the RDA are considered from individuals, part-nerships, limited companies, co-operatives or charitable trusts as either owners or tenants. Tenants must have a fixed-term lease with at least five years left to run and written consent for the proposed works from their landlord.

The amount of the grant is at the discretion of the RDA. Application must be made and approved before work starts and grants would normally be paid on completion of the work.

Uses of redundant outbuildings have become quite varied. Eligible projects are:

- manufacturing
- crafts or service industries
- office premises
- tourism and leisure (but not bed-and-breakfast, self-catering, agricultural or horticultural uses)
- retail outlets.

For details of your local RDA contact the Department of Trade and Industry (DTI)★.

One expanding business area is the conversion of barns into 'playbarns' – children's indoor play areas, that is, multi-level, soft play equipment jungles which allow children to let off steam safely. More and more buildings are being converted to this use (most of the playbarns are franchises) but – be warned – the insurance premiums are very steep and the staff levels have to be high because the Children Act requires that children be carefully supervised, even though all these playbarns state that parents must supervise their own children.

Other popular conversions are little garden centres (which, although horticultural, qualify under the retail eligibility section for Redundant Building grants), tropical fish centres, craft centres, indoor bowling, indoor cricket and small manufacturing units.

The key criteria are:

- the building for which the grant is needed must be completely unused or unusable in its current state for the purpose(s) the applicant proposes
- the proposed conversion or refurbishment project must enable the building to be used for business purposes.

On a more modest level you could, of course, rent out any outbuildings, including garages (much sought after in urban areas), greenhouses, sheds and stables – anything, in fact, that you do not use but would be of value to someone else.

When looking at properties with a view to buying them, you should never discount the land and outbuildings. If contemplating a move from town to country, you might feel that any land is too much to cope with and you are never going to use the stables that are in the second field. But someone will – and those outbuildings could bring you in some money. For example, there are over 1,000 farmers who offer hospitality to visitors, either in the farmhouse supplying bed, breakfast and evening meals, or in self-catering cottages or converted farm buildings. These enterprising farmers are members of Farm Stay UK Ltd★, which exists to advise members on successful farm tourism. You don't have to be a farmer to develop those outbuildings or derelict cottages into a tourism enterprise.

CASE HISTORY: Jessica

Jessica is a farmer's widow and she owns a farm of some 100 acres in North Yorkshire. The farm used to raise beef but suffered a decline due to the BSE crisis and the death of Jessica's husband. Jessica has no children, owns the farm outright and does not want to sell it, so she decided to make the land pay for itself in other ways. She set up a caravan park with her brother-in-law in one of the lower fields: they invested £30,000 to install amenities – electricity, water – and built some toilet and shower blocks. Jessica decided to run the site shop herself and she employs a local girl to help her. Another field is let out for fairs, shows and markets. Business for this has increased in the past two years and an event is held in that field every month or so. The woodland has been rented out to a local shooting club, mostly wealthy businessmen who like to target shoot in the woods. There is a large wooden barn, which has a preservation order on it. Jessica has decided to renovate it and install heating and other amenities so that it can be rented out for functions. She has applied for planning permission to tarmac part of an adjoining field to use as a car park. She is currently investigating other ways in which she can capitalise on her land and thus never have to move from her home.

Making the most of your land assets

Farm Diversification Scheme

This is part of the England Rural Development Programme run by Department for the Environment, Food and Rural Affairs (DEFRA)★. A total of £152 million EU has been allocated for the period April 2001 to the end of 2006. Most of the money will be allocated to upgrading and diversifying farming practices while keeping the farms operating as agricultural units. Part of the money, however, is there for the development of tourist and craft activities on-farm and financial help is also available for non-farmers, that is, rural businesses or rural community groups.

In Scotland, the Scottish Executive Environment and Rural Affairs Department (SEERAD)★ offers grant assistance for farmers who want to diversify into any kind of business. The conditions, however, are that applicants have to have farmed full- or part-time for at least two years.

What about trees?

Suppose you have a redundant farm or a lot of land which, although it provides a wonderful view, does not actually contribute to the paying of the bills. You could, of course, as many landowners do, rent out fields to farmers, to plant crops or keep livestock, rent to horse, pony and donkey owners, or rent it out for sports to be played. But what about trees?

The Forestry Commission★ awards grants for establishing and looking after woodlands and forests.

The aims of the Woodland Grant Scheme are:

- to encourage people to create new woodlands and forests to:
  - increase the production of wood
  - improve the landscape
  - provide new habitats for wildlife, and
  - offer opportunities for recreation and sport
- to encourage good management of forests and woodlands, including their well-timed regeneration; in particular, looking after the needs of ancient and semi-natural woodlands
- to provide jobs and improve the economy of rural areas and other areas with few other sources of economic activity
- to provide uses for land other than agriculture.

Grants for the creation of new woodlands (providing your application met all the necessary criteria) are currently as follows:

Rate of grant	Conifers	Broadleaves
Woods less than 10 hectares (ha)	£700 per ha	£1,350 per ha
Woods more than 10 ha	£700 per ha	£1,050 per ha

Grants are paid in two instalments – 70 per cent when planting is finished and 30 per cent after five years. You must maintain the area to the satisfaction of the Forestry Commission for at least ten years.

The Farm Woodland Premium Scheme is designed to enhance the environment through the planting of farm woodlands, in particular to improve the landscape, provide new habitats and increase biodiversity. The scheme offers a variety of payments depending on the size of the proposed woodland, whether or not it is on set-aside land, and other factors.

The Forest Authority (part of the Forestry Commission) takes the planning and management of woodland very seriously. A variety of factors must be considered: the existing land, sources of water, prevailing wildlife, open ground, recreational potential and so on. An information pack is available from the Forestry Commission.

Wind farms

One of the most interesting but also the most controversial uses of redundant farmland in recent years has been the establishment of wind farms. As yet there are relatively few wind farms in the UK, mainly because many local communities have opposed their construction. If you are interested in installing a wind farm on your land contact the British Wind Energy Association★. For more information about wind farms and other alternative sources of power, read *The Which? Guide to the Energy-saving Home*.

Animal establishments

Using land to set up animal-related businesses is very popular, and riding stables and kennels/catteries are the most common choices. If you decide to open a kennels or cattery you will need to apply to your local Environmental Health Department for a licence. If you opt for a riding establishment you will need a licence from your local authority. Remember that the regulations covering such licences will be strict.

Caravan sites

Caravan sites need to be licensed by the local authority and, in most cases, require planning permission. You may not require planning permission for a seasonal touring caravan site but you most certainly will for a permanent residential site or a site where you own caravans that are permanently on site and rented out to the public.

A caravan site, of any kind, must have a satisfactory mains water supply, waste water disposal, sewage disposal, refuse disposal, sufficient and satisfactory fire-fighting appliances, safe storage facilities for liquified petroleum gas, fully inspected electricity supply, and adequate toilet and washing facilities.

Location for TV and film

If you think that your property's greatest asset is that it is beautiful, ancient, unusual, remote, tiny, vast – in other words just extraordinary – then it may be worth compiling a portfolio of photographs of your home and/or garden and sending it to several film and television production companies for consideration as a location. Interiors are just as sought-after as exteriors; you may have original wood panelling and beams in your home that would make a wonderful background shot for some TV drama. Sometimes a piece of land, without the modern eyesores of pylons, aircraft, telephone poles and tarmac road, is what a location company is looking for, on which to shoot a period drama. Most television and film companies do not advertise for locations but hire a Locations Manager for each production, whose job it is to find the right location.

If you want to mailshot film and TV companies with the particulars of your home then you can find comprehensive listings in two books in particular, *The Blue Book of British Broadcasting* and the *BFI Film and TV Handbook*. An easier way would be just to contact one of the many locations agencies that are listed on the Internet. In addition, register with your local authority: most councils nowadays have a website which promotes film and TV locations in their area because they wish to promote the economy of the area generally.

Location work can be lucrative, but it is also a tremendous upheaval to your life, with film crews swarming all over the place at all kinds of hours.

With some careful preparation and knowledge of and compliance with local authority by-laws and regulations it is possible to make your bricks and mortar, grass and paddock work for you. It will not be easy and the rewards may be a long time in coming, but more often than not the benefits outweigh the disadvantages.

Chapter 14

Employing others

The time will finally come, if you are successful and the business takes off, when you have to expand your operation and employ someone else. It may be that your home is the business – you take paying guests, you grow crops on the land, you rent your outbuildings as workshops and so on – and therefore it has been a family venture from the start.

For others, however, who may have been enjoying the luxury (for it is a luxury) of working for themselves and by themselves in their own home, the trauma of having to become an employer can be considerable, particularly if you want to continue to be based in your home. If you have been working for the last year in the converted spare bedroom, which makes a very nice office/craft room/workshop/despatch room but only has enough space for you, what are you going to do about housing another working person? After all, it may be that you chose your current occupation precisely because it would allow you to work at home and so to have to move out and set up an office/workshop somewhere else would defeat the object of the whole exercise and add considerably to costs.

Apart from the practicalities, you should consider the personal issues. You have got used to being on your own, working to your own routine, not having to think about anyone else, or explain what needs doing. You may have to give up working irregular hours in order to supervise an employee who works 'normal' hours. Of course, you may be working 24 hours a day and desperately need help but that may not make the prospect of sharing your space, particularly in your own home, with someone else any easier. If the thought of it truly depresses you, then think about the options.

What options are there?

You need to consider all the possibilities – from doing nothing to becoming a fully fledged employer and all the stages in between.

Carry on as you are

This is probably not an option unless you are the second-income generator and you are able to make an easy decision not to expand your activities. If you just want a paying hobby, some spare money in retirement or an enjoyable but reasonably lucrative pastime, you can carry on in your splendid isolation and not worry about finding the right sort of staff.

If your family is relying on the money you earn from home, however, you may have no option but to get some help. You do not necessarily have to appoint a permanent employee – becoming an employer is something that you can do in easy stages.

Involve your family more

You may be able to employ your wife, husband, son, daughter, mother, father, anyone in the family who has the time, the interest and the capabilities to do some work for you. At least you know each other and it is not like having a stranger coming to work in your home. You should be able to trust members of your family to do their best for you and the situation should be considerably more relaxed than that of traditional employer/employee.

CASE HISTORY: Christina

Christina is a freelance public relations consultant. She found that using an office services bureau and an answerphone was just not enough to give her the required amount of credibility with clients. She was having difficulty finding the right person to handle all her secretarial work when her widowed mother suggested stepping in to fill the post temporarily. Christina's mother had assisted her father in his business activities all her life. After working for her daughter for two months it was apparent that the arrangement worked so well that she is now employed full-time as her daughter's secretary.

There are dangers, though, in employing family members. For a start, it is most certainly not the way to shore up a crumbling marriage. If a relationship is already under stress, the added strain of the uncertainties of self-employment and the unnatural situation of you and your spouse trying to be employer and employee will undoubtedly drive the final nail into the coffin.

There may be the temptation of employing your teenage children because they are having difficulty getting a job elsewhere. This is a mistake unless they are genuinely interested in your business. There is nothing worse than employing sullen offspring who resent the fact that they have been railroaded into a career in which they are not interested and are expected to be grateful to boot. It is a 'no-win' situation: you end up by becoming more and more frustrated with each other, each feeling obliged to stick it out because it is 'family'.

Employing one or other parent could be just as stressful. Most parents and most adult 'children' would not be able to handle the role reversal of the child employing the parent and telling him or her what to do. However, if you have a good relationship with your parents and one or other is capable of acting as your secretary, accountant or 'other pair of hands', then make the most of it.

Employ friends

Think about this very carefully before you do it. Employing a friend can be the quickest way to say goodbye to a great friendship. Friends who become employees can often resent the suddenly formal nature of the working relationship. Friends who become employers are disappointed that the friend with whom they thought they had so much in common does not view the business with the same degree of importance as they do.

One way that a friendship might endure through a working situation is if the two of you became equal partners in a venture at the outset. It would be unlikely to work if you, having worked alone for a year or more, took your friend on as a partner. The relationship and partnership would never survive your inability to adapt from working alone and making all the decisions to sharing everything.

Use a bureau or a lone operator

This is probably the best option for the self-employed person who is cautiously expanding. An office services bureau can be your secretary, receptionist, bookkeeper, mailroom and more, all rolled into one. If you have one conveniently close to your home (look in the *Yellow Pages*) even better. It is simple for you to drop off work and pick it up the next day, although it still requires you to be highly organised, since you need to plan the daily/weekly work for the bureau.

A good bureau can offer a variety of useful services: typing (audio, copy, word processing), data processing, addressing labels and filling envelopes for mailshots, printing, binding reports, desktop publishing, receiving and sending faxes, being an answering service and so on.

However, if it is just typing, data processing or invoicing that is needed, perhaps the best option would be an individual who also works from home, offering those very services. Check in your local papers, parish magazines or on bulletin boards in local shops. You may find someone who can pop in and pick up your work, then deliver it back to you.

Hire a temp occasionally

If you have a situation where paperwork gets on top of you now and then, you could hire a temporary secretary from time to time from an employment or recruitment agency. This is less daunting than taking on someone full-time as you know you are only going to be employing that person for a short period. It is a good way of gradually getting used to being an employer and, indeed, having someone working alongside you.

Subcontract

Subcontracting is a common way of dealing with sudden overloads of work in certain trades, such as building and clothing. It is always worth 'networking' with other people in your area who have similar skills; it lays the foundations of a good working relationship so that, at some point, you can approach someone and subcontract certain parts of your work to them.

Use outworkers

If you want to continue to use your own home as a base but do not want any employees working from there and you also do not want

---

CASE HISTORY: Daniella

Daniella designs and hand-prints fabrics and makes clothing from them. She got a very large order from a chain of fashion stores and decided she could not cope alone. She rang round all of the people she had been at college with and found that three of them were still looking for work. She could not afford to employ them but she offered them subcontract work. She rented machines for them and then supplied the printed fabric and a copy of the clothing pattern. Her subcontractors then cut and sewed the garments on her behalf. She could not have used outworkers because she needed skilled designers/cutters like herself to be able to duplicate her work exactly.

---

or cannot afford to rent an office, warehouse or factory, taking on outworkers may be one solution. You can use outworkers (see Chapter 3) as long as it is practical and it complies with any relevant regulations. There are some situations where it would not be feasible – for example, if you made cakes for a living and you were swamped with orders, you could get outworkers to bake cakes for you but unless their kitchens were of the standard required by the Environmental Health Department, you would have to have the outworkers bake in your own kitchen.

Most employers, certainly those just starting out, prefer outworkers to be self-employed so that the employer does not have to get involved in National Insurance and tax. If you pay an outworker less than £89 per week there is no liability for National Insurance for you or your outworker. But, strictly speaking, outworkers can be classed as self-employed only if they satisfy certain criteria (see Chapter 7). Also, the Inland Revenue may not regard anyone as self-employed who has no real management over their own work.

Finding suitable workers for your line of business may not be easy. You may make clothing and know plenty of people who sew but who are not skilled machinists with experience of making clothing or parts of clothing to exacting commercial specifications. You may have to advertise or go through a JobCentre to get some staff.

If any special equipment is needed you should, as the employer, provide it. You will also have to insure it, making sure that it is fully covered even though it is not on your premises, and maintain it so that it meets the legal safety requirements. You may also have to spend some time at the outset training your outworkers to deal with the equipment you have provided for them.

Finding efficient and reliable workers is a matter of trial and error. One of the drawbacks of outworkers is that you are not there to supervise them and, although you are probably paying them by results (so much per unit completed or per hundred), you have no guarantee that this will be enough of an incentive to make them work hard for you. You could insist on a probationary period of, say, three months and see whether things work out. The majority of outworkers work from home because they are tied to the home through disability, illness or a family. Therefore all sorts of things can happen such as a period of worse health, children falling ill, school holidays and family demands in general which affect the quantity of work and, possibly, the quality. You have to be able to assess whether each outworker is giving you what you need in the end.

It takes some time for a team of outworkers to be trained and to settle down into an efficient working unit. For this reason you should not rush to use unknown outworkers just to see you through a particularly busy patch.

Take a partner who also works from home

This kind of arrangement works particularly well if you have complementary but not identical skills – that way you both feel that you are not being submerged by the other and you both bring something different and valuable to the business. It is a way of expanding and diversifying without actually becoming an employer. It is especially suited to consultants, who spend a lot of their working week away from their 'desks' and might meet up once a week to discuss developments. It is also suitable for craftsmen and women, who often prefer to work alone in their workshops. Two carpenters might join forces in this way, one making tables and chairs, the other making cabinets and drawers. It could be a permanent partnership or a joint venture just for a specific project. Either way, a clear contract is essential if disputes are to be avoided.

CASE HISTORY: Imran

Imran runs his own computer services bureau from home. His particular interest is in designing programs, software training and dealing with computer viruses. However, as he was increasingly being asked if he provided technical maintenance and repair for the hardware, he decided to find a partner who would handle this. He advertised in various computer magazines and eventually found Richard. They both operate from their own homes but under the same company name. Imran's wife continues to make appointments with clients. She then rings Richard and Imran to tell them where their next jobs are. Most of the time they work in different places on different projects.

Take on an apprentice

If you do not need to work alone and you enjoy explaining and teaching your work to others, you could consider taking on an apprentice or trainee. You may be able to send your apprentice on a government training scheme. Consult your local Learning and Skills Council (LSC)★ or Local Enterprise Council (LEC)★ in Scotland for further information.

Your trainee/apprentice does not have to be a school-leaver. The government also encourages older men and women, particularly in former coal and steel areas, to retrain for employment, and many early retirers are looking for a new direction in life and would willingly sign up as an apprentice. Taking on an apprentice/trainee should never be considered as a form of cheap labour – that sort of attitude will do nothing but harm to the working relationship between you and your helper. If the person has promise and could shape up into the ideal employee or eventual partner, you want to do everything to make sure that you keep him or her. This means being fair in all ways – working practices, quality of training and money.

Taking on your first employee

Before you try to find your employee you have to decide exactly what you want that person to do and be very clear about it. What will be his or her duties and responsibilities? Does the job require any qualifications? Do you require the employee to drive? Are keyboard skills essential? Do you want him or her to develop a new part of the business or clear up the mess in the paperwork caused by your struggling alone? A candidate who applies for a position with you expecting it to be one thing and finding that it is another will be very resentful. For example, if you run a catering business from your home, the applicant who hopes for 'hands-on' catering work is going to be disappointed if you do not make it plain that you are looking for a secretary and not a fellow chef.

Another consideration is personality. Will your employee be required to deal with the public? If so, an outgoing and pleasant nature is essential. You do not want to end up with complaints from customers about the surly treatment they received from your staff. If he or she is going to be working with you all day and you are a bit of a loner, you will want someone quiet and reserved. Does appearance matter in your line of work? Will your employee be representing your business to the outside world? Will your customers expect a certain dress code? Think carefully about such matters before you hire your staff.

When you advertise the job, whether through a publication, shop window, JobCentre, employment agency or in a school or college, you need to put in as much information about the job and your requirements as possible. You may not, by law, state a preference for anyone of a particular gender, religion, ethnic background or physical ability in your advertisement, nor should you discriminate when the applicants come forward.

When you receive the applications, take note of their presentation if this is relevant to the job. There is no point in interviewing someone as a potential secretary if he or she has untidy handwriting or sloppy typing and cannot spell or punctuate. If you are hiring someone for their specialist skills you need to see examples of their work. You can also make the job offer subject to the receipt of satisfactory references. Always take up references. Employees' and employers' rights and regulations are covered in detail in *The Which? Guide to Employment*.

Contracts of employment

All employees, whether full- or part-time, are entitled to a written Statement of Particulars of employment. This lays down the terms and conditions of the job in question and cannot be changed by either party without adequate consultation. The statement should be given to an employee within two months of commencement of employment. It is advisable for the employee to see the terms and conditions of employment as a whole prior to accepting employment. Further discussion of this and other employee rights is in Chapter 3.

The written Statement of Particulars must include the following:

- full names of both parties
- job title
- date the employment will start and, if the employee is hired for a specific period, the date the employment will finish
- place of work
- rate and frequency of pay
- hours of work
- holiday entitlement – amount to be taken and if with pay
- notice period
- sick pay details
- pension arrangements
- disciplinary procedures, and who to appeal to if dissatisfied with procedures or in the event of a grievance.

You may wish to include additional important matters in the contract, such as a confidentiality clause (that is, your employee must not disclose any of your or your clients' business information to any other party). An employee may wish to negotiate over his or her terms of employment, so do not necessarily expect the first draft of the contract to be the final one.

ACAS (Advisory, Conciliation and Arbitration Service)* will give free advice on drawing up contracts of employment.

Employment law

There is a great deal of employment legislation to be adhered to. Having to cope with the ever-increasing laws has frightened many first-time employers, and may even have made some of them shy away from expansion. The entitlements of all employees are laid out in full in Chapter 3. In this chapter we will just run briefly through the legislation in order to give some indication of what you can expect. It is probably best to read a more detailed book on the subject of employment, such as the *Which? Guide to Employment* and *The Company Secretary's Factbook* published by Gee.

A brief outline of key legislation is as follows.

Recruitment

- **Sex Discrimination Act 1975** Employers must not discriminate on the grounds of gender or marital status.
- **Race Relations Act 1976** Employers must not discriminate on the grounds of colour, race, ethnic origin or religion.
- **Disability Discrimination Act 1995** Employers must not discriminate against disabled candidates and must make 'reasonable adjustments' to jobs where there is a suitable candidate with a disability.
- **Asylum and Immigration Act 1996** It is an offence to employ someone who does not have the right to work in the UK.
- **Rehabilitation of Offenders Act 1974** Prohibits an employer from taking past offences into account if the maximum sentence passed was not more than 30 months.
- **Equal Pay Act 1970 and Regulations 1983** Men and women must receive equal terms and conditions including pay for like work.
- **Employment Act 1990 and Employment Relations Act 1999** Employers must not discriminate against applicants on the grounds of membership or non-membership of a trade union, neither must employers compile blacklists of union members or activists with a view to denying them employment.
- **Data Protection Act 1998** Employers must follow the standards laid down for collecting and processing personal data.
- **Police Act 1997** Some employees should be checked for past criminal activity through the Criminal Records Bureau.

Employment through personal service companies

In April 2001, the government changed the tax treatment of those individuals who worked as freelance consultants or as temporary staff. This was because many individuals were, in fact, working for one employer full-time, but invoicing as a self-employed contractor or service company, thus claiming the additional tax benefits of being self-employed. The responsibility for determining employment status rests with the worker but it would be advisable, as a new employer, to read the Inland Revenue booklet *Are your workers employed or self-employed?*.

Dismissal

There is a great deal of employment legislation which applies to the management of employees once they are working for you, but the area that causes employers the most grief is how to get rid of an unsatisfactory employee without becoming involved in lengthy tribunal proceedings.

Employees are entitled to a minimum period of notice as follows:

Service	Notice entitlement
1 month–2 years	1 week
2 years	2 weeks
3 years and so on	3 weeks
12 or more	12 weeks maximum

However, it may have been agreed in the contract of employment that the minimum period of notice will be longer than the statutory minimum.

An employee can claim wrongful dismissal if he or she is dismissed without notice or justification.

Under the law, there are certain circumstances which qualify as **automatically unfair dismissal**. These are:

- sex, race or disability discrimination
- pregnancy, childbirth or taking maternity leave
- trade union membership or refusal to belong to a trade union or trade union activities
- taking appropriate action for health and safety reasons
- acting as an employee trustee of a pension scheme
- acting or proposing to act as an employee representative
- asserting a statutory right
- a refusal on the part of a protected or opted-out shop worker or betting shop worker to work on a Sunday
- a refusal on the part of an employee to opt out of the Working Time Regulations
- a 'qualifying disclosure' under the Public Interest Disclosure Act 1998 (giving out information on the company that is in the public interest, for example, hidden environmental pollution).

There are five **'fair' reasons allowed for dismissal**:

- lack of capability or qualifications – lack of capability can cover long-term sickness problems and persistent absenteeism
- bad conduct – this can cover poor timekeeping, absenteeism, drug and alcohol abuse, smoking in a non-smoking environment, violence and dishonesty
- redundancy
- contravention of some other law – for example a sales rep who loses his or her driving licence because of drink/driving
- 'some other substantial reason' – the main use of this, apparently, has been the defence of a business reorganisation where employees have lost their jobs as part of a slimming-down exercise, but it appears to be a negotiable reason when it comes to a tribunal.

An employer should follow an agreed disciplinary procedure before dismissing an employee. The Advisory, Conciliation and Arbitration Service★ (ACAS) provides guidelines of the procedures that should be included in any employer's disciplinary procedure. For more information, employers can consult *Discipline at Work*, an advisory handbook from ACAS.

Failure by the employer to follow such a procedure can result in the employee, if he or she has been in the same employment for over one year, presenting a claim for unfair dismissal to an employment tribunal and asking for compensation. At present this compensation may be awarded under three separate headings.

- **Basic award** This should be calculated by multiplying a figure by the average weekly earnings, which is at present capped at £260. The maximum award is £7,800. The figure necessary to calculate the Basic Award can be obtained from a 'ready-reckoner' table on the DTI website *www.dti.gov.uk*.
- **Compensation for loss** This compensates the employee for earnings lost between the date of dismissal and the tribunal hearing. It also covers potential future losses, pension rights and loss of other statutory rights. The maximum that can be awarded is £53,500. Note that there is no maximum amount for cases involving sex, race or disability discrimination or public disclosure.
- **Additional compensation for refusal to reinstate or re-engage** If a tribunal orders an employer to reinstate or

re-engage the employee in question and the employer refuses, the tribunal can make an additional award of between 26 and 52 weeks' pay to the employee.

Employers may find it useful to consult a leaflet entitled *Fair and Unfair Dismissal: A Guide for Employers* (PL714), available from the DTI Publications Orderline★.

Redundant employees may claim a tax-free statutory redundancy payment provided they have the appropriate qualifying period of employment, which is two years' continuous service. The statutory amount for employees aged over 18 or under normal retirement age is calculated in the same way as for the Basic Award, with reference to the DTI ready-reckoner table (see above).

For the purposes of calculating the statutory redundancy payment a week's pay is currently capped at £260. The maximum service that can be taken into account is 20 years and the greatest amount of redundancy pay which is payable is 30 weeks. The maximum payable is therefore £7,800.

The Which? Guide to Employment covers redundancy and dismissal procedures in depth. Further information is also available at JobCentres and on the Department of Trade and Industry (DTI) website★.

Tax and National Insurance

All the information and the necessary forms for first-time employers can be found in the Inland Revenue's *New Employer's Starter Pack*.

You need to contact your PAYE tax office (which may be different from the tax office that deals with your business) and fill in a form to tell them that you have now employed someone. Each payday you must work out the tax and National Insurance charges due with the help of a set of tax and NI tables given to you by the PAYE tax office. The deductions you make from your employee's pay are then paid over to the PAYE tax office every month. At the end of the year you have to do a summary which tells the tax office how much each employee has earned and how much tax and National Insurance you have deducted.

That is the *basic* system. There are, of course, forms to fill in and the Inland Revenue will have to give you PAYE codes for each employee which show how much the individual employee's tax allowances amount to. The Inland Revenue tries to be as helpful as possible to new employers and will talk you through the system if you wish.

Keeping employees

Once you have employees and you are happy with them, you want to keep them, and this requires more than a little effort on your part. Everyone appreciates being told if they are:

- doing a good job
- behaving responsibly
- learning the ropes quickly and thoroughly
- being a great help to you
- helping the business to develop.

You must make time to assess your employees' development and to guide them if they have difficulty learning particular skills or dealing with certain tasks.

If you have one treasured employee or a small team of excellent workers, consider rewarding them. It does not have to be cash bonuses – it could just be an outing that you pay for, perhaps a meal or a visit to the theatre.

Make any criticisms of staff constructive. Never lose your temper – it is not productive. If you are plunged into a crisis do not waste time trying to apportion blame; direct your energies instead to overcoming the crisis, then, when it has all died down, institute a quiet investigation into what went wrong. Never humiliate a member of staff in front of his or her colleagues as you will lose everybody's respect that way. If you have a bone to pick with someone take them away quietly for a private chat.

If you can, make your employees' work interesting. It is not always possible in the case of outworkers doing mundane, repetitive jobs, of course. In that case, try to be fair about money and understand that, if your profit margins can bear it, people need to be rewarded for doing difficult, unfulfilling jobs.

Listen to your employees: some of the best money-making ideas have come from members of staff. Also heed what they have to say about procedures and routines within your business. You may have done it your way for such a long time you cannot see the wood for the trees. A fresh mind applies itself to the job and suddenly certain flaws in the system become apparent.

Do not be jealous of a new employee. That may sound a silly thing to say but it is a common feeling among lone entrepreneurs who have nursed their 'baby' from concept to profitability. The first employee may be full of eagerness and new ideas and the employer initially may resent any 'interference'.

Above all, communicate with your employees. Tell them how the business is doing, explain any problems, reassure them about future orders and contracts, explain your philosophy and your hopes. This is very important if you have just one employee who, perhaps, stands in for you when you are not there. He or she needs to be able to think as you do, to deal with any problems or exploit any opportunities that may arise while you are away. While you do not want to give an employee the impression that he or she can make important decisions without referring to you, you do want someone who will take a bit of responsibility and initiative in your absence.

Human relationships are a tricky business at the best of times. Just remember that being an employer does not make you a different person from the one who started out earning money from home in a very modest way. If a particular association, whether with employee, colleague or client, fails to work out, accept the situation and end the relationship as simply as you can.

Addresses

All organisations, associations and government offices marked with an asterisk in the text are listed below. Your local reference library will have information on associations for specific lines of work and regional bodies that are too numerous to mention here.

AbilityNet
Tel: (0800) 269 545
Fax: (01926) 407425
Email: enquiries@abilitynet.co.uk
Website: www.abilitynet.co.uk

ADAS
Woodthorne
Wergs Road
Wolverhampton
WV6 8TQ
Tel: (01902) 754190
Fax: (01902) 743602
Website: www.adas.co.uk

Advertising Standards Authority (ASA)
Brook House
2 Torrington Place
London WC1E 7HW
Tel: 020-7580 5555
Fax: 020-7631 3051
Email: enquiries@asa.org.uk
Website: www.asa.org.uk

Advisory, Conciliation and Arbitration Service (ACAS)
Head Office
Brandon House
180 Borough High Street
London SE1 1LW
National Helpline: (0845) 747 4747
Website: www.acas.org.uk

Arts Council of England
2 Pear Tree Court
London EC1R ODS
Tel: 020-7608 6100
Fax: 020-7608 4100
Email: enquiries@artscouncil.org.uk
Website: www.artscouncil.org.uk

Arts Council of Wales
ACW Central Office
9 Museum Place
Cardiff CF10 3NX
Tel: 029-2037 6500
Fax: 029-2022 1447
Email: info@artswales.org.uk
Website: www.artswales.org.uk

Association of British Insurers (ABI)
51 Gresham Street
London EC2V 7HQ
Tel: 020-7600 3333
Fax: 020-7696 8999
Email: info@abi.org.uk
Website: www.abi.org.uk

Association of Chartered Certified Accountants (ACCA)
29 Lincoln's Inn Fields
London WC2A 3EE
Tel: 020-7369 7000
Email: info@accaglobal.com
Website: www.acca.co.uk

Association of Disabled Professionals
BCM ADP
London WC1N 3XX
Tel: 020-7700 0646
Fax: 023-9224 1420
Email: AssDisProf@aol.com
Website: www.adp.org.uk

Association of Taxation Technicians
12 Upper Belgrave Street
London SW1X 8BB
Tel: 020-7235 2544
Fax: 020-7235 2562
Email: info@att.org.uk
Website: www.att.org.uk

British Agents Register
24 Mount Parade
Harrogate
North Yorkshire HG1 1BP
Tel: (01423) 560608
Fax: (01423) 561204
Email: info@agentsregister.com
Website: www.agentsregister.com

British Chambers of Commerce
50 Broadway
St James's Park
London SW1H 0RG
Tel: 020-7152 4046
Fax: 020-7152 4145
Email: info@britishchambers.org.uk
Website: www.chamberonline.co.uk

British Franchise Association
Thames View
Newtown Road
Henley-on-Thames
Oxfordshire RG9 1HG
Tel: (01491) 578050
Fax: (01491) 573517
Email: mailroom@british-
franchise.org.uk
Website: www.british-franchise.org.uk

**British Insurance Brokers Association
(BIBA)**
14 Bevis Marks
London EC3A 7NT
Tel: 020-7623 9043
Fax: 020-7626 9676
Email: enquiries@biba.org.uk
Website: www.biba.org.uk

British Standards Institution
389 Chiswick High Road
London W4 4AL
Tel: 020-8996 9000
Fax: 020-8996 7400
Email: cservices@bsi-global.com
Website: www.bsi.org.uk

British Wind Energy Association
Renewable Energy House
1 Aztec Row
Berners Road
London N1 0PW
Tel: 020-7689 1960
Fax: 020-7689 1969
Email: info@bwea.com
Website: www.bwea.com

BT
Customer Service: (0800) 800150
Internet Sales: (0800) 800001
Website: www.bt.com

Business Connect (Wales)
Tregormen Business Park
Nelson Road
Ystrad Mynach
CS82 7FN
Tel: (0845) 796 9798
Fax: 029-2082 8775
Website: www.businessconnect.org.uk

Business Link Hertfordshire
45 Grosvenor Road
St Albans
Hertfordshire AL1 3AW
Tel: (01727) 813533
Fax: (01727) 813706

Business Link Signpost Line
Tel: (0845) 604 5678
Fax: 020-7010 1041
Email: info@bl4london.com
240 Business Links open throughout England

Central Office of Information
COI Communications
Hercules House
Hercules Road
London SE1 7DU
Tel: 020-7928 2345
Fax: 020-7928 5037
Email: coi@coi.gsi.gov.uk
Website: www.coi.gov.uk

Chartered Institute of Patent Agents
(CIPA)
95 Chancery Lane
London WC2A 1DT
Tel: 020-7405 9450
Fax: 020-7430 0471
Email: mail@cipa.org.uk
Website: www.cipa.org.uk

Chartered Institute of Taxation
12 Upper Belgrave Street
London SW1X 8BB
Tel: 020-7235 9381
Fax: 020-7235 2562
Email: post@ciot.org.uk
Website: www.tax.org.uk

CheckSURE Ltd
Merlin House
Brunel Road
Theale
Berkshire RG7 4AB
Tel: (08708) 408034
Fax: (07092) 311942
Email: sales@checksure.biz
Website: www.checksure.biz

Companies House (England, Wales and Scotland)
21 Bloomsbury Street
London WC1B 3XD
Tel: (0870) 333 3636
Fax: 029-2038 0517
Email: enquiries@companieshouse.gov.uk
Website: www.companieshouse.gov.uk

Companies Registry (Northern Ireland)
IDB House
64 Chichester Street
Belfast BT1 4JX
Tel: 028-9023 4488
Fax: 028-9054 4888
Email: info.companiesregistry@detini.gov.uk
Website: www.companiesregistry-ni.gov.uk

Consumers' Association
2 Marylebone Road
London NW1 4DF
Tel: 020-7486 5544
Fax: 020-7770 7600
Website: www.which.net

Corporate Venturing UK Ltd
40–42 Cannon Street
London EC4N 6JJ
Tel: 020-7246 0751
Fax: 020-7246 0766
Email: info@corporateventuringuk.org
Website: www.corporateventuringuk.org

Crafts Council
44A Pentonville Road
London N1 9BY
Tel: 020-7278 7700
Fax: 020-7837 6891
Website: www.craftscouncil.org.uk

HM Customs and Excise
Alexander House
21 Victoria Avenue
Southend on Sea
Essex SS99 1AA
National Advice Service:
(0845) 010 9000
Website: www.hmce.gov.uk

Department for Education and Skills
(DfES)
Sanctuary Buildings
Great Smith Street
London SW1P 3BT
Tel: (0870) 000 2288
Fax: (01928) 794248
Email: info@dfes.gsi.gov.uk
Website: www.dfes.gov.uk

Department for the Environment, Food and Rural Affairs (DEFRA)
Ergon House
17 Smith Square
London SW1P 3JR
Tel: 020-7238 6000
Email: helpline@defra.gsi.gov.uk
Website: www.defra.gov.uk

Department of Trade and Industry (DTI)
Enquiry Unit
1 Victoria Street
London SW1H 0ET
Tel: 020-7215 5000
Fax: 020-7222 0612
Email: dti.enquiries@dti.gsi.gov.uk
Website: www.dti.gov.uk

DTI Publications Orderline
Admail 528
London SW1W 8YT
Tel: (0870) 1502 500
Fax: (0870) 1502 333
Email: publications@dti.gsi.gov.uk
Website: www.dti.gov.uk

**Department for Transport, Local
Government and the Regions (DTLR)**
Eland House
Bressenden Place
London SW1E 5DO
Tel: 020-7944 8300
Website: www.dft.gov.uk

Department for Work and Pensions
Correspondence Unit
Room 540
The Adelphi
1–11 John Adam Street
London WC2N 6HT
Tel: 020-7712 2171
Fax: 020-7712 2386
Website: www.dwp.gov.uk

Direct Mail Information Service
5 Carlisle Street
London W1V 6JX
Tel: 020-7494 0483
Fax: 020-7494 0455
Email: info@dmis.co.uk
Website: www.dmis.co.uk

Direct Marketing Association
DMA House
70 Margaret Street
London W1W 8SS
Tel: 020-7291 3300
Fax: 020-7323 4165
Email: dma@dma.org.uk
Website: www.dma.org.uk

Direct Selling Association
29 Floral Street
London WC2E 9DP
Tel: 020-7497 1234
Fax: 020-7497 3144
Email: ukdsa@globalnet.co.uk
Website: www.dsa.org.uk

Disability Alliance
Universal House
88–94 Wentworth Street
London E1 7SA
Tel: 020-7247 8776
Fax: 020-7247 8765
Email: office.da@dial.pipex.com
Website: www.disabilityalliance.org

Disability Rights Commission
Freepost MID 02164
Stratford upon Avon CV37 9BR
Helpline: (0845) 762 2633
Fax: (0845) 777 8878
Email: enquiry@drc-gb.org
Website: www.drc-gb.org

Disabled Entrepreneurs Network
Email: info@disabled-entrepreneurs.net
Website: www.disabled-entrepreneurs.net

**Employment Opportunities for People
with Disabilities**
123 Minories
London EC3N 1NT
Tel: 020-7481 2727
Fax: 020-7481 9797
Email: eopps.ho@care4free.net
Website: www.opportunities.org.uk

English Tourism Council (ETC)
Thames Tower
Black's Road
London W6 9EL
Tel: 020-8563 3000
Fax: 020-8563 0302
Website: www.englishtourism.org.uk

Euro Info Centres
Website: www.europa.eu.int

European Investment Fund
43 Avenue JF Kennedy
L-2968 Luxembourg
Tel: 352 42 66 88 100
Fax: 352 42 66 88 200
Email: info@eif.org
Website: www.eif.org

European Social Fund
Website: www.esfnews.org.uk

Farm Stay UK Ltd
National Agricultural Centre
Stoneleigh Park
Kenilworth
Warwickshire CV8 2LG
Tel: 024-7669 6909
Fax: 024-7669 6630
Email: admin@farmstayuk.co.uk
Website: www.farmstayuk.co.uk

Fax Preference Service
DMA House
70 Margaret Street
London W1W 8SS
Tel: 020-7291 3320
Fax: 020-7323 4226
Email: fps@dma.org.uk
Website: www.fpsonline.org.uk

Finance and Leasing Association
2nd Floor
Imperial House
15–19 Kingsway
London WC2B 6UN
Tel: 020-7836 6511
Fax: 020-7420 9600
Email: info@fla.org.uk
Website: www.fla.org.uk

Financial Ombudsman Service
South Quay Plaza
183 Marsh Wall
London E14 9SR
Helpline: (0845) 080 1800
Fax: 020-7964 1001
Email: complaint.info@financial-
ombudsman.org.uk
Website: www.financial-
ombudsman.org.uk

Financial Services Authority
25 The North Colonnade
Canary Wharf
London E14 5HS
Tel: 020-7676 1000
Fax: 020-7676 1099
Email: enquiries@fsa.co.uk
Website: www.fsa.gov.uk

Food from Britain
4th Floor
Manning House
22 Carlisle Place
London SW1P 1JA
Tel: 020-7233 5111
Fax: 020-7233 9515
Email: info@foodfrombritain.com
Website: www.foodfrombritain.com

Food Standards Agency
Aviation House
125 Kingsway
London WC2B 6NH
Tel: 020-7276 8000
Email: helpline@foodstandards.gsi.gov.uk
Website: www.foodstandards.gov.uk

Forestry Commission
231 Corstophine Road
Edinburgh EH12 7AT
Tel: 0131-334 0303
Fax: 0131-334 3047
Email: enquiries@forestry.gsi.gov.uk
Website: www.forestry.gov.uk

Health and Safety Executive
HSE Infoline
Caerphilly Business Park
Caerphilly CF83 3GG
Tel: (0870) 1545500
Fax: 029-2085 9260
Email:
hseinformationservices@natbrit.com
Website: www.hse.gov.uk
Look in the phone book for your local office

285

Highlands and Islands Enterprise
Cowan House
Inverness Retail and Business Park
Inverness IV2 7GF
Tel: (01463) 234171
Fax: (01463) 244469
Email: hie.general@hient.co.uk
Website: www.hie.co.uk

Home Business Alliance
Freepost ANG3155
March
Cambridgeshire PE15 9BR
Tel: (0870) 749 6321
Fax: (0870) 749 6322
Website: www.homebusiness.org.uk

ICT Marketing
Corner House
Barn Street
Haverfordwest SA61 1BW
Tel: (01437) 766441
Fax: (01437) 766173
Email: info@ictenterprise.co.uk
Website: www.ictenterprise.co.uk

Inland Revenue
Somerset House
Strand
London WC2R 1LB
Enquiry Line: 020-7667 4001
Website: www.inlandrevenue.gov.uk

Institute of Chartered Accountants in England and Wales (ICAEW)
PO Box 433
Chartered Accountants Hall
Moorgate Place
London EC2P 2BJ
Tel: 020-7920 8100
Fax: 020-7920 0547
Website: www.icaew.co.uk

Institute of Chartered Accountants in Ireland (ICAI)
Chartered Accountants House
87–89 Pembroke Road
Ballsbridge
Dublin 4
Republic of Ireland
Tel : 00 353 1 637 7200
Fax: 00 353 1 668 0842
Email: ca@icai.ie
Website: www.icai.ie

Institute of Chartered Accountants of Scotland (ICAS)
CA House
21 Haymarket Yards
Edinburgh EH12 5BH
Tel: 0131-347 0100
Fax: 0131-347 0105
Email: icas@icas.org.uk
Website: www.icas.org.uk

Institute of Directors (IoD)
116 Pall Mall
London SW1Y 5ED
Tel: 020-7839 1233
Fax: 020-7930 1949
Email: enquiries@iod.com
Website: www.iod.com

Learning and Skills Council (LSC)
Cheylesmore House
Quinton Road
Coventry CV1 2WT
Tel: (0845) 019 4170
Fax: 024-7682 3675
Email: info@lsc.gov.uk
Website: www.lsc.gov.uk

LINC Scotland
Queens House
19 St Vincent Street
Glasgow G1 2DT
Tel: 0141-221 3321
Fax: 0141-221 2909
Email: info@lincscot.co.uk
Website: www.lincscot.co.uk/index2htm

Local Enterprise Councils (LECs)
Scottish Enterprise
5 Atlantic Quay
150 Broomielaw
Glasgow G2 8LU
Tel: 0141-248 2700
Fax: 0141-221 3217
Email: enquiries@scotent.co.uk
Website: www.scottish-enterprise.com

Livewire (Shell/Livewire)
Hawthorn House
Forth Banks
Newcastle Upon Tyne
NE1 3SG
Tel: (0845) 757 3252
Website: www.shell-livewire.org

Mail Order Traders Association
Drury House
19 Water Street
Liverpool L2 ORP
Tel: 0151-227 9456
Fax: 0151-227 9678

Mailing Preference Service
DMA House
70 Margaret Street
London W1W 8SS
Tel: 020-7291 3320
Fax: 020-7323 4226
Email: mpsonline@dma.org.uk
Website: www.mpsonline.org.uk

Manufacturers' Agents' Association (MAA)
Unit 16
Thrales End
Harpenden
Herts AL5 3NS
Tel: (01582) 767618
Fax: (01582) 766092
Email: prw@themaa.co.uk
Website: www.themaa.co.uk

Market Research Society
15 Northburgh Street
London EC1V 0JR
Tel: 020-7490 4911
Fax: 020-7490 0608
Email: info@mrs.org.uk
Website: www.mrs.org.uk

National Association of Farmers' Markets
South Vaults
Green Park Station
Green Park Road
Bath BA1 1JB
Tel: (01225) 787914
Fax: (01225) 460840
Email: nafm@farmersmarkets.net
Website: www.farmersmarkets.net

National Bureau for Students with Disabilities (SKILL)
Chapter House
18–20 Crucifix Lane
London SE1 3JW
Information line: (0800) 328 5050
Tel: 020-7657 2337
Fax: 020-7450 0650
Email: skill@skill.org.uk
Website: www.skill.org.uk

National Business Angels Network
40–42 Cannon Street
London EC4N 6JJ
Information hotline: 020-7329 4141
Tel: 020-7329 2929
Fax: 020-7329 2626
Email: info@bestmatch.co.uk
Website: www.bestmatch.co.uk

National Farmers Union (NFU)
Agriculture House
164 Shaftesbury Avenue
London WC2H 8HL
Tel: 020-7331 7200
Fax: 020-7331 7401
Email: nfu@nfu.org.uk
Website: www.nfu.org.uk

National Federation of Enterprise Agencies
Trinity Gardens
9-11 Bromham Road
Bedford MK40 2UQ
Tel/Fax: (01234) 354055
Email: enquiries@nfea.com
Website: www.nfea.com

National Group on Homeworking
Office 26
30–38 Dock Street
Leeds LS10 1JF
Advice Line: (0800) 174095
Fax: 0113-246 5616
Email: homeworking@gn.apc.org
Website: www.homeworking.gn.apc.org

National Newspapers Mail Order Protection Scheme (MOPS)
18a King Street
Maidenhead
Berkshire SL6 1EF
Tel: (01628) 641930
Fax: (01628) 637112
Email: enquiries@mops.org.uk
Web site: www.mops.org.uk

NESTA
Fishmongers' Chambers
110 Upper Thames Street
London EC4R 3TW
Tel: 020-7645 9500
Fax: 020-7645 9535
Email: nesta@nesta.org.uk
Website: www.nesta.org.uk

Newspaper Society
Bloomsbury House
74–77 Great Russell Street
London WC1B 3DA
Tel: 020-7636 7014
Fax: 020-7631 5119
Email: ns@newspapersoc.org.uk
Website: www.newspapersociety.org.uk

NTL
NTL House
Bartley Wood Business Park
Bartley Way
Hook
Hampshire RG27 9UP
Tel: (01256) 752000
Fax: (01256) 754100
Website: www.ntl.com

Office of Fair Trading
Fleetbank House
2–6 Salisbury Square
London EC4Y 8JX
Tel: (0845) 722 4499
Fax: 020-7211 8877
Email: enquiries@oft.gov.gsi.uk
Website: www.oft.gov.uk

Office of the Information Commissioner
Wycliffe House
Water Lane
Wilmslow
Cheshire SK9 5AF
Tel: (01625) 545745
Fax: (01625) 524510
Email: data@dataprotection.gov.uk
Website: www.dataprotection.gov.uk

Patent Office
Concept House
Cardiff Road
Newport
South Wales NP9 1RH
Tel: (0845) 950 0505
Fax: (01633) 814444
Email: enquiries@patent.gov.uk
Website: www.patent.gov.uk

Periodical Publishers Association
Queens House
28 Kingsway
London WC2B 6JR
Tel: 020-7404 4166
Fax: 020-7404 4167
Email: info1@ppa.co.uk
Website: www.ppa.co.uk

Prince's Trust
18 Park Square East
London NW1 4LH
Tel: 020-7543 1234
Fax: 020-7543 1200
Website: www.princes-trust.org.uk

Prince's Scottish Youth Business Trust
6th Floor
Mercantile Chambers
53 Bothwell Street
Glasgow G2 6TS
Tel: 0141-248 4999
Fax: 0141-248 4836
Email: firststep@psybt.org.uk
Website: www.psybt.org.uk

Profunding
Suite 1.02
St Mary's Centre
Oystershell Lane
Newcastle upon Tyne NE4 5QS
Tel: 0191-232 6942
Fax: 0191-232 6936
Email: info@fundinginformation.org
Website: www.fundinginformation.org

Royal Association for Disability and Rehabilitation (RADAR)
12 City Forum
250 City Road
London EC1V 8AF
Tel: 020-7250 3222
Fax: 020-7250 0212
Email: radar@radar.org.uk
Website: www.radar.org.uk

Royal Mail
Enquiries: (08457) 740740
Sales centre: (08457) 950950
Website: www.royalmail.com

Scottish Arts Council
12 Manor Place
Edinburgh EH3 7DD
Tel: 0131-226 6051
Fax: 0131-225 9833
Email: help.desk@scottisharts.org.uk
Website: www.sac.org.uk

Scottish Enterprise
5 Atlantic Quay
150 Broomielaw
Glasgow G2 8LU
Tel: (0845) 607 8787
Fax: 0141-221 3217
Email: network.helpline@scotent.co.uk
Website: www.scottish-enterprise.com

Scottish Executive Environment and Rural Affairs Department (SEERAD)
Longman House
28 Longman Road
Inverness IVF 1SF
Tel: (01463) 234141
Fax: (01463) 714697
Email:
seerad.inverness@scotland.gsi.gov.uk
Website: www.scotland.gov.uk

Scottish Organic Producers Association (SOPA)
Scottish Organic Centre
10th Avenue
Royal Highland Centre
Ingliston
Edinburgh EH28 8NF
Tel: 0131-335 6606
Fax: 0131-335 6607
Email: sopa@sfqc.co.uk
Website: www.sopa.org.uk

Scottish Tourist Board
Contact Scottish Enterprise for tourism business support

Shaw Trust
Information Resource
Shaw House
Epsom Square
White Horse Business Park
Trowbridge
Wiltshire BA14 0XJ
Tel: (01255) 716300
Fax: (01255) 716334
Email: stir@shaw-trust.org.uk
Website: www.shaw-trust.org.uk

Shetland Enterprise
Toll Clock Shopping Centre
26 North Road
Lerwick
Shetland ZE1 0DE
Tel: (01595) 693177
Fax: (01595) 693208
Email: shetland@hient.co.uk
Website: www.hie.co.uk

SIPP Provider Group
Francis Moore
Shortsmead
Alvediston
Salisbury SP5 5LD
Tel: (01722) 781028
Fax: (01722) 781009
Email: clientservicing@epml.co.uk
Website : www.sipp-provider-group.org.uk

The Small Business Service
Kingsgate House
66–74 Victoria Street
London SW1E 6SW
Tel: (0845) 600 9006
Website: www.sbs.gov.uk
www.businesslink.org

Soil Association
Bristol House
40–56 Victoria Street
Bristol BS1 6BY
Tel: 0117-929 0661
Fax: 0117-925 2504
Email: info@soilassociation.org
Website: www.soilassociation.org

Teaching Company Scheme
Brunel House
Faringdon
Oxon SN7 7YR
Tel: (01367) 245200
Fax: (01367) 242831
Email: office@tcsoffice.org.uk
Website: www.tcsonline.org.uk

Telewest
Sales enquiries: (0800) 953 5383
Website: www.telewest.co.uk

The Telework Association (TCA)
Wren Telecottage
Kenilworth
Warwickshire
CV8 2RR
Tel: (0800) 616008
Fax: (01453) 836174
Email: info@telework.org.uk
Website: www.telework.org.uk

TradePartners UK
Kingsgate House
66–74 Victoria Street
London SW1E 6SW
Tel: 020-7215 5444
Fax: 020-7215 2482
Website: www.tradepartners.gov.uk

UK Intellectual Property on the Internet
Website:
www.intellectual-property.gov.uk

UK Telephone Preference Service
(To clean telephone sales lists of people who have elected not to receive unsolicited phone calls)
DMA House
70 Margaret Street
London W1W 8SS
Tel: 020-7291 3320
Fax: 020-7323 4226
Email: tpsonline@dma.org.uk
Website: www.tpsonline.org.uk

United Kingdom Register of Organic Food Standards (UKROFS)
Contact DEFRA (see above)

Wales Tourist Board
Brunel House
2 Fitzalan Road
Cardiff CF24 0UY
Tel: 029-2049 9909
Fax: 029-2048 5031
Email:
walestouristboard@tourism.gov.uk
Website: www.wtbonline.gov.uk

WI (Women's Institute) Country Markets Ltd
Dunstan House
Dunstan Road
Sheepbridge
Chesterfield S41 9QD
Tel: (01246) 261508
Fax: (01246) 268208
Email: info@wimarkets.co.uk
Website: www.wimarkets.co.uk

Women in Business
Website: www.womeninbusiness.co.uk

Work Global
Pairc House
Habost
South Lochs
Isle of Lewis HS2 9QB
Tel: (01851) 880225
Fax: (01851) 880386
Email: enquiries@work-global.com
Website: www.work-global.com

Index